FUNDAMENTALS OF
Mainstream Buddhism

FUNDAMENTALS OF
Mainstream
Buddhism

PUBLISHED IN ASSOCIATION WITH THE
BUDDHIST SOCIETY

ERIC CHEETHAM

Charles E. Tuttle Co., Inc.
Boston • Rutland, Vermont • Tokyo

Published by Charles E. Tuttle Company, Inc.
of Rutland, Vermont and Tokyo, Japan, with editorial offices at
153 Milk Street, Boston, Massachusetts 02109

The body of this work was originally published as four booklets in
1987 by the Buddhist Society, London.

Library of Congress Cataloging-in-Publication Data

Cheetham, Eric.
    Fundamentals of mainstream Buddhism / Eric Cheetham.
        p. cm.   — (Tuttle library of enlightenment)
    Includes bibliographical references and index.
    ISBN 0–8048–3008–8 (pbk.)
    1. Buddhism—Doctrines. I. Title. II. Series.
BQ4150.C487 1994
294.3—dc20   94–34899
                                                         CIP

Design by Jill Winitzer

    3   5 6 9 10 8 6 4 2

Printed in the United States
(EB)

CONTENTS

FOREWORD TO THE ORIGINAL EDITION

The Buddhist Society is proud to present this series of booklets by Eric Cheetham. They are designed to follow the Society's introductory or correspondence courses. Familiarity with the basic principles of Buddhism is therefore assumed.

The Buddhist Teachings address human beings; they advocate specific attitudes on how to orientate in this world—outer and inner—in which we are born, suffer seeming bondage on a wheel of endless cyclical dissatisfaction and unfulfillment, and die. Out of this suffering, the Buddha points the Way that leads from delusion to genuine insight—seeing all things the way they really are—an insight to which he himself awakened by means of dedicated practice. The erstwhile Prince Gautama became the ascetic Gautama, and on awakening from the delusions that beset us human beings, became the Buddha, the Awakened One, all-wise and all-compassionate. He then spent the rest of his life teaching the way of release to like-minded others. This Way is the way out of suffering: that is the grand theme, the grand message of Buddhism, whether played on a solitary reed-flute or fully orchestrated into great symphonies.

Westerners responding to these melodies and their message do well to acquaint themselves with the "key" in which the music is composed. For it is other than, and foreign to, our way of thinking. The great monotheistic religions of the West have either crumbled at the advent of science, or turned their back to time and development and retreated into fundamentalism. Being "book" religions, their dogmas and commandments were revealed, once and for all, by the divinity who is the sole creator of all that is and who transcends his creation absolutely. This imprint has shaped the very ways we think and perceive, and is reflected in the very structure of our languages. In Western religions, "historicity" is an essential feature because divine revelation is to be believed to the letter.

This is utterly foreign to Buddhism which, in common with other great Eastern religions, knows of no sole, divine, transcendent creator. For what the "life" of the Buddha spells out, is not—repeat, not—the authenticated biography of an historical person, but a map indispensable for the stages of the Way that is to be trodden. In Buddhism, the sense of divinity is seen as inherent in all that is, as the ground of all being, Buddha-Nature, Nirvana. These, and other such terms in the great orchestration, stand for something that itself is beyond expression. To be re-linked with it leads out of suffering, out of this our world of Samsara. Those so minded may follow the Way indicated and rediscover for themselves, step by step, this ancient Way and music.

The pursuit of this Way requires strength, the discipline of sustained application, and such directional pointers as the Noble Eightfold Path, the Precepts, and the Paramitas. Such pointers comprise a necessary map to ascertain whether one's feet are still on the Buddha's Way. There is a variety of such maps, such as the Wheel of Change, the Twelve-linked Chain of Dependent Origination, and the Three Realms as the abode of all living beings. Buddhist teachings constantly refer to these and other frameworks, and we need real familiarity with them as inner reference points that lead away from our prevalent concern with "I, me, mine."

The Teachings explicitly warn against taking these frameworks as an outer locality. Rather, the Buddha and those great ones who in the chain of generations devoted their lives to following his Way have all found or re-discovered these universal structures in their own hearts. This re-discovery, following the Buddha, equals Deliverance. Hence—and this is of particular importance for Westerners conditioned to belief in doctrines—believing or not believing are not issues on the Way to Deliverance but are rather, like any other pair of opposites, contributors to delusion.

What Mister Cheetham presents in these pages is Mainstream Buddhism—traditional teachings basic to all schools of Buddhism, whether of the southern or northern persuasion. He is not concerned here with the local variations of the various schools. As Westerners we need to be careful with such individual variations, for many of them, though of interest, are meant to be evocative rather than factual. Their importance comes when one of these manifold variations, one of the many Buddhist "orchestrations," touches our heart and incites us to follow the Way.

It is the Buddha, all-wise and all-compassionate, who points the Way; but it is we ourselves who must walk it. The teachings also advise us not to waste this fleeting life. To Buddhists, Deliverance from the Wheel is possible only from the human state. Having the rare boon (or good Karma) to be born with a human body, we are encouraged to make strenuous "right" effort on the Buddha's Way towards the Awakening that opens the heart to behold all things as they really are. To become that insight and so to be always living it, compassionately and helpfully partaking in what is—that is the teaching of all the Buddhas.

—Myokyo-ni
August 1985

INTRODUCTION

Between 1985 and 1988 the Buddhist Society in London published a series of interconnected booklets by this writer for the purpose of establishing a reliable foundation for the study and practice of basic Buddhism. These four booklets, entitled *Fundamentals of Mainstream Buddhism*, were followed by another four called *Outline of Indian Mahāyāna,* completed in 1993, and all are associated with ongoing lecture and practice classes at the Society.

As the original booklets attempted to demonstrate, the crucial importance of foundation doctrine and practice is both practical and historical. The practical importance needs no emphasis, other than to say that those who wish to put the Buddhist teachings into practice need to have some assurance that what they embark upon is truly Buddhist and not some hybrid of uncertain parentage. Historically speaking, all later developments of the Teachings, to be valid Buddhism, had to retain their doctrinal links with the earliest corpus of teaching, and in most cases their particular identities arose as a result of a close attention to parts of that original teaching.

In consequence, it becomes necessary to bring those original teachings into clear focus, not only for their own sake and for right practice, but in order to understand and in some degree to evaluate whether later developments preserve the original intentions of the Buddha's methods concerning ends and means. Such evaluations may also include an idea of authenticity, of the value of modifications deemed necessary for later times and different circumstances.

All of this requires what may be called a database of well-established foundation doctrine and practice drawn from the earliest known strata of Buddhist tradition, authenticated by actual Buddhist masters of the time and subject to a minimum of inter-sectarian dispute. These are the criteria that guided the compilation of the first four booklets and that led to the use of the phrase "Mainstream Buddhism" in the title. That phrase is intended to describe a collection of the earliest Buddhist teachings on which the substance of Indian Buddhism is based.

In order to make this database of mainstream teaching available to a wider public, those first four booklets have here been combined into a single volume, with minor editing required by the new format. The essential matter of the four introductory chapters of the booklets are amalgamated in the present Introduction so as to preserve the explanations of some of the new perspectives employed in the special terminology of the texts. In almost all other respects the expositions and the comment remain as they were in the original.

In conformity with these criteria, one of the major concerns in this presentation of the fundamental Buddhist teachings has been to pay close attention to how the subjects are elucidated in the early Buddhist texts. This requires not only attending closely to the textual treatment but employing the original explanations as much as possible, and conveying them in plain English.

Moreover, no attempt is made to select what may or may not be acceptable to Western tastes in philosophy and religion, because doing so invariably distorts the original meaning and intention and defeats the purpose of trying to gain contact with the Teaching as taught. This is very much the case in our traditional presentation of the subject of Samsara, the continuous round of births and deaths of all the worlds and all the beings in those worlds. Western writers sometimes dismiss the ancient world view of the concentric system of mountains, seas, continents, heavens, and hells as so much archaic folklore having no bearing on the "core" of the Teaching. This selected core is thus presented shorn of its original context and background; unfortunately, much of the original power and cohesion is thereby neutralized. Far from helping in the necessary process of assimilation, this selective method is likely to hinder it by omitting the thrust and direction of the basic themes and so failing to convey its immediacy and personal impact to the reader. The present expositions will therefore try to preserve as much of the original material as possible.

Another special characteristic of *Fundamentals of Mainstream Buddhism* is that some of the source material is drawn from the texts of Indian Buddhism as well as from the better known scriptures in Pali. These mainland Indian Buddhist writings, including those of the great Indian master Vasubandhu, have been made accessible in recent years through translations and studies by Belgian and French scholars such as L. de la Vallée Poussin and A. Bareau. A result of this broadening of attention and source works has been the possibility of distilling a general consensus of basic Buddhist doctrine as it was understood and accepted by the majority of Indian Buddhists during the first phase of development, i.e., during the first four centuries after the Buddha's death. This whole spectrum of early Buddhism in India and Sri Lanka is referred to as Mainstream

Buddhism, though in fact the mainstream of Buddhist thought and ideals continued on through Indian Mahayana and beyond. Because this conceit of Mainstream Buddhism arises from comparatively recent scholarship, a brief explanation of what is involved is in order.

Much Western understanding of basic Buddhist teaching has been derived from English (and other) translations of Pali language scriptures that were written and preserved in Ceylon (now Sri Lanka). But as most of us know, Sakyamuni Buddha was born and died in North India, where his principal contemporaries and first followers also lived. For these immediate followers and subsequent teachers Ceylon was virtually unknown, and for several centuries after the death of the Buddha it remained so. Only during the reign of the Indian Buddhist Emperor Asoka, two and a half centuries later, did Ceylon enter Buddhist history by receiving Asoka's monk missionaries, who could recite and maintain the Dharma (teaching) and Vinaya (regimen) as accepted by Asoka's court. Those recitations and monastic disciplines have been preserved, with a degree of development and some significant breaks, until the present day.

Since the discovery of the Pali scriptures by Europeans in the 19th century, numerous other Buddhist scriptures and texts have come to light, representing the main body of Indian Buddhism centered upon the Buddhist "homeland" of North India. These have been translated into several European languages, and their historical provenance has been closely studied. The overall picture that we now have, although far from complete, shows clearly that the Pali scriptures, albeit a full and precious record of ancient teaching, are the canon of but one school of early Buddhism, called the Theravada. There were eventually at least seventeen other schools of Buddhism on the mainland, some of them older than the Theravada and having scriptural canons in the Sanskrit language of North India.

By comparative analysis of this textual material it can be shown that differing factions of the Buddhist community were diverging at very early dates, even to the extent of engaging in disputes over doctrine. Such records of events, however biased, together with the existence of other legitimate canons of scripture originating from the heartland of Buddhism in India, make it virtually impossible to accept that the canonical collection in the Pali language of the Theravada school is the only complete and exclusively valid version of the Buddha's teaching.

Fortunately for our purposes, although there are marked differences in certain matters, there is a remarkable degree of consensus about basic aims, methods, and topics among all of these original schools of Buddhism. This consensus, which will be followed wherever possible in this book, is as much a part of the "Mainstream" concept as the location and collective identity of the schools themselves. Taken as a whole, the mainland schools in particular are mainstream because all the original strands of doctrinal interpretation and later development are found in their scriptures and commentaries. When combined with the canon of the Theravadins, the mainland records preserve all the first known recitations of the Buddha's remembered words. Our treatment of basic Buddhist themes takes advantage of this wider perspective and of the accessible Indian texts that we call Mainstream Buddhism. It also uses the ancient expositions of Indian masters as well as the more familiar references in the Pali texts.

A further matter needing some comment and directly bearing on both the content and method of this book's expositions is the intrinsic strangeness to us of Oriental modes of thought and expression. This lack of ready comprehensibility is further compounded by the many warnings in the early texts that the Dharma is subtle, deep, profound, to be seen and understood only by the wise, etc. There was even some hesitation by the Buddha himself on how to teach it at all to the world. On other occasions we are told quite forcefully that our own cupidity, ignorance, and prejudice blind us to our own true situation and prevent us from acquiring the undistracted, acute concentration necessary for even a tolerable understanding of the pregnant meanings and precise directions of this Teaching.

Faced as some of us are with just fragments of this highly sophisticated and integrated teaching system, we must be constantly aware of the dangers of misconstruing its proper meaning and import simply because of our unfamiliarity with its general outlook, its suppositions, and its highly technical vocabulary. If we also attempt to disengage parts of it from the original body and then interpret the parts in our own way, we are inviting distorted views, frustrated intent, or worse. This problem of accurate comprehension is not special to our day and age. Examples of quite large-scale misunderstandings in history are now known in considerable detail. Even highly accomplished Asians of the past got it all wrong, sometimes for the same reasons that Westerners now err—i.e., because of over-selective attention to attractive fragments without due regard to the whole.

For all these reasons our approach to the Dharma in the West should always be respectful. It is not there to be plundered indiscriminately. It should be carefully investigated, as it was given and on its own terms. Before we can hope to adapt it to our modes of thought and behavior, we must first adapt to it. In this way the Dharma can perform one of its most vital functions.

Not only does the Dharma explain and teach; a knowledge of its range of contents and some understanding of its underlying intentions act as vital regulators of all practice. In other words, the "how" has always to stand in the correct relationship to the "why," the ultimate aim must constantly guide and direct the method and means.

In a very small and limited way, *Fundamentals of Mainstream Buddhism* aims to present the fundamental elements of the Dharma within this context. The book is non-specialist in that it omits all such scholarly paraphernalia as references and cross-references. The language is as straightforward as the complexity of the subject allows and the author's skill permits. At the same time the vocabulary, although non-technical, tries to reproduce the original terminology as often as possible without encumbering the exposition with over-detailed passages. To assist in this, and to facilitate relatively painless recognition of key words, the original Sanskrit or Pali terminology is frequently given in brackets and placed in the body of the narrative. There should thus be no doubt as to the intended meaning of the English phraseology.

The sequence in which the major subjects are presented attempts to preserve the original context of the Buddha's message. In Part One the ancient world view of Samsara, with its pre-Buddhist connotations of everlasting rebirth and the perceived need to find a way out of this terrible predicament, is outlined. Into this great arena of turmoil the Indian princeling was born who would achieve Buddhahood and solve the great riddle of how to live against the dark background of perpetual, repetitive existence.

Contrary to the widespread notion among Westerners that the life of the Buddha is of only passing interest when compared to the practice of the teachings, the early Indian Buddhists constantly remembered and contemplated the events of that life. For them, the principal events of the biography formed an integral part of the Teaching, as their monuments and literature testify. Again, the selection of only parts of the story and the discarding of what seem to be mere legendary intrusions deprive us of the meaning and import that emerges from the whole. To help correct this, in Part Two the author has adopted the role of an ancient story teller who, without disturbing or embellishing the story itself, pauses from time to time to draw attention to relevant features. Similar considerations apply to the fundamental teachings, which begin with the last chapter of Part Two and continue through the rest of the book. The aim is to preserve as much as possible of the original modes of expression. A fruitful re-interpretation in modern terms for modern conditions is only valid if we know with some accuracy what was really discussed and explained by the ancient Masters. It is they, after all, who knew what was necessary to come to grips with what the Buddha taught.

Parts Three and Four of this work explore the basic topics of the Buddha's teaching in some detail. This is necessary because the Buddha penetrated the innermost workings of human existence within the world system of Samsara, and having himself realized and attained release from its burdens of suffering, he then set out detailed explanations and instructions to his followers to enable them to do the same. It can hardly be expected that such a momentous achievement can be replicated by attending to a few pithy sayings and some vague generalizations. Such recondite and baffling matters as the nature and destiny of life require a precision of expression and special modes of communication even for one who has gained the answers, let alone one who seeks them. This precision of detail, set within a special mode of graduated training aimed at producing the ability to rightly understand what is expressed, is the realm of Abhidharma. This word, meaning "higher teaching" or "special teaching," is the name given to a section of the canon of scripture that contains extended explanations of the Buddha's brief or profound sayings. It also expounds critical matters with the necessary fullness. Some of the major schools of Indian Buddhism held that the separate sections of the Abhidharma were composed by recognized Arhats (those who had actually gained the goals of the Buddha's instructions), who grouped together similar topics supported by examples of the Buddha's words and then elucidated them systematically.

It does seem that the word Abhidharma arouses very mixed feelings in the minds of Western students of Buddhism. Perhaps this is because Abhidharma is thought to resemble philosophical theorizing rather than direct teaching. If so, those feelings badly misconstrue the purpose of such material. Perhaps unfamiliarity with the detail, as well as a lack of attention to the evident struggle for precision in matters that are erudite at the least, are mistaken for our own habits of hair-splitting. On the other hand, Abhidharma texts are perhaps deliberately set aside and relegated because of sheer ignorance of their real purpose. Hopefully it will be shown herein how invaluable they are to those who really want to know what the Dharma is about.

Another way of looking at the purpose of Abhidharma is to recall that the overall intention of the entire body of teaching is to provide the means to lay down the burden of suffering and to put a stop to the endless recurrences of painful existence. For this to be fully and finally achieved, the whole internal structure of each individual locked into the chain of cause and effect has to be dismantled piece by piece. The end result of this process is the demolition of the entire "house," so that the accomplished Arhat can say, as did the Buddha before him:

> Countless are the births wherein I have circled and run seeking, but not finding, the builder of the house; ill is birth again and again.
> Now thou art seen, thou builder of the house; never again shalt thou build [me] a house. All thy rafters are broken, shattered the roof-plate; my thought is divested of the samkharas; the extinction of craving has been won.
> —Dhannnapadavv.153–54
> (from "Buddhist Texts," p. 79)

The "house" whose roof is shattered is the product of countless separate actions and misconceptions. In short, the structure is complex and long-standing. To attempt demolition by brute force and ignorance invites great risk of injury without producing much impact on the structure. The building has to be examined carefully and reduced with the skill of a surveyor or architect. The effective demolition requires what we might call professional knowledge of such things as weight-bearing walls, roof beams and struts, as well as stairway construction. One does not, for example, start by removing the staircase, which would only make the upper levels more difficult to reach. For all that, one has to get inside the house as well as study whatever plans are available. Now the "plans" of all the parts and layout, as well as their method of construction and the effective sequence of demolition, are all the province and the substance of traditional Abhidharma. This being so, some present-day prejudices, based on the mistaken idea that the practice of the Dharma renders theoretical studies irrelevant and unnecessary, are ironical, to say the least. For it is in the traditional Abhidharma texts that the practices of the Path are carefully described. They are in fact the major manuals of doctrine and practice, and they specify the preliminaries required before the Path can be even approached.

The reader who now proceeds to the doctrinal sections that follow will be getting inside the structure guided by some of the ancient plans and will thus be introduced to Abhidharma topics through the detailed expositions. But a word of warning. Although the doctrinal expositions of the texts use concept and logic, what is afoot in much of the Abhidharma is reasoning founded upon intense introspective experience, following Sakyamuni's directions. Efforts are clearly made to preserve logical integrity where this does not subvert the reality of the "beyond." The detail clarifies inner processes that when mastered and perfected transcend worldly knowledge altogether and supplant it with quite another variety.

But while the plans and maps of approach are indispensable, no one in his right mind would believe that tracing the route on a map is the equivalent of travelling the terrain in person. Nevertheless, the prudent traveller consults his maps with care before he steps out in any direction. And the maps we are about to unfold and consult are like any other route map. They show the road and its stages in bold print while the features of the surrounding countryside are left indistinct and faded. The towns, the landscape, even the inhabitants are not the concern here; only the road through it all.

The exposition of the fundamentals of Mainstream Buddhism culminates with a stage-by-stage presentation of the

Path to Nirvana in five successive phases. That is followed by an outline of the ancient scheme of the three ways of attainment, in which the differences in stature and accomplishment among the Indian schools are discussed to distinguish the Buddha from the Arhat achievers who followed him. Finally, the conclusion consists of comments on the whole scheme from the perspective of today and is followed by a series of lists of certain key elements of the Path as well as a glossary and index of terms and formulas.

The question may well be asked, "How can someone who has not travelled this Path himself describe it in any worthwhile detail?" It is a fair and valid question. This book deals with the very highest levels of the religious life as conceived by Indian Buddhists in the first centuries after Sakyamuni's Parinirvana. What can any modern Western author have to say about such matters that is not mere theorizing on something that is totally beyond his own experience and knowledge? The answer is that a number of the original Indian Arhats have themselves described this Path in considerable detail, and their instructions have been preserved and handed down in manuals of doctrine and practice. These manuals, together with the sutras of the Buddha's recorded teaching, have been collated by other Indian masters for the express purpose of perpetuating the correct and verified stages of the Path. For example, the scriptural canon of the Sarvastivadins contains works accredited to Sariputra, Mapdgalyayana, and Katyayaniputra, all of them recognized Ahrats. Later on, Vasubandhu, perhaps one of the greatest of the Indian Hinayana masters of the golden age, studied and practiced under Sarvastivadin tutors so as to gain authenticity for his magnum opus, the Abidharmakosa. It is from teachers and mentors that this author draws the detail that fills the later sections of this book.

Accordingly, both the outline and detail of the Path are reformulations of the Indian doctrines themselves drawn from various sutras and suttas as well as from explanations found in Vasubandhu's *Abhidharmakosa.* The reader may know already that Vasubandu's work, which incorporates the doctrines of several schools, came to supersede almost all other Abhidharmas in mainland India soon after its appearance. It became the recognized authority on all aspects of Sarvastivadin/Vaibhasika orthodoxy as well as for many of the important variants. As such it commands our respect. This school in particular produced its own line of teaching masters, such as Sangharaksa, Sanghabhadra, and Vasumitra, as well as a reputation for the practice of dhyana and the Path of Purity. Its reputation and some of its teaching masters travelled from Kashmir into China and western Tibet, where their work did much to establish new centers of orthodox doctrine and practice. Vasubandhu's great summary of this body of diverse teaching is not only authoritative for Indian Buddhist practice in general, but in combination with the sutra texts themselves represents a consensus view of the Mainstream Indian Hinayana Buddhism this book sets out. Needless to say, the Pali commentaries, especially Buddhaghosa's *Visuddhamagga,* agree with this Mainstream consensus on major issues. Variant views and opinions on certain points are contained in such works as the *Kathavatthu* of the Pali Canon.

It has to be emphasized that the Path described herein is the Path to Nirvana culminating in the state of Arhat. It is distinct from and precedes other Paths such as the Bodhisattva Path, which belongs to a later period of Indian Buddhist doctrine. As will be seen, the whole range and orientation of the elaborated fourth noble Truth well merits its designation as the Path of

Purity. Its motivation, aims, and means are directed toward the rapid destruction of all the causes of suffering. To this end, rebirth itself is identified as the prime target, to be totally eradicated so as to bring the whole of Samsara to a stop for the successful practitioner.

Thus the Path to Nirvana requires the progressive extrication of the noble disciple from all entanglements of all the worlds. Throughout this process, his gradually purified Dharma stream becomes confined to increasingly intense meditative states within which no mundane passions and vices can gain a footing. Here, in the upper stages of the Path proper, i.e., in the Path of the Saints, the disciple reaches the level of no further training and is then within reach of the final exit, Nirvana. For such a radically purified being all the outflows of kharmic ripening are either dried up or blocked off. That particular stream of Dharmas becomes so attenuated that, for some, rebirth into our mundane realm is impossible and his last existence takes place in the meditative realms from which Nirvana is more readily accessible. Such a Path is indeed noble and admirable for its utter dedication to the route and goal first re-discovered by Sakyamuni Buddha and marked out for those desiring to pass through the "gates of the Immortal."

This Path of Purity is a matter of total dedication and a full-time occupation that supersedes all ties of blood or affection. It is impervious to half-measures, and although it begins in the ordinary surroundings of lay life, its upper levels are more readily attained within the cloister. The price of travelling this Path is high and non-negotiable, but the reward is the "jewel without price," the Deathless Nirvana.

As already stated, footnotes have been set aside in the interest of undisturbed and uncluttered attention to the subject matter. Instead of page-by-page references a list of source works is appended. These are either works used as textual authority or consulted for expert opinion on accuracy of presentation. This list of reference works and texts, incidentally, covers the entire range of Mainstream Buddhadharma, as well as the known history of its foundation and development in India.

—Eric Cheetham
1994

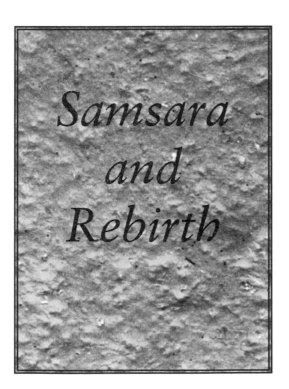

Samsara and Rebirth

P
A
R
T
·
O
N
E

1. PREVIEW

The connected topics of Samsara and rebirth are in several ways the outer gateways to the Dharma. Firstly, they were the "given" factors or general outlook that existed at the time of Sakyamuni Buddha's life and teaching in north India around 580 B.C. From a quite different point of view they are, as perceived by Indian Buddhism, the most immediate and vital matters to be considered by anyone approaching the Dharma for guidance and instruction.

Let us begin by considering Samsara and rebirth as ingredients of the worldview of Sakyamuni's India. Most readers will know that Samsara is a word denoting the mundane world, which is always characterized in Buddhist teaching by suffering, disturbance, and painful change. In recent years this word has acquired such familiarity that one can sometimes come across the phrase "this samsaric world" in books about the Dharma. It is evidently assumed that everyone knows what that means. Indeed it is very likely that the general reader will understand the phrase in the sense of "this world of suffering" and in so doing he will be correct—in part.

The meaning that the word Samsara is supposed to convey was well understood by all members of ancient Buddhist and Indian culture. For them it was part of their inherited view of the world and would require little or no further explanation; some-

3

what in the same way as the medieval European would readily comprehend the world "Christendom." However, the full meaning of Samsara needs to be laid out in detail for non-Indians, just as the intended meaning of the word Christendom needs to be explained to non-Europeans. Both words have a train of physical, geographical, ethical, and religious elements that are rarely specified.

For the inhabitants of India prior to and during Sakyamuni's lifetime, Samsara denoted the physical world of their continent, the surrounding oceans and other continents, the habitations of the gods around and above them, and the lower orders of animals and spirits. Below these were the realms of dire punishment, where evil-doers suffered the reward of their crimes in hell. Within this framework beings of all kinds passed successively through the various levels of existence by a process of transmigration controlled either naturally, by the deeds they performed, or at the will or whim of the gods.

The highest god, Brahma, was thought to be the originator or creator of the whole animated world, and he and the other gods expected and demanded offerings and worship from the humans they had created. Just as humans can be influenced or coerced by gifts of special value, so could the boons of long life, success, or progeny be enticed from the gods by special offerings at their designated altars. The knowledge of what was beloved of particular gods and the precise manner of the acceptable offering was the domain of the priesthood, and that knowledge and technique was generally considered worthy of suitable gifts to the officiating priest.

The priesthood also had what might be described as a secret weapon. It had long been believed that the gods could be compelled to certain courses of action by magical means. Naturally the priests kept this method strictly to themselves, though it was on offer to those who could afford the high price. This usually meant only kings, who richly rewarded the priesthood to ensure their victory in battle or intrigue. In such cases elaborate public or semi-public rituals were performed, whose magical words and actions literally bound the god or gods to deliver the goods.

There was another secret teaching of this early period, and this was highly prized and unknown to all but a few of the elite of priestly ascetics. This was the discovery by ancient holy men that the practice of certain rigorous meditative techniques could project a future birth into the realm of the gods. By such practices a man could in fact become a god, could even displace an already existing and "reigning" god if his concentrated meditation and purity of life were powerful enough. The supreme consummation of this process was actually taught and practiced during Sakyamuni's lifetime by an ascetic called Mahavira, who maintained that the final secret was the complete release from Samsara altogether.

A severely austere self-denial was required, for this, coupled with total inactivity and intense interior concentration, resulted in the stopping of all further transmigration. The released saint was thereafter neither human, god, nor spirit; the whole realm of Samsara was left behind and this purified essence ascended to the summit of the universe. Those who followed Mahavira's teaching became known as the Jainas and they still flourish in India today, though few of them are ascetics. These first Jainas were contemporaries of Sakyamuni Buddha, and their teachings illustrate very clearly the general climate of ideas that existed at that time.

The most important of these teachings was yoga. Yoga is so ancient in India that its origins are lost in legend and obscurity. Certainly yoga methods and philosophy were already extremely ancient in Sakyamuni's time. All the religious practices, even the priestly ritual, involved some yoga techniques, either of posture or of mental concentration. It was just such total control of bodily functions, together with refined methods of concentrating and directing the mind, that provided the instrument used to explore the realms of the gods. The Jaina ascetics used yoga techniques to an extreme degree to fulfill their ultimate aim of preventing further worldly existence and gaining such essential purity that they could rise to the summit of the universe and remain there in undisturbed bliss forever.

This supreme attainment of the Jainas took many births to accomplish, but each successive incarnation so strengthened the desire for renunciation that finally the Jaina was ready for the grim effort of his last birth. When the moment arrived the Jaina saint withdrew into total solitude, took up a standing posture naked and motionless, and remained thus without food or drink until he died. This extreme asceticism was required to prevent the karmic process of the world from flowing into his body through the senses, food, and mind. It was just these inflows of subtle substance that sustained the unending flow of repeated existences in the lower realms. These inflows had to be shut out, their traces purged for final release and ascent. The huge statues of Jaina Tirthankaras in India depict this final act of motionless self-extinction with great power.

Here, then, we have an elite vanguard ignoring the gods and their service, utterly rejecting all the known realms of existence, and by means of an extreme yogic asceticism, propelling themselves up and out of the worlds of transmigration to the very limit of the universe. Because of its purged purity, their spirit-essence remained impervious to further influence from any of the mundane processes and so enjoyed the bliss of no further existences in eternity. All this was part of the accumulated knowledge of Sakyamuni's time, and from the detail of his early biographies, it seems highly likely that he embarked on a similar course of extreme asceticism before he abandoned it to pursue his Enlightenment.

From this brief résumé of ancient Indian thought and practice it can be seen that Samsara was widely understood to involve the higher and lower realms of existence as well as humankind. It can also be seen that the ordinary man's uncertainty as to his future was to some extent relieved by service to the gods with the assistance of priest-specialists. But already the more perceptive and determined explorers of the worlds had gained the knowledge that even the most favored of human stations was unstable and liable to catastrophe, so that entry, even invasion, of the god's domain was better and more satisfying.

Despite this, the most resourceful came to believe and to demonstrate that the highest ideal of all was to get free of Samsara altogether by gaining a blissful non-existence at the top of the world. In short, the whole of Samsara in its heights and depths was accessible to human endeavor by the process of transmigration. But for some, the highest good was to stop the whole process and gain complete exit from the entire system. So much for the general outlook in Sakyamuni's time.

The other point of view concerning Samsara and rebirth falls firmly within the range of the Buddha's teaching and refers to those who wish to approach that teaching for personal assistance. In this case it is of no consequence whether one is of ancient, medieval or modern times; nor does it matter whether one is of this or that culture or society. The supreme and perfect wisdom and the direct perception of reality that Sakyamuni Buddha attained by his Enlightenment surpasses all the gods and is unaffected by time or space.

It was as a part of this exhaustive penetration of the mysteries of existence that Sakyamuni saw, without error, the whole of Samsara in all its realms, throughout its entire range in the past, the present, and the future. This immediate and total perception enabled the Buddha to correct the errors of his predecessors and his contemporaries. The true nature of Samsara was revealed to him; the gods did not create it and they did not, could not, control it. Nor was there an unchanging, indestructible essence that transmigrated.

But in its main outline, in its general structure and content, Sakyamuni's revelation was a valid picture with one overriding addition: it was far worse than any of the previous speculation and partial views had imagined. He perceived the unseen tyranny of existence in Samsara and confirmed the Jaina views concerning the imperative need for a way out. But he also saw that his forerunners in the exploration for escape were deluded into thinking they had attained it. All remained bound to repeated existence, even those at the top of the world, for although their undisturbed life spans were to be measured in immense ages, they were not and never would be free of renewed life when the reward of their efforts became exhausted.

It is of course the rebirth aspect of Samsara that was then and is now the most immediate concern at the stage of an initial approach to the Dharma. For those in the past or in the present, born into a culture where the idea of rebirth is inherent, various preliminary Dharma teachings are appropriate without further ado. Those of us not so culturally prepared need to get this ancient theme into sharp focus right at the beginning. Although the idea of rebirth is not unknown in the West, it is so often confused with reincarnation that the specifically Buddhist interpretation is difficult to extricate. At this early stage, however, the distinction between rebirth and reincarnation and the connection of rebirth to Samsara do not matter, because what is at issue is rather more general.

Crucial is the hidden and unperceived fact that our present form and circumstances of life are part of an uninterrupted series of separate existences that stretch back into the distant past and will continue on into the interminable future. It is clear that this belief was widespread in ancient India, not only among the elite ascetics, some of whom perceived their own and others' previous births, but also among the populace at large. The various teachings connected with entry into the realm of the gods, or more prosaically, the service and offerings to the gods to secure boons of good rebirth as well as mundane success, testify that the idea of rebirth was part of the fabric of society. Even the front-runners who sought the final exit recognized that a long series of interrelated human births were necessary before one could aspire to "the top floor." A constant and uninterrupted flow of beings living in the different stratified levels and passing on from one to another was of the very essence of the world-view called Samsara. The scheme of things, rewards and punishments, human conditions in high or low estate, all had their reason for existence in this cosmic flux of inter-connected events and states. The conclusive evidence of Sakyamuni Buddha's supreme Enlightenment confirmed and endorsed the essential elements of the process of Samsara and rebirth. Of course, Sakyamuni did not have to spell out the disposition of Samsara or argue the fact of rebirth; all that was common knowledge. But he certainly spelled out for all time the continuous burden of repeated birth and the possibility of laying down that burden. For Westerners, then, rebirth and its intimate connection with Samsara are far more than a cultural characteristic to be viewed at long distance.

This symbolic representation of Samsara as the Wheel of rebirth and death depicts the six destinies within the outer rim of the twelve stages of "Arising Due to Conditioning." The whole Wheel is gripped firmly by Mara the God of death.

2. Samsara
and Rebirth

What, then, is the full and extended meaning of Samsara in Buddhism, and what is the connection with rebirth? Because a considerable amount of detail is required to answer these questions, we shall first provide a brief general description and follow that with the essential detail.

According to one of the Sanskrit/English dictionaries the original or pre-Buddhist meaning of the Sanskrit word Samsara was:

> . . . going or wandering through, undergoing transmigration . . . course, passage, passing through a succession of states, circuit of mundane existence the world. . . .

The connection with rebirth is immediately apparent. The idea of wandering through the world in a succession of states or of connected lives is explicit in the definition of the word itself. A convenient metaphor that conveys the idea quite closely is that of an *arena* with *performers*.

Imagine an arena or Roman-style amphitheater with a perpetual succession of performers coming into the central area and

passing out of it after their "act" is complete. Ranks of spectators line the terraces to watch, encourage, or condemn. After
their "act," the performers pass down to the underground cellars or take their places among the spectators on the terraces.
Sometimes the performers are required to return to the arena
without a break to act out a continuous succession of activities.
At other times they descend to the cellars and to captivity in
darkness for long periods before emerging to the light again for
further exertions. If they perform well, they can take their places
among the spectators for long periods of comparative ease until
their turn comes again to descend to the cellars prior to another
bout of work in the central arena.

The arena itself is a closed structure. No one can get out of it
or away from it. All the performers are inexorably driven through
it and under it, or they enjoy temporary respite on its terraces
before resuming the center stage again and again. Ages pass, and
at intervals of enormous length natural catastrophes occur, overwhelming and destroying the amphitheater by fire, flood, or tempest. Even this does not put a final end to the constant uproar of
the continuous performances. Before each catastrophe occurs, the
whole "cast" is shepherded to a place of safe confinement to
await the rebuilding of another exactly similar amphitheater.
When all is renewed, the whole process starts again, and the cap-
tives are once more thrust out into the center, onto the terraces,
or down to the cellars to continue the interminable circuits until
the next catastrophe. And so on, to infinity.

This is a mere symbol of that terrible, awe-inspiring, never-
ending round of existence that was fully and directly perceived by
Sakyamuni Buddha during that night, long ago, when he attained
supreme and perfect Enlightenment. His contemporaries and
predecessors who had attempted the exploration of this vast

construction did not or could not get the whole picture within their focus. Some of them thought it was enough to gain the support of the spectators (the gods) to ensure an easy passage across the arena. Others thought the best thing to do was to gain a helping hand out of the center and onto the terraces (realms of the gods), or even to storm the barriers and unseat the principal spectators (Sakra, Indra, etc.). The more perceptive and discriminating observers found the goings-on nauseating and disgusting and found a way to the topmost tier of the auditorium, where the din and the dust were most distant. There they thought themselves to be safe and undisturbed, and for immense periods of time they were. But their vision was limited, and they were mistaken in believing that they had gained the ultimate heights of eternal disinvolvement. Only a Buddha can perceive the whole ghastly panorama that condemns all participants to endless cycles of repetitive performance. All that, expressed in metaphor, is in the meaning of the one word, Samsara.

THE ARENA OF THE STRUCTURE AND DURATION OF THE WORLD-SYSTEM (LOKADHATU)

Now let us add the traditional details, first of the structure of the so-called arena with its physical components and its periods of endurance and repeated dissolutions. Details of the denizens of the various realms will then follow, as will a description of their appearance and lengths of life. These denizens are the so-called performers.

The Structure

Imagine a circular, flat-bottomed pan, rather like a frying pan with no handle. The pan bottom consists of ocean waters, and at the outer edge of the pan rise concentric circles of mountain ridges interspersed with seas. The outermost rim (the lip of the frying pan) is a circular range of mountains, higher than the other, inner, ranges and enclosing the whole area. From the center of the pan rises a single gigantic mountain peak dwarfing all the rest. This is *Mount Meru,* or Sumeru, the pivot or axis of the world and abode of the gods.

Disposed at each of the cardinal points around Mount Meru are the *Four Continents.* Starting at the southern area, the continent of Jambudvipa, triangular shaped, with the *Himalaya* range of mountains marking its northern boundary. The legendary *Lake Anavatapta r*ests high up in the mountains near the base of Mount Meru. This southern continent is what we know as India.

In the eastern direction is the continent called Purvavideha, which is shaped as a half moon. In the western direction is *Godaniya,* a continent in the shape of the full moon. In the northern direction is the continent of *Uttarakuru,* which is square in shape. All four continents are inhabited by humans of various types and colors.

Below the surface of Jambudvipa, and plunging to unfathomable depths, are the *Eight Tiers of Hell.* Here there are sixteen abodes of dire retribution: eight tiers of hot burning torment side by side with eight cold, freezing abodes. The lowest and the worst of the hot hells is *Avici,* said to be 20,000 leagues under Jambudvipa.

Returning to Mount Meru, we find that the topmost peak is terraced. This is the heaven of the *Caturmaharaja* (the four Great Kings), sometimes called the Protectors of the Dharma. *Sun and Moon* revolve around the peak, shedding light and heat by day and cool illumination by night.

Higher still, on the summit itself, is the highest physical heaven, called *Trayastrimsa* (Heaven of the Thirty-Three). Here lives Sakra, king of the lower gods. Above the summit are four more "aerial" heavens, the first and the lowest of which is *Yama*. Above that is the *Tusita*, the heaven where Maitreya resides. Here all the final-stage Bodhisattvas arrive before embarking upon their last birth into Jambudvipa, where they attain supreme Enlightenment. Above that again is the heaven of the *Nirmanavati*, while highest of all the "aerial" heavens is *Paranirmitavasavarti*.

All these locations—from the hells, continents, and mountains up to Mount Meru with its plume of aerial heavens—make up the realm of all the passions, called *Kamadhatu*. This huge composite of lower heaven, earth, and the nether regions is the first and lowest of the three-layer configuration that in total comprises this whole world-system (this Saha-World or Lokadhatu).

The second of the three layers starts above the highest aerial heaven and is called *Rupadhatu* (Realm of Form). It consists of seventeen separate heavens in ascending order and falls into four sections, which correspond exactly with the four *dhyanas* (jhanas in Pali), or meditative absorptions. The first three sections corresponding to the first three dhyanas have three distinct heavens each, while the fourth and highest dhyana has eight heavens, the topmost being the *Akanistha*, which is the peak of the second layer, Rupadhatu. It is among these heavens of the four dhyanas, in Rupadhatu, that the king of all the gods, Brahma, is found.

Surmounting the second layer is the third, called *Arupyadhatu* (Realm of No Form). In this most remote and ethereal region are four heavens. The first, and lowest, is *Akasanantyayatana* (Realm of Continuous Space). Above that

15

is the *Vijnananantyayatana* (Realm of Continuous Consciousness). Thirdly, and higher again, is the *Akimcanyayatana* (Realm of Continuous Nothingness). Fourthly, and highest of all, is the *Naivasamjnanasamjnayatana* (Realm of Neither Perception Nor Non-Perception). This last is also referred to as *Bhavagra*, the it is the outermost limit of the Universe, beyond is nothing other than further, similarly constructed universes vast distances away in each of the ten directions of space.

These three realms or layers of Kamadhatu, Rupadhatu, and Arupyadhatu are often referred to as the *Tri-dhatu* (*Three Realms*). The word *Tri-dhatu*, or *Tridhatuka* (*Belonging to the Three Realms*), is regularly used as a synonym for Samsara. The Tri-dhatu with all their stratified levels are the amphitheater, the arena, the closed structure within which and through which everything happens and repeats itself over and over again.

Duration

The Buddhist assertion that impermanence (anityata) governs all things and beings applies also to the very structure of the world-system. Not only are the various component realms of limited duration, the whole three-tiered universe is periodically destroyed and renewed. Staggering time scales are applied to these events. In some cases, to calculate according to the formulas given produces figures of millions of years. The subtlety of the scheme is that the inhabitants of long-lasting realms of the gods also have long spans of life, and for them terrestrial time is experienced in expanded form to match. Their days and nights, for example, last for hundreds of years each in our earthly time. The end result is that all beings in the system follow the same pattern of existence; they are born, grow and develop, decline, and finally die, thereafter producing further patterns. And always, because the arc of birth and death is constant in all the realms, the perpetual change and loss produces distress and suffering, intense and savage in some of the lower orders, far less so with the gods. Even with the gods, however, the final decline and fall from the heavenly abodes is pitiful.

Ancient Indian time periods, including the Buddhist, differ from ours in the computation of the year and the months. They also differed by using a large scale unit to measure (or rather to describe) immense eons of time. This unit is called the *kalpa*. The kalpa is said to consist of 320 million years. It is subdivided into *Antarakalpas*, which last 16 million years each, so that there are twenty antaras to one kalpa. The largest unit of time is the *Mahakalpa*, which is said to comprise four kalpas, or 1,280 million years.

The whole world-system is said to last for three kalpas, which is the equivalent of 960 million years. A partial destruction occurs after every kalpa. Although these vast stretches of time are difficult for us to grasp, they are not so very different from modern conceptions of geological and planetary time scales. The partial destructions occur regularly and are preceded or presaged by certain signs and conditions. As the end of the kalpa approaches, the length of human life spans diminishes and there are prolonged periods of widespread war, famine, and disease. The actual mode of destruction and collapse involves three of the basic elements. The most frequent mode of destruction is by fire. Out of the regular cycle of sixty-four destructive sequences, fire occurs forty-nine times. The other fifteen are by flood and wind.

Much of the detail is too complicated to concern ourselves with here, but the gist of it is that war, famine, and disease engulf first the continent of Jambudvipa and then the other continents in succession. These catastrophes depopulate the human world, whose inhabitants are all reborn into Rupadhatu (Realm of Form). The animal and infernal realms follow suit, swelling the ranks of the gods of the heaven worlds of the higher dhyanas. Soon after this, seven suns appear in the sky, one after the other, until all seven are blazing together. At that point the continents, the seas, and even Mount Meru ignite; everything roars into flame. The whole of Kamadhatu, up to and including the realms of the lower god and the heavens of the first dhyana, are totally consumed by fire. Then there is a long pause.

When the natural world recovers its old form, as it always does, the higher gods whose life span has expired begin to be reborn again into the continents as humans of five thousand years duration. Gradually the mode of life coarsens in regard to food, sensation, and activity as the new kalpa proceeds, and in consequence human life span shortens.

Soon animal life reappears, and infernal realms are reconstituted, as retribution demands, until all is restored as before, until the next disintegration. If the end of kalpa destruction is by flood, then all is reduced up to and including the second dhyana of Rupadhatu. In the most severe case, destruction by wind, everything is demolished up to and including the third dhyana. Thus the superior gods of the fourth dhyana and those of the unconscious realm are left untouched. These upper realms are only reduced in the unimaginable cataclysm of the end of the Mahakalpa.

Thus it can be seen that the first part of the ancient Buddhist credo, "All formations are impermanent . . . ," is meant to apply literally to the entire universe with all its inhabitants and even its very physical structure.

THE PERFORMERS OR THE MODES OF EXISTENCE (GATIS)

We now turn to the various classes of beings who exist within this stratified world of three layers. It is perhaps more accurate to describe their modes of existence at different levels of the strata. The distinction is important, because whereas the conditions that obtain at each stratum remain constant within limits, the beings who reside there are only passing through and will in time experience the mode of life of all the strata, from the highest to the lowest. Whichever way we look at it, these are the *performers* who wander up and down the tiers of the Tri-dhatu structure.

The Destinies (Gatis)

Five kinds of existence (sometimes six) are possible within the closed structure of the Tri-dhatu, the so-called arena. Proceeding from the upper tiers to the lower, there are the *gods* (deva), sometimes with a sub-class of gods called the *Asuras*, who are always at war with each other. As we have seen, a variety of gods inhabit the upper levels of Mount Meru through the whole realm of Rupadhatu to the highest realms of the Arupyadhatu. At the terrestrial level there are *humans* (manusa), *animals* (tiryak), and *disembodied spirits* (preta), which roam about cemeteries and wild places. Below the surface of the earth are the two classes of *infernal beings* (naraka), either hot or cold.

All five or six are open to any being of any class by rebirth. The determining factor producing rebirth from one particular class into any other is the quality of the karmically reproductive seeds in the being about to die. More will be said about this process later. One exception to this general principle are humans who gain temporary residence in the heavens by meditational practice and yogic techniques. Another exception concerns humans who, again by employing yogic techniques, acquire so-called magic powers (rddhis) and project a subtle replica of themselves into any of the modes of existence. As with the meditational techniques, these visitations are temporary and involve considerable risk to the unwary.

Among the five or six modes of existence are *four kinds of birth*. The first is birth from the womb, as is the case with humans and other mammals. Second is birth from an egg, as is the case with birds and reptiles, while third is birth from moisture, as with worms and flies. Last is apparitional birth, the simple appearance in a body of attenuated elements without an intermediary, as with some of the gods, the disembodied spirits, and the intermediate beings between death and rebirth.

Sexual activity resulting in womb-birth remains a feature of the heavens of the lower gods in Kamadhatu. These gods enjoy the sexual favors of the *Apsarases*, female goddesses of stunning beauty and superb musical and amorous skills. Children born of such unions are said to arrive developed to the equivalent of five or six years old. When they have time to spare from dalliance with the captivating Apsarases, the gods of the Heaven of the Thirty-Three (on top of Mount Meru) are said to observe the behavior of men and other beings. Sakra and his retinue review the actions of men below on a regular basis. This accounts for the many instances in the Buddhist sutras where the gods intervene in worldly affairs. It should in fact be remembered that it was the gods who first knew that the Buddha had attained his Enlightenment; they had even helped the struggling Bodhisattva at certain critical points in his career.

Duration of Life

Lengths of life vary enormously between the various modes of existence, and their variations further depend on the degree of an individual's progress through the three kalpa life span of the world-system. It is all rather complex, but a few examples will illustrate comparative life expectancies.

At the early phase of the new kalpa, humans live for an incredible 80,000 years. This span shortens progressively as the kalpa proceeds until life lasts for a hundred years or less.

The life spans of animals are not specified, so that they may be presumed to be short and unpleasant.

Pretas have life spans extending over thousands of years.

Infernal beings suffering the punishments of hell have lives lasting from thousands of years in the lesser abodes up to millions of years in the great hells such as Avici.

The gods of Kamadhatu, i.e., those living on the terraces of Mount Meru or in the aerial domains immediately above it, have lives lasting 500 or 1,000 years on the mountain, or up to 16,000 years in the aerial regions.

The gods of Rupadhatu in the first dhyana have a life span of 160 million years and have bodies measuring half a league. Those in the other three dhyanas live up to 640 million years and have bodies measuring 250 leagues.

The lives of the gods of Arupyadhatu outlast the material part of the world-system of living, They live for the full span of the Mahakalpa and have "bodies" extending to 1,000 leagues.

The Lower Destinies (Durgati) or the Fall to Lower States

Before leaving this section on the modes of existence in Samsara, we must emphasize an aspect of rebirth that is clearly part of the Buddha's teaching but that has been set aside or glossed over in some Western interpretations. This concerns the possibility of humans falling into the lower destinies of animals, pretas, or hell-beings after death. The Dharma across its whole range is quite unambiguous on this matter. Humans can and do descend to the lower destinies after death if their past and present deeds so warrant.

Here we have another case where selective exposition ignores unpalatable elements and can misrepresent the Teaching as given. Whatever we may think of this aspect of the Teaching, whether we dislike it or disown it, it is clear and unmistakable. A few examples may suffice:

In the *Anguttara Nikava* in Pali we find the Buddha explaining to his monks that just as there are few pleasant parks, groves, and lakes in India and many dense jungles, precipitous mountains, and raging rivers, there are just as few cases of men being reborn as men. Far more numerous are the cases of men being reborn as animals and hell-beings.

In the *Majjhima Nikaya* in Pali we find the Buddha telling Sariputra that he, the Buddha, knows and comprehends five destinies open to humans after death and the break up of the body. They are the destinies of hell, animals, disembodied spirits, men, and gods. After death, and according to one's present quality of life, rebirth takes place in any of the five.

In the *Sutta Nipata*, one of the most ancient texts of the Pali Canon, we read the Buddha telling Puma that for those having wrong views one of two things are in store, either rebirth in hell or as an animal.

A later Pali text, *The Stanzas of Dharmika Subhut*i, which derives from a Sanskrit original said to be composed by Asvagosha, specifies in great detail the retributive rebirth that follows from various human actions. Thirty-two verses are devoted to human activities resulting in rebirth in hell. They reveal that seven kinds of action produce rebirth as animals and contain fifteen verses on rebirth as disembodied spirits.

The great Mahayana master Nagarjuna wrote what he called the "Friendly Epistle" to his patron the king, in which he sets out the "good life" and warns of the dire consequences of wrongdoing. Three of these verses tell of human actions that result in an animal rebirth.

Finally from this brief selection, in the Tibetan glossary of Sanskrit terms called the *Mahavyutpatti* there are quoted 127 different types of animal destinies reserved for evil men.

The Decline of the Dharma

The last of the teachings concerning duration of life is the life span of the Dharma itself and the eons that produce Buddhas in the world and those that do not.

Of the successive eons (kalpa) comprising the continuous life of the world-system, the Bhadra kalpa, or auspicious eon, is especially favorable for the birth and teaching of a Buddha. During the 320 million years of this kalpa, as many as 1,000 Buddhas will appear in succession. We are now supposed to be living in such a Bhadra kalpa, and the last Buddha, Sakyamuni, has been preceded by other Buddhas and will be succeeded by many more. Next to appear will be Maitreya, who even now resides in the Tusita heaven (one of the aerial realms of the gods of Kamadhatu) awaiting the right time to descend to his chosen birth in India. Then he will repeat the life cycle of the previous Buddhas, achieve full Enlightenment at the very same spot under a Bodhi tree, teach his Dharma, establish a new Samgha, and pass away into Nirvana.

23

It follows from this that the other kalpas are either totally devoid of Buddhas or have immense periods without any. And as the Dharma of each successive Buddha follows a regular pattern of decline and total disappearance, so it is that such kalpas are without any trace of Dharma for equally immense periods. Not only are the other kalpas without Buddhas and without Dharma, but *this* kalpa has long periods when the Dharma of the last Buddha has died out and the new Buddha has not yet appeared to rediscover it.

This brings us to the three-stage decline of each and every Dharma dispensation. After each Buddha gains full Enlightenment, he teaches the same doctrine and practices as all his predecessors have, thus re-opening the Way. He guides his many followers to the full realization of the fruits of the practice and ensures the transmission of the Teaching after his death. This period is called *Saddharma* and involves purity of practice and actual attaining of its full results. This is the time when Arhats abound and the promise of the fruit of the Path can be be fulfilled in this one life. The length of this first period is variously given as 500, 1,000, or even 5,000 years.

The second period is called the *Counterfeit Dharma* (pratirupaka Dharma) and follows immediately upon the end of the first. At this stage the sutra texts (the records of the Teaching and the means of transmission) are lost or ignored. The practice becomes mixed, partly valid and in accord with the Teaching and partly not. Consequently, the proper fruits of the practice are not realized. Although practice continues, there is an inability to achieve the right result. Full realization therefore becomes very rare, and the Teaching itself becomes inaccessible and constantly open to misinterpretation. This second period is said to last for varying lengths of time, sometimes 500, 1,000, or even 5,000 years.

Then comes the *Final Period* (pascima Dharma). During this stage the sutra texts disappear altogether, doctrinal squabbles ensue, and there is little practice. The remaining practice is unsupported by any Teaching and so fades out due to uncertainties of aims and methods. At the end of this third period all Dharma is lost. The texts have disappeared or are inaccessible, the teaching lines have died out, and no one can remember a word of Dharma. Even the name Dharma at last fades from memory. The long era of waiting begins. And while the waiting lasts there is no way out of Samsara. The "gates of the immortal" quietly and firmly close, and a new Buddha is needed to re-discover the lost Way and re-open them.

3. Review

N ow this detailed picture of Samsara and rebirth can be considered as a whole. From this perspective, these two related topics occupy a vitally important place in the integrated scheme of the Dharma (Teaching).

Let us begin with the negative or dark side of the subject. Sakyamuni Buddha, before his Enlightenment, chose birth into the ancient Indian society that already had a consensus of given knowledge about the structure of the universe. This was peopled by gods, men, and lower beings who transmigrated up and down through the various levels. Some of the more persistent and sensitive religious leaders and philosophical explorers were repelled by the prospect of interminable bondage to an ultimately pointless succession of existences, and they became convinced that they had found a way out. By extremes of yogic discipline and self-extinction, they probed to the very limits of the world-structure, beyond even the abodes of the highest gods. There, at the top of the world, they achieved a quasi-eternal state of peaceful bliss, separated from the turmoil and the suffering of the lower realms. This, for them, was the highest good, the true goal of religion, and the only safe haven.

The Buddha's years of search prior to his Enlightenment led him first of all to teachers of this kind. They instructed him in the techniques necessary to attain these highest abodes of peace. But once he had mastered them, he found they were wanting in the critical matter of impermanence; he decided they were not a final, stable, or reliable refuge from infinitely repeated existences. Only when he gained the supreme and unsurpassed wisdom and knowledge under the Bodhi tree did he penetrate the full dimensions of Samsara. Only then did he know for certain that he had laid bare the innermost workings of the world-process and that he was free of it forever. In the brilliant, steady light of full comprehension the Buddha saw directly ". . . as if there were two houses with doors and a man with vision standing between them might see people entering . . . and leaving . . . and going back and forth. . . ." In his insight, he perceived that all, even those in the highest abodes of bliss, were subject to repeated rebirth, even though their lives might last for many millennia. Samsara was thus worse than the earlier masters had thought. Even the great cataclysm at the end of the Mahakalpa was only a pause in the never-ending flood of birth and death.

The flood is a very suitable simile for the onward roaring tempest of Samsara. The Buddha sometimes described his Teaching as a safe crossing to the other shore on a strong raft. On other occasions he referred to the need for his monks to be islands unto themselves. Undoubtedly the early Teaching to his first disciples was concerned with how to put a definitive end to the rebirth process, how to escape finally and safely from the flood of Samsara. His first five converts after the initial preaching at the Benares Deer Park all became Arhats. All were in their last birth, whose substrate of rebirth is destroyed.

Samsara, then, consisting of a three-layered structure with five or six realms of living beings, is in a constant state of turmoil, anguish, and tumultuous onward flow. Without pause, beings are passing through human, godlike, or punishment realms, mostly without any idea of what is happening to them. Ignorance of their condition and of the causes that underlie it fuels the process and prevents these beings from recognizing their terrible plight. Viewed across its whole length and depth, Samsara is thus a gigantic cosmic flood of events, of beings heaving and tumbling in perpetual pandemonium. Yet within the seeming confusion all is strictly governed by mysterious internal forces that determine repeating patterns of growth, decline, and dissolution.

Many times the Buddha spoke to his monks on this topic, and the tenor of his remarks was always the same; always he emphasized the enormity of the burden that each one of us unknowingly carries. Once while at Sravasti he told his monks that Samsara is a world without end or beginning. Not all the sticks and twigs of the Indian continent could equal the number of mothers and fathers one man has had in his long series of existences. Another time he said it was not easy to find a being who has not formerly been one's mother, father, brother, sister, son, or daughter. Then to stress the point he said that each of his monks had shed floods of tears for misery and disease, tears greater in volume than the waters of all the oceans. Finally, he said, the cairn of bones resulting from one man's innumerable deaths in only one kalpa would rise as high as Vulture Peak mountain at Rajagrha.

The effect of bringing this great panorama into clear view can at first be quite shattering. Even an intimation of the extent of one's past existences can suddenly be felt as a crushing burden. The endless prospect of future passage through the lower realms, even if punctuated by pleasant interludes among the

Apsarases, can produce moments of paralyzing fear. What must it be like, then, to become aware of the same fate awaiting all beings, even the gods themselves?

European civilization is not entirely without hints of this cosmic drama. The final scenes of the burning of Valhalla in the "Twilight of the Gods" from the legends of the Ring of the Nibelungen, so powerfully re-created in Wagner's opera, seem to stir ancestral memories of the far older Indian ideas. Once seen or even dimly perceived the need to escape becomes paramount. In its original basic outline, that is just what the Buddha's teaching is, a Way of escape from such bondage, a Way to put an end to Samsara, a Way to the Nirvana that supervenes when Samsara is eventually switched off. Existence becomes a nightmare from which one awakes, or a horror film in which one is the eternal victim but which is suddenly stopped dead in its tracks. All attempts to cross this Flood must begin by perceiving, understanding, and being aware of the fact of the Flood itself. This is the beginning of the "right views" that arouse energy, resolve, and preparation.

This leads us to the positive or bright side of this picture. Once the whole of the dark aspect is brought into view, the sense and sanity of the Way of release is clear, and its attraction is potent. Most importantly, one understands what it means to be human, to be living in the Bhadra kalpa of 1,000 Buddhas, to have made contact with the Dharma of the most recent Buddha, Sakyamuni, and now to have the flood of Samsara and rebirth spelled out in detail. The knowledge of all that can serve as a seed of future effort or as a spur to effort already undertaken. Effort for what? Effort to secure relief from the burden and to turn toward the means of achieving that relief.

For the doctrine and practice of the Buddhadharma has just

that as its first-degree purpose. Relief from the burden is not the whole story by any means, but the primary requirement is the knowledge of how things really stand for us. That knowledge, once gained and assimilated, converts to energy (a convertible currency!), to motivation and stamina for seeking out and taking hold of the Teaching that was delivered and preserved for this very purpose.

The knowledge that triggers off that energy and motivation is locked up in the extended meaning of a single Sanskrit word, Samsara. Samsara is a key term in Buddhist teaching. But there are many other such key terms in the original languages of the Buddhadharma, all of them having extensive meanings and related motivations locked up in single words or short phrases that need to be opened up and laid out. All this was well understood by the ancient Indian masters but sadly is often misunderstood in Western circles. The widespread reluctance and resistance to considering the purpose and content of special terminology is still a noticeable characteristic of modern Western opinion (with a few honorable exceptions) on Buddhist exposition. Somehow the terminology is seen as an adjunct to scholarship; scholarship to word chopping; and word chopping to dead-end philosophy. The current insistence on simple, preferably single syllable words as equivalents for Sanskrit or Pali "power-pack terms" is bordering on the foolish and is certainly self-depriving. As we have seen, it is impossible to suggest a simple English word for Samsara that conveys all of its dimensions. And the sooner we realize that it is not only impossible but highly undesirable to try to find such a word, the better we can be on the lookout for such special words and their powerful locked up meanings.

Throughout this book other key terms will emerge and display some of their content. Such special terms must stand out in high relief and must not be submerged and lost among their fellows. For those of us who read and study Dharma as part of its practice, the recognition of key terms and consideration of their contents is an indispensable factor in acquiring more of the knowledge convertible into energy. It is just this combination that slowly builds, with other ingredients, into that very special Buddhist quality, Wisdom (prajna). All this is the positive, bright aspect of the full, vast, and terrifying image contained in the word Samsara.

It is interesting to see in some early Buddhist Pali texts that there were doubters then, even when confronted by the Buddha "in person." Just as now, none of us knows certainly and infallibly that there is such a thing as rebirth, let alone that there exists the intimidating paraphernalia of the Indian world-system. And we have no immediate means at our disposal to verify it. However, as a Pali text of the *Majjhima Nikaya* has it, an intelligent man can reflect on it and liken the situation to placing a wager or throwing the dice. In either case no certain verification or forecast is possible in advance.

This text also records that the Buddha visited the village of Sala and conversed with Brahmin householders. He posited the case of an intelligent man who observes and listens to various teachers, some of whom say there are no existences for man other than the present one. Other teachers say that future life exists and that right behavior now secures future advantage. In this case the Buddha discounts those Arhats and ascetics who have realized and perceived the continuous chain of existences "through the higher knowledge" and does not offer his own direct confirmation. Here he adopts the standpoint of the ordinary man who is naturally skeptical or who just is unaware that such "higher knowledge" exists. The Buddha argues that whether there is rebirth or not it is better to wager that there is. To behave well, whether or not we assume an afterlife reward, is to be happier and of good repute in the present life. Even if there is no afterlife, such a man loses nothing after death. If there is an afterlife he will certainly gain. The opposite course brings troubles and ill-repute in the present life, and if there is an afterlife, he is reborn in a lower destiny of punishment. The man with the "lucky throw" is the one who, not knowing for certain, "puts his money on" those who teach the rewards of an afterlife. Such a man behaves well; it so happens he believes in what is really the case; and he enjoys the respect of others. After death he will be reborn in the heavens and avoid the realms of punishment.

Of course, that is a clever simplification, and simplifications, if based on ignorance, are invariably dangerous, especially in such weighty matters. In his wisdom, however, the Buddha was putting up a simple argument in favor of individual safety in the face of an uncertain and potentially threatening situation. The argument should not be lost on us.

In the next part, this book will convey the story of Sakyamuni's life, with detail and anecdotes from traditional sources, against the background of this concept of Samsara. Perhaps some of legendary, and therefore questionable, incidents and circumstances of his life will take on meaning in the context that he too had to enter the same arena as everyone else. And once he appeared in the center of that arena, the gods at least had some idea of what was afoot. Just as in the last act of a gripping drama the audience is hushed into rapt expectancy, the gods watching from the "terraces" followed every move with attention. Some of them called out admonition and encouragement and even intervened at critical points to ensure the central character's success. But one of the most powerful gods was implacably opposed and missed no opportunity to raise obstacles.

As straightforward epic drama, Sakyamuni's life is unsurpassed, but there is much more to this story than mere entertainment. The times had ripened to the point where another Conqueror (Jina) could take the field, once more search out the Gates of the Immortal, and show the Way for those able to follow.

DIAGRAMMATIC SCHEME OF THE WORLD SYSTEM (LOKADHATU, TRI-DHATU)

In this diagram of the three-layered world structure, all the locations are given their Sanskrit names, some of which will be familiar and some not. The diagram is intended to supplement the descriptions given in the sections on the arena and the performers. It may also be of some service in identifying particular locations when they are referred to in other works on this subject.

ENGLISH EQUIVALENTS OF SANSKRIT NAMES

Bhavagra: Highest existence

Naivasamjnanasamjnayatana: Realm of neither perception
          nor non-perception

Akimcanyayatana: Realm of continuous nothingness

Vijnananantyayatana: Realm of continuous consciousness

Akasanantyayatana: Realm of continuous space

Akanistha: Supreme heaven

Sudarsana: Perfect vision

Sudrsa: Perfect form

Atapa: Heatless

Avrha: Passionless

Brhatphala: Great results

Punyaprasara: Fortunate progress

Anabhraka: Cloudless

Subhakrtsna: Universal beauty
Apramanasubha: Infinite beauty
Paritifasubha: Lesser beautv
Abhasvara: Universal light
Apramanabha: Infinite light
Parittabha: Lesser light
Mahabrahman: Great Brahma
Brahmapurohita: Brahma-serving
Brahmakayika: Brahma-bodied
Paranirmitavasavarti: Dominant over transformations
Nirmanarati: Pleasure in transformations
Tusita: Contented
Yama: [Proper name of a god]
Trayastrimsa: Thirty-three
Caturmaharaja: Four Great Kings
Uttarakuru: [Name of northern continent]
Purvavideha: [Name of eastern continent]
Jambudvipa: Island of jambu [name of India]
Godaniya: [Name of western continent]

HOT HELLS	COLD HELLS
Samjiva: Constant revival	*Arbuda*: Swelling
Kalasutra: Black chain	*Nirarbuda*: Shrinking
Samghata: Stone slabs	*Atata*: Teeth-chattering cold
Raurava: Howling	*Hahava*: Shivering cold
Maharaurava: Great howling	*Huhuva*: Shuddering cold
Tapana: Burning heat	*Utpala*: Bursting
Pratapana: Fiery lake	*Padma*: Lotus
Avici: Uninterrupted	*Mahapadma*: Great Lotus

The World System

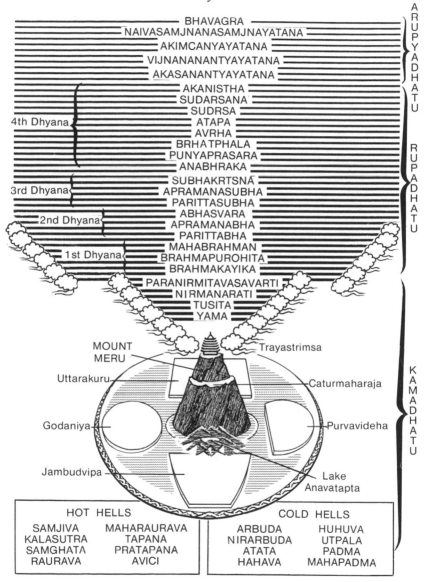

BHAVAGRA
NAIVASAMJNANASAMJNAYATANA
AKIMCANYAYATANA
VIJNANANANTYAYATANA
AKASANANTYAYATANA

ARUPYADHATU

AKANISTHA
SUDARSANA
SUDRSA
4th Dhyana — ATAPA
AVRHA
BRHATPHALA
PUNYAPRASARA
ANABHRAKA

3rd Dhyana — SUBHAKRTSNA
APRAMANASUBHA
PARITTASUBHA

2nd Dhyana — ABHASVARA
APRAMANABHA
PARITTABHA

1st Dhyana — MAHABRAHMAN
BRAHMAPUROHITA
BRAHMAKAYIKA

RUPADHATU

PARANIRMITAVASAVARTI
NIRMANARATI
TUSITA
YAMA

MOUNT MERU — Trayastrimsa
Uttarakuru — Caturmaharaja
Godaniya — Purvavideha
Jambudvipa — Lake Anavatapta

KAMADHATU

HOT HELLS		COLD HELLS	
SAMJIVA	MAHARAURAVA	ARBUDA	HUHUVA
KALASUTRA	TAPANA	NIRARBUDA	UTPALA
SAMGHATA	PRATAPANA	ATATA	PADMA
RAURAVA	AVICI	HAHAVA	MAHAPADMA

The Life
of
Sakyamuni
Buddha

PART TWO

4. Preparations

As we have seen in the discussion of Samsara and rebirth, the appearance of a Buddha in the world is an event that has occurred before and will occur again. Even so, the vast stretches of time involved in each of the kalpas means that, although one thousand successive Buddhas will appear in our present favorable kalpa, there are long intervals between these Buddhas when the Teaching has died out and nothing of it remains.

If we recall that one kalpa lasts for over 300 million years, even a succession of one thousand Buddhas, equally spaced, would produce intervals of 300,000 years between each. Given that the Teaching of Sakyamuni Buddha will decline in three equal stages of 500, 1,000, or perhaps even 5,000 years, we are still left with a minimum "empty" period of 285,000 years. Even if we assume that the Bhadra (favorable) kalpa refers to an "antarakalpa" of only 16 million years, one of the empty intervals between a Buddha and his Teaching is large enough to swallow all of our recorded history and prehistory as well. This would be the minimum case of 1,000 Buddhas appearing successively over 16 million years, producing equal gaps of 16,000 years. The three-stage decline of the Dharma after each Buddha in, say, 1,000-year stages would leave us with intervals of 13,000 years with no Dharma at all.

It is notoriously difficult to be precise in matters of this kind, and even in the two possibilities given above there are unanswered questions. Are we right, for example, to assume equal intervals between each Buddha? Whatever the right calculations may be, we can be certain that all authorities affirm the existence of enormous stretches of time during the life of a world-system when no Buddhas appear and no Dharma at all survives from the previous dispensation. From such a perspective the ancient texts do not exaggerate when they tell us that the appearance of Buddhas is a rare event, and that to live in an era when their Teaching is accessible is equally rare.

There is another aspect to this rarity. The attainment of Buddhahood is not a matter of a single lifetime's effort. As we shall see, Sakyamuni attained full Enlightenment at about the age of thirty-five, having begun his homeless life about six years earlier. We would be very much mistaken, however, if we imagined that Enlightenment was gained by this Indian prince of rather sensitive but determined character in a mere seven years of even the most arduous and dedicated striving.

No real understanding of the final achievement of Enlightenment is possible unless the immense preparation over eons of time is taken into account. The beginning of the chain of events and experience that culminated under the Bodhi tree goes back, not just beyond our present kalpa, but beyond the origin of the present world-system of three kalpas. The explanatory works of Indian Buddhist masters make it plain that at least three incalculable eons are required to bring to proper maturity a being capable of full and complete Enlightenment. An incalculable eon (asamkheva kalpa) is described as a period required for the appearance of at least 75,000 Buddhas. And it takes three of these!

Sakyamuni himself emphasized this when recounting how he gained the first of the special super-knowledges of his En-lightenment. In the Pali account of the *Majjhima Nikaya* he says:

> I remembered my former existence such as
> one birth [up to] a hundred thousand births;
> many cycles of dissolution of the universe,
> many of its evolution, many of its dissolution
> and evolution. . . .

Armed with some idea of what is involved in these "cycles" (see Part One), we can appreciate the immensity of time and past experience intended to be conveyed. This is just one of the awesome powers of an Enlightened Buddha, and examples of his immense "hindsight" are recorded throughout the range of the ancient texts. All of this means that the attainment of full and perfect Enlightenment by each successive Buddha is the crowning achievement of a vast and immeasurable sequence of existences, all intent upon the ultimate goal and all advancing toward it over enormous tracts of time and through innumerable forms and stages of life. Perhaps the most striking example of one of the earliest stages of this grand march up the evolutionary scale is the occasion when Sakyamuni Buddha explained why he sometimes smiles. After observing the activity of certain insects he said:

> From generation to generation I have
> hitherto been a poor little insect, but little by
> little I accumulated good roots and I have now
> attained to the great wisdom and I have

become a Buddha. . . . All beings can also
become as I am.

A whole corpus of very ancient texts called *Jatakas* have
been put together from the scattered anecdotes of Sakyamuni's
previous existences. In these Sakyamuni tells how he was once a
lion, an elephant, a monkey, an antelope, a peacock, a hare, a
dog, and other animals. During all this time he accumulated
"good roots." These stories have sometimes been described by
Western writers as mere legends for the entertainment and edification of illiterate peasantry. Doubtless they were so used, but
they also formed part of the well-understood progress of a being
who, from the most far reaching depths of time, moved on, existence after existence, toward that final consummation under the
Bodhi tree.

It is against such a background that the life story of
Sakyamuni Buddha should be seen. Indeed, it is only within such
a context that all the traditional elements of that life can be
understood in their true light. As we proceed to unfold the
recorded sequence of those events, this background should be
borne in mind. This way, many of the so-called legendary and
mythical parts of the story can reveal their intended implications. As a consequence, Sakyamuni's life will be seen to be not
just history but sacred biography.

THE LINEAGE OF PREVIOUS BUDDHAS

We see, then, that many Buddhas have appeared before
Sakyamuni and many will follow him. In certain older texts we
find eight Buddhas mentioned by name: Dipamkara, Vipasyin,
Sikhin, and Visvabhu of an earlier kalpa, and Krakucchanda,
Kanakamuni, Kasyapa, and the latest, Sakyamuni, in the present

kalpa. In other texts twenty-five previous Buddhas are named, including Pusya and an ancient Sakyamuni of a long past kalpa.

It is in the time of a previous kalpa, during the life of the Buddha Dipamkara, that a crucial point was reached in the development of the being who eventually became our Buddha, Sakyamuni. The story is told in several texts, but the Indian teacher Asvaghosa (circa second century A.D.) gives much of the detail in his work called the *Buddhacarita*. The outline of the incident is that a wandering scholar called Megha (sometimes Sumedha) came to the city of Dipavati. He found it in festive array and inquired what the city was celebrating. The citizens told him they were awaiting the arrival of the Buddha Dipamkara, who was about to enter the city on a visit. Megha, who had never heard of a Buddha before, was strangely moved by this news, and so after buying some flowers to present as an offering, he joined the throng already gathered to welcome this Buddha.

Soon there were welcoming cries from the onlookers, and Megha then saw the Buddha Dipamkara walking slowly down the street towards where he waited. The serene majesty of that Buddha's appearance, with a strange glowing light playing about his whole body, impressed Megha greatly. At once Megha conceived the idea of becoming like him. Just as Dipamkara came within reach, Megha and other onlookers threw their flowers to the path in front of him. But all those flowers remained hovering in the air above that Buddha's head.

At the sight of this, Megha pushed through the crowd and threw himself at Dipamkara's feet, causing him to pause. With his long hair Megha reverently wiped the Buddha's feet and formed an ardent wish that he too would become such a Buddha. Dipamkara looked down at the prostrate form of

Megha and in a moment perceived, with his Buddha powers, the whole of Megha's past lives and future births. The Buddha smiled, and with Megha bowed at his feet in the dust of the road, he announced to the crowd that this young student would, in eons to come, become another Buddha with the name of Sakyamuni.

Nothing more is recorded of Megha after that, but this event became the archetype of the prediction of Bodhisattvas to future Buddhahood, and many examples of Sakyamuni's predictions occur in the Mahayana sutras. According to one ancient source, this city of a past eon, called Dipavati, became known in Sakvamuni's time as Nagarahara, situated near the modern city of Jelallabad in Afghanistan.

THE RIPENING OF THE BODHISATTVA DESTINED TO BECOME THE BUDDHA SAKYAMUNI

From the moment of Dipamkara's prediction, the student Megha was launched on a trail of exertions and trials over a whole incalculable kalpa. From then on he always gained a human birth and never again fell into the lower realms of existence. Many of the human Jataka tales belong to this immense period devoted to perfecting the moral virtues.

For example to perfect the quality of giving (dana), this being as Prince Visvantara gave away his family and kingdom at Varsapura; as King Sibi gave his flesh to save a pigeon at Girarai; as Candrapabha gave his head at Taksasila; and as Prince Mahasattva gave his body to the hungry tigress on the upper Indus. Then as Ksantivadin he silently endured having all his limbs cut off by an enraged king at Mangalapura in order to perfect the quality of patience (ksanti).

To fulfill the perfection of energy he visited a Buddha of the past called Pusya, who was then residing in a mountain cave. Standing outside for seven days and nights on one leg, he praised that Buddha continuously in spontaneous verses. Finally, under the Buddha Kasyapa of the present kalpa, he lived out his penultimate existence as the ascetic Jyotipala before gaining the Tusita heaven as a fully matured Bodhisattva. There he awaited the ripening of causes and conditions on earth before selecting the time and place for his final birth. At that time he would achieve full and perfect Enlightenment and become the Buddha Sakyamuni, thus fulfilling Dipamkara's prediction of a previous era.

It is at this point that the story of our historical Buddha can rightfully commence. It is only when we are aware of the immense prehistory bringing to fruition a truly purified and vastly experienced being that we can fully appreciate the story of "our" Buddha's life.

Before starting that story, notice the succession of previous Buddhas who travelled a path similar to Sakyamuni's. Our position today within this vast framework means that many hundreds of Buddhas are yet to appear to fulfill the quota of 1,000 Buddhas for the current kalpa. That being so, and given that each Buddha is preceded by infinitely long lines of development and training, then the seeds and elements of at least some of those future Buddhas are around us *now*.

Certainly while Sakyamuni's Teaching dispensation lasts there is opportunity and necessity for these already existing "lines of development" to intensify their practices and experience. The next Buddha-to-come, Maitreya, is said even now to reside in the Tusita heaven, waiting, as Sakyamuni did before him, for the proper time and place for his final birth. For such a great number of forthcoming Buddhas to be sustained there must be, somewhere in the world, a being approaching the stage of Jyotipala, that is, the human birth just before entering the Tusita where he will gain the place vacated by Maitreya's assumption of his final form. In like manner there needs to be a Megha and others suitably advanced to receive Maitreya Buddha's prediction in due time. All this flows from understanding the original perspective of Sakyamuni Buddha's biography.

5. THE BIRTH AND YOUTH OF SAKYAMUNI BUDDHA

The ancient Sanskrit and Pali literatures are in close agreement on the events and manner of Sakyamuni's birth. The story begins in the Tusita heaven, where the great Bodhisattva examined the world below to select the proper time and place for his final birth. He decided upon the city of Kapilavastu, capital of the Sakya clan, the site of which has been identified in northeast India on the border with Nepal. The king or chief of the Sakya clan, Suddhodana, and his wife, Maya, were chosen as fitting parents.

Then the great Bodhisattva descended from the Tusita heaven, fully conscious and aware, and entered Maya's womb. Certain accounts tell how the great Bodhisattva adopted the form of a white elephant that appeared to Queen Maya in a dream and entered her womb through her side. Her pregnancy ran the normal course, except that the baby was fully equipped with all his limbs and sense organs throughout the gestation period.

As the time for birth approached, while Queen Maya was travelling with her retinue, she rested a short way from the capital, in a pleasure park called Lumbini. There, standing under a tree and holding onto a branch for support, she gave birth. The great Bodhisattva emerged from her right side without causing his mother any pain or discomfort. As he emerged, four gods from the Brahma heavens received him into a net and presented him, standing, to his mother. Two streams of water poured from the sky onto mother and child as a token of purification, even though neither was stained with any impurity. While the gods held a white parasol over him and carried for him other symbols of royalty, the newborn child walked seven steps toward the north and said in a loud voice that this was his last birth into the world. Modern scholars have calculated that this birth took place about the year 563 B.C. Ancient traditions from Sri Lanka (Ceylon), China, and Tibet maintain variant dates, some of them considerably earlier.

Very shortly after giving birth, Queen Maya died and was reborn into the Trayastrimsa heaven. Her sister Mahaprajapati took over care of the child and brought him up as her own. He was given the personal name of Siddhartha and had the family name of Gautama.

When the child was born, an ascetic called Asita, dwelling in the Himalaya mountains, perceived by his supernatural powers that the gods were raising an extraordinary commotion, waving their garments and rejoicing. Seeking the cause of this celestial delight, he surveyed the area with his special vision and soon perceived the shining brilliance surrounding the newborn child at Kapilavastu.

Asita decided to go and visit him. After travelling to the capital and being received with respect by the king, Asita asked to see the child, who was just then asleep. As if aware of an important visitor, the baby awoke and was shown by his father to the visitor. With his supernatural power of vision Asita immediately saw that the child's body was endowed with the thirty-two special marks of a great man, as well as the eighty minor marks. He therefore venerated the child by bowing and walking around him clockwise. Then he took the child in his arms and stood in silent contemplation. The king and his courtiers were astonished and distressed to see the old ascetic begin to shed tears. The king asked what was the meaning of such grief. Did this portend some calamity for the boy in the future?

Not at all, Asita replied. This child, he said, has only two possible destinies. If he remains a householder he will become a world emperor (Cakravartin); if he takes up the homeless life he will become a fully Enlightened Buddha who will lead countless beings to salvation. Asita himself wept because although his proficiency in the higher meditational practices assured him of rebirth in the Brahma-heavens, he would pass away before hearing and being able to follow the supreme doctrine that this new Buddha would preach.

When questioned about his certainty, Asita enumerated the thirty-two and the eighty special marks that the child possessed and that testified to his enormous accumulation of meritorious acts in past existences. The volume and quality of the signs confirmed that the child was a special being in his last birth and had only two possible destinies.

In the various texts there follow lists of these special marks, which for brevity's sake are not fully reproduced here. A few can be given from each group, and from these it will be seen that some are rather strange. Among the thirty-two major marks there are: a protuberance on the top of the head; hands that hang to his knees when he is standing up straight; palms and soles are marked with wheels of 1,000 spokes; fingers and toes that are webbed or netted; a long and very large tongue; and curled white hair between the eyebrows. Among the eighty minor marks are: a body that emits light; large, long eyes the color of a blue lotus; and hairs of the head that all together coil like a conch.

So the king was reassured and produced suitable gifts to Asita. Then the ascetic departed for his hermitage in the Himalayas.

Only two major incidents are preserved about the boyhood of Prince Siddhartha, and it is uncertain in what order they occurred. In what is perhaps the best known, we find the young boy, in the care of his nursemaids, accompanying his father to a state ritual. One source describes this as a ceremonial plowing of the land by the king to ensure good crops. While this was in progress, the boy was placed under a shady tree, where his attendants left him alone while they went and watched the spectacle.

The quiet and rare solitude were used by Siddartha to sit up straight on his cushions and observe his own breathing. Without effort or instruction he soon attained one of the meditative absorptions (dhvana). He remained motionless and recollected throughout the whole time he was unattended. Evidently several hours elapsed, because the sun moved around and the shadows cast by the surrounding trees moved accordingly. However, when his minders returned they found him still deep in meditation and protected by his tree, whose shade had not moved. All were astounded by the miraculous event, and they hurried to tell the king the news. Of course the king was both pleased and disturbed because he recalled the prediction made by Asita.

In the second boyhood incident he was taken to the local temple by his aunt and foster mother, Mahaprajapati. This may have happened when he was quite young. In any case he could by then converse. It seems that such a presentation of young children at the temple was a custom of the time and place; it may have been a form of ceremonial seeking the blessing of the gods and inviting their protection for the prince.

During the preparations the boy asked his aunt where they were going. He was told he was to enter the temple and pay the customary respect and honor to the gods. To the discomfort of his aunt the boy smiled and replied that he had already been acknowledged by the gods as their superior and so entitled to their respect but that he was quite willing to go in conformity with custom. So they went, but the moment Siddhartha's feet crossed the threshold of the temple, all the images of the gods, including Siva, Brahma, and Sakra, assumed bodily forms, came down from their shrines, and offered praise to the boy Bodhisattva.

Before moving on to the next stage of the story it is worthwhile to note certain significant features. If we are to understand that everyone in the entourage either witnessed or knew about the unusual circumstances of the child's birth and so took seriously the predictions of Asita, it was surely clear from the beginning that this was a birth of great moment. His family and retainers were thus aware of the child's special status and exalted destiny.

The accounts also make it clear that at this point the child Siddhartha himself retained some of the characteristics of his former pursuits and was conscious of what he really was and had been. On the other hand, the special bodily marks perceived by Asita were evidently invisible to others; by their nature they were not fully developed in a young child. At first, then, it was common knowledge that Siddhartha was far more than his father's son, and no doubt Suddhodana wanted and expected the boy's destiny to be that of a world-ruling emperor.

EARLY LIFE OF PLEASURE AND MARRIAGE

At pains to make sure that his son's destiny should be that of royal power, King Suddhodana took care that the boy should have no wish to leave home. His father provided the youth with three separate palaces, in which he spent the varying seasons of the year. His food and garments were the very finest and even his retainers and servants were fed luxuries unheard of by the commonality. Each of the palaces was filled with precious things, and he was pampered and entertained by a host of female musicians and concubines. In short, all the pleasures of the arts and senses were at his disposal, and there is nothing in the accounts to suggest that he did not drink his fill of everything provided.

Only one thing was forbidden him. He was never allowed to leave his palaces and go at will among the people and the city. Not that there was evidence of any inclination to do so. Thus, for the years prior to manhood he seemed totally preoccupied with his own pleasure and the company of his personal retainers and servants. When in his father's opinion the time came for him to marry, Suddhodana invited all the nearby princes and aristocratic families to propose their daughters for matrimonial (and, of course, political) alliance. But the neighboring peoples had a poor opinion of this prince who displayed no interest in the manly arts and who devoted his time to idle luxury and dalliance. How could one so cosseted and confined to the company of women and servants be expected to lead a kingdom and defend it from its enemies? So ran the general opinion, and no ladies of rank were offered.

The king was quite downcast and humiliated and asked his son whether he could demonstrate any skills in the warrior arts. To this the prince replied that he could show his ability with the great bow. When it was brought to him, it was unstrung; normally the combined effort of several strong men was required to string it ready for use. With apparent ease the young prince strung the bow unaided and then struck the taut string with a stick. The resulting sound reverberated through the city and caused consternation among the populace. After this the prince accompanied his father to the practice butts and showed his prowess in shooting with the great bow so that the citizens could be assured that he was more than proficient in the arts of war.

After this, fears for his competence were allayed and numerous ladies of rank were suggested as candidates for marriage with the prince. Of all the candidates Yasodhara was chosen, and she married Siddhartha and became his chief consort. Some versions of the story name her as Gopa or Gopaka, but in any case she and all the ladies of pleasure provided the prince with a life of luxurious sensual pleasure untouched by any of the cares and anxieties of the world. So passed the prince's early manhood until he was about twenty-eight or twenty-nine. Then, as he showed no sign at all of embarking on his true destiny, the gods decided to intervene.

INTERVENTION OF THE GODS
AND THE GREAT RENUNCIATION

It came about that the prince began to feel restless confined to his palaces. He therefore proposed a pleasure excursion to a royal park on the outskirts of the city. The king, his father, agreed, but ensured beforehand that all cripples, beggars, and other afflicted persons were removed from the streets and that the route was swept clean and lined with happy people demonstrating affection for his son.

Riding in the state chariot and accompanied by his charioteer, the prince emerged from his palace and rode along the
streets to the delight of the populace. At this point the gods
arranged for one of their number to assume the guise of an old
and decrepit man. As the princely chariot progressed through
the city, this apparition came into full view of the prince and his
charioteer. Siddhartha saw the bent and trembling figure, gray
haired and hobbling along, grasping a stick for support. The
prince was struck with astonishment, because never before had
he seen anyone of advanced age and infirm with years.

Turning to his charioteer, he asked what sort of person this
was. On being told that this was a case of age and infirmity and
that it was the common lot of all, the prince was suddenly aware
that old age awaited everyone. He grieved that the people
should be in such a festive mood despite the evidence of their
ultimate fate.

Deeply perturbed, he abandoned his drive to the park and
returned quickly to the palace. His father, surprised at the sudden return of his son, inquired the reason. On learning what had
happened, he resolved to redouble his efforts to avoid any repetition that might turn his son's mind from the pleasures of home
life.

The gods, however, had taken a decisive hand in the affair,
and after a while they aroused in the prince's mind the desire to
travel again. On two further occasions Siddhartha went out into
the city with his charioteer, and on each journey the gods produced an apparition that he could not avoid seeing. Once it was
a sick man, unable to walk, being carried along while crying in
pain and anguish. After that it was a corpse, lifeless with the pal-
lor of death, being borne along to the funeral pyre. Each time
there was the same astonished shock, the same questions, the

same sudden turnaround of the chariot and flight back to the palace in alarm and agitation.

From then on he took no delight in the favors of his women attendants, nor did he even show much interest in the fact that his wife was far advanced in pregnancy. All was blighted by his sudden perception that the beauty of women and the strength of men were doomed always to the shambles of wasting age, disease, and death.

His thoughts began to turn toward the idea of abandoning all to search for a cure for this universal affliction. Much oppressed by these somber reflections, he decided on another chariot ride for some diversion in the open air. For the fourth time he and his charioteer ventured out into the city and this time the gods delivered the *coup de grace*. They manifested a vision of a wandering mendicant, who approached the chariot and on being questioned extolled the virtues of the homeless life, without possessions, intent only on gaining the supreme goal of final release.

Once more the prince turned the chariot around, but this time he had seen a practical example of an alternative life. Pondering deeply, he returned to the palace and, quite exhausted, fell upon his bed and slept. When he awoke he looked around at his female attendants, who, relieved for a while from the perpetual task of diverting and entertaining their lord, had fallen into a relaxed stupor. Caught off-guard, the prince saw them unobserved, and they presented a picture of motley disarray. All had slumped down in unaffected positions of bodily exposure and in a disheveled state. Siddhartha, in an unusual mood of high sensitivity, was revolted by what appeared to him as a disgusting exhibition. At that moment all desire died. As if to press home an advantage, news was just then brought to him that Yasodhara had given birth to his son. Immediately he made his resolve to abandon the home life before his newborn son added to the bonds of affection and involvement.

Calling his charioteer to saddle his horse, the prince paid a last visit to his wife and son. Both were asleep, so he quietly and at length gazed on them both. Then he went down to the court-yard to mount his horse and depart. The faithful charioteer insisted on going with his master and refused to be dissuaded. At this point two opposing celestial powers exerted their influ-ence simultaneously. First came Mara, the god of desire and death, who promised that within seven days the prince would become a world-ruling emperor if only he stayed where he was. Briefly and impatiently the prince refused. Mara then promised he would henceforth follow him like a shadow, awaiting the first moment of weakness to confound him. Other gods then put all the palace guards to sleep, muffled the horse's hooves, and silently opened the palace gates, letting the prince go forth in what has become known as the Great Renunciation.

Again a moment's pause is appropriate to ponder these events, for without doubt we are involved here not only in his-torical events but also in religious or sacred drama. And like all sacred drama the purpose has several strands. In addition to our growing acquaintance with the story of the great Bodhisattva in his last earthly life, we also see that gods of the higher realms are actively involved in that story, for and against. This is where the dramatic range is spread out to include beings of the world-sys-tem at large and so some of the elements of the Life become loaded with extra significance.

To start with, recall how the child and youth are aware of special powers and destiny while the young man and husband seem to lose sight of them. The combined effects of his enforced isolation from the everyday world and his total immersion in sensual pleasure, in a luxurious, indolent mode of life, were only too successful. The prince in his gilded cage seems to suffer a memory blank. It is as if all his sensitivities, feelings, and capacities were totally absorbed, admitting no interest or concern other than his own pleasure and the continuous round of "artful" engagements.

The various accounts of Asita's prediction conclude that there was enough uncertainty between the alternatives to convince the boy's father that, if only the desire to leave home could be averted in his son, the favored destiny would ensue. The god Mara's last-minute attempt to head off the prince serves to confirm that then there really were two alternatives. If the achievement of Buddhahood had been a certainty, and been understood to be so by his family, then the elaborate attempts to guide him away from it would have been pointless.

Then there is the intervention of the gods. As mentioned above, Suddhodana's strategy was working all too well. Note it well: even a being of such vast maturity and dedication as this great Bodhisattva seems to have been hypnotized by the concentrated dazzle of a one-sided display of Samsara's beauty and delight to the senses. We should certainly not overlook that it took four separate visions produced by the gods, each vision more powerful than its predecessor, to shake the great Bodhisattva out of his stupor of contented lethargy. It is entirely proper to wonder what might have happened without such a drastic intervention by the gods.

We are thus left in no doubt as to the difficulty of turning "against the stream" and of the immense binding power that Samsara exerts, even for beings having the skill and equipment, amassed over eons of experience, for striving against it. Here it can be seen that a combination of necessary ingredients is indispensable. A perfect coincidence of causes (the Bodhisattva's innate merit and power) and of ambient conditions (the gods' attentive following of events and their positive assistance) are required to bring about an end result that has been in the making for ages.

Of course, there are other ways of interpreting these events. The early Mahayana view, expressed in the *Suramgamasamadhi* sutra, has it that the great Bodhisattva at this time before the "shock" of the Four Signs was already perfectly enlightened and was merely acting out an elaborate charade for the purpose of "ripening" beings. Some of the higher gods were fully aware of this "deception." As they said: "The Bodisattva is not really attached to royalty and pleasure, even now he causes the Wheel of the Law to turn."

Whichever view we are inclined to accept, the events are clearly meant to convey a significance beyond what is required to make the story intelligible. The opinion of the *Mahayana* sutra is a case in point. This is yet another reason for not tampering too drastically with the traditional elements of this biography, and for not using bits and pieces tailor-made to suit the modern view of the possible and the impossible.

TEACHERS, AUSTERITIES, AND ENLIGHTENMENT

On leaving the palace, Siddhartha and his charioteer travelled southeast into the night. At a distance safe from pursuit they stopped. There the prince cut off his hair and gave his fine jewels and soft clothing to the charioteer to take back, with his horse, to Kapilavastu. Several times the charioteer tried to dissuade him from leaving home and family, but he was firmly

Austerities of the Buddha. *Drawing from a fourth century Gandhara Grey schist figure*

rejected. When he finally took his leave, Siddhartha sent with him a message for his father not to grieve for him, as they would quickly meet again if the goal of the conquest of old age and death could be gained. Failure in this meant their final separation; he would never give up. The charioteer then rode back to the palace and the prince, now shaven and simply clothed, went off in search of teachers who could help him in his quest.

There seems to have been little difficulty in finding them, for the great Bodhisattva (we should no longer refer to him as Siddhartha) soon came upon a body of wandering disciples led by their master. He is named in the Pali version as Alara Kalama. It is clear from the narrative that Alara presided over a considerable company of followers who practiced a form of meditation that reached up to the highest levels of Samsara. The Bodhisattva, having approached the teacher, requested permission to join him and "to practice the religious life" under his guidance. He was accepted and was taught Alara's system of meditation. When the Bodhisattva asked the teacher what were the limits of the meditation being taught, the answer was "the attainment of the state of nothingness." Such a name is very close to one of the upper levels of Arupyadhatu (Formless Realm) and is part of the topmost range of the three-tiered Indian world-system.

The Bodhisattva very soon learned both the doctrine and practice of this meditation and was totally proficient at it. On further questioning, Alara perceived that the Bodhisattva was his equal in the realization of that doctrine and offered him the joint leadership of the company of disciples. The Bodhisattva declined. He saw that this highly refined practice had a fatal flaw. Peaceful and remote from ordinary affairs though it might be, it was still subject to unavoidable decline into decrepitude and death. So the Bodhisattva left that company and wandered on to continue his search.

Again the Bodhisattva sought out a teacher of repute. This time he attached himself to one called Uddaka Ramaputta. A similar procedure followed. First the Bodhisattva asked what the limits of the teaching and practice were. He was told it was the state of "neither consciousness nor unconsciousness." In fact, this was one stage higher than that of his previous teacher and equivalent to the very summit of the world-system. Once again the Bodhisattva, exerting his power, very soon gained the realization of that meditation and became the equal of his second teacher. As before, the full extent of his teacher's range still failed to meet the ultimate criterion. An offer of partnership was again made and declined, and once more the Bodhisattva abandoned the company.

This time he went on alone without seeking any more teachers. His wanderings led him southward into the old kingdom of Magadha and eventually to the banks of the river Nairanjana. Here he began to explore the limits of yoga-based experience. Here, too, he was joined by five other wandering ascetics who, impressed by the strenuous nature of his yogic efforts, stayed with him in the expectation of being the first to hear whatever revelation should eventually be revealed by this ardent practitioner.

Back in the palace at Kapilavastu, the charioteer's news of the prince's departure brought consternation and grief. Despite all his well-intentioned efforts, the king's precautions and preventive measures had failed. But the king was at least reassured that his son was well. Some of the Sanskrit sources record that he sent out messengers regularly to seek out his whereabouts and to report back with news. Later on, this thirst for tidings was to have sorry consequences, as we shall see.

Having separated himself from all teachers, the Bodhisattva now embarked on the most severe practices "to restrain . . . the mind. . . ." He reduced his food to a single seed or grain of rice per day. He suppressed his breathing until during periods of meditation he stopped his breath completely and suffered violent pains in consequence. These extremes of self-discipline must have continued for a considerable time, for he was reduced to just skin and bone. So wasted and motionless did he become that the gods, who were watching his progress intently, became alarmed at the thought that he might be dead. Other gods perceived that he was very close to death and approached him with the offer of celestial food just to keep alive. The Bodhisattva refused this on the grounds that it would be a covert act and thus a falsehood. Yet the true knowledge of the deathless state eluded him. Even the very limits of yoga practice failed to produce the wisdom and insight that he sought.

Then, exhausted and starved as he was, the memory came to him of the time in his early youth when he sat quietly under a tree while his father performed a state ceremonial. He recalled how, without austerities of any kind, he had attained a high degree of concentrated meditation devoid of all passion and distraction. It occurred to him that the better way would be in that direction. Certainly he was convinced that the most severe austerities were a dead end and that no purpose was to be served in continuing them. To do so meant certain death from debility and exhaustion, and to die meant to be reborn, repeating the whole sorry process all over again. This new conviction prompted him to take food once more, to build up his strength for this different approach.

It was just prior to this decision that Mara, the god of passion and death, approached him again, and seeing he was close to death, pressed him to give up the fruitless struggle and return home. With reasoning and guile, Mara said that by leading a life of generosity and good deeds he could achieve both human and divine happiness. But if he persisted, Mara threatened, such an army would be raised against him that he would be utterly destroyed. The Bodhisattva, knowing Mara's purpose, brushed him aside and promised Mara that soon he would conquer all of his armies and reach the supreme goal. Mara withdrew.

Then the Bodhisattva went down to the river to bathe. In his emaciated state this was a slow and painful process. Afterwards, as he made his way back up the bank to his seat, he was observed by a passing peasant's daughter named either Sujata or Nandabala. Again the gods intervened and prompted her to fetch a bowl of rich milk-rice and make an offering of it to the Bodhisattva. This she did and with it he resumed taking food. His five mendicant companions, on seeing this, decided he had given up the struggle completely and that by taking food again after his long efforts in austerities he was admitting defeat. They therefore left him and continued their own wanderings. In all, this period of ascetic striving, culminating in near-death and the loss of his companions, lasted over six years.

After regaining his strength the Bodhisattva moved off one evening and came to the Bodhi tree, where he gathered grasses and prepared his seat under its shade. On seating himself cross-legged and upright, he vowed not to rise from that seat until he had gained the supreme wisdom. Now Mara appeared to him with a whole army of terrifying monsters. Aided by his sons and daughters, all personifications of pride, lust, and greed, he attempted to shake the seated Bodhisattva's resolve and then destroy him. The monsters and the rest were all launched at the Bodhisattva under the tree, but none was able to reach him. Mara then challenged the great Bodhisattva to show proof of his past lineage of merit, which enabled him to so disregard all the conditions and restraints of Mara's realm.

The great Bodhisattva silently reached out with his right hand and touched the earth on which he sat. As if in answer, the earth rumbled and roared, quaked and shook to such a degree

The Buddha as Teacher. *A drawing from a fourth century Gandhara grey schist figure*

that all of Mara's cohorts were terrified, fell to the ground, and disappeared. Mara himself, repulsed and downcast, fled.

But he was not yet quite done. He now resolved to distress the father of the Bodhisattva. Appearing then to Suddhodana the King, Mara offered news of his son, and then reported that the Bodhisattva had died that very day. On hearing this the king collapsed, and the wives (in this version both Yasodhara and Gopaka are mentioned) sank down in tears. The king lamented that neither of Asita's predictions for the child had been fulfilled and that he had therefore lied. Once more the gods took a hand, and one of them appeared to the court to announce that Asita had not lied, Mara was the liar. Indeed, the king's son had just now attained to supreme and perfect Enlightenment. The king, the wives, and all the inhabitants of Kapilavastu expressed great joy, and the city was bedecked as if for a festival.

It was just as the gods had reported. On the dispersal of Mara and his hordes, the great Bodhisattva, as night drew on, sat undisturbed under the Bodhi tree. Deep in meditation he entered successively each of the four absorptions (dhyana). Having reached and established the fourth and highest of these meditations, he saw a series of profound insights unfold.

During the course of that night, he at first perceived directly and clearly his own births and deaths in all his previous existences. Everything was plainly revealed in every detail, from his very earliest aspirations and even his sub-human modes of life. Then, as the insight deepened, he turned his attention to the world at large. Samsara as a whole was then perceived directly with all its beings passing away here and being reborn there, according to their accumulated deeds. The entire stratified world-system, from its lowest hells up to the abodes of the highest gods, appeared to him plainly "as though reflected in a spotless mirror. . . . " Finally, the true nature of the world and all its beings was revealed. The causes and hidden patterns opened out to the pure, concentrated, and perfected vision of the great Bodhisattva.

These profound penetrations were later codified into two major formulas: the Four Noble Truths and the Twelve Links of Arising Due to Conditions. The gaining of that supreme knowledge and wisdom made the great Bodhisattva into a fully enlightened Buddha. The last stages of this completion of an age-old path are described in some *Abhidharma* texts as consisting of thirty-four moments of perfect vision that both stop forever the last traces of defilement and penetrate to ultimate reality. At the same time they convey the knowledge that Buddhahood has been gained, rebirth of any kind extinguished, and the Way justified.

The gods were the first to see that a new Buddha had arisen in the world, and soon all the gods were rejoicing in their heavens as the Buddha Sakyamuni quietly rested under the Bodhi tree.

Ancient Buddhist commentators have long pondered, and sometimes elaborated upon, these momentous events. There is little doubt that the Buddha's innumerable followers through the ages are meant so to ponder them. In times past the storytellers of Asia pointed out the various themes and their special significance to gatherings of illiterate but attentive listeners. Elsewhere scribes and exegetes scratched away at their birch bark or leaves, recording in erudite detail the lessons and implications of this or that part of the story.

Here, all that can be done is to draw attention to some of the threads and to present some information on the background of time and place. For example, the abandoning of the home life and the search for teachers should be seen within the context of the cultural and religious ferment of the times. At this period (circa 530 B.C.) in north India, wandering mendicant teachers of religion and philosophy were commonplace. There were also several established religious sects in existence, and early Buddhist texts enumerate six different competing systems together with their leaders or principal exponents. Almost certainly there were more than this, as well as innumerable individual visionaries, magicians, and yoga practitioners of one sort or another.

The majority were perpetual wanderers and mendicants; they travelled from place to place, attracting followers here or losing them there, all of them preaching their view of the world and ultimate reality or simply entertaining the locals with tricks or astounding them with their ascetic rigors. In modern times several major religio-philosophies have been identified with this milieu. Among them were the Sankhyas, whose teachings derived from the already ancient Vedas and Upanishads. There were also the Jainas, sometimes referred to in the Buddhist texts as the "naked ascetics" (nirgrantha), a well-established religious society with a large lay following and a saintly leader, Mahavira, who lived and taught at roughly the same time as the Buddha Sakyamuni.

In the northern and northeastern areas of India, within which all these events took place, the caste system and the Brahmanical religion were not as all-pervasive as in the more westerly regions. Here, along the banks of the lower Ganges, were a number of petty kingdoms and republics where no single religious body was predominant. Consequently, all over this vast area were teachers of all kinds with their disciples. In general they lived an austere life of begging or, more easily, a life of accepting gifts from pupils or of earning proceeds through public preaching or debate with opponents.

The fact that the great Bodhisattva fled from home in a southeasterly direction brought him into the heart of this domain of conflicting inquiry. Thus the great Bodhisattva was repeating a mode of life that he had adopted many times in his past existences—as Megha during the time of Dipamkara and as

Jyotipala in the life prior to his residence in the Tusita. Because of this, it is not so surprising that he should very quickly master the techniques and the teachings of his two preceptors. What we seem to have here is a revision or a refurbishing of skills and capacities already latent but dulled by his princely life of luxurious idleness.

With regard to the early teachers themselves, from the descriptions of their meditational practices it is likely that they were followers of the Jaina system. Both practices seem to have a remarkable similarity to the very highest levels of the commonly held world-system. And it was just this "top of the world" that Jaina saints aimed ultimately to achieve. Not only was it to be reached in meditation but a "pure" death was sought that would result in the saint's "life monad" rising to that summit of the world, there to remain in blissful peace for ever. In this context the great Bodhisattva is shown as gaining and discarding the most sublime achievements of his most spiritually advanced contemporaries. Some texts of the *Abhidharma*, when explaining these matters at a later date, warn that these highest levels of Samsara, attained by the practice of "absence of perception" (asamjnisamapatti), were a dead end, a wrong path misleading even the most skilled and advanced ascetic into quiescent states mistaken for the final release of Nirvana.

Another feature of this sacred drama that needs to be underlined is the several interventions of the gods in this final stage of the Bodhisattva's career. After their crucial and decisive assistance in bringing about the Great Renunciation, in the final assault on "the gates of the immortal," the gods are at first absent. It is as if they watched with bated breath as the great Bodhisattva approached ever nearer his goal. As impotent observers and occasional helpers they demonstrate their inferior status to the great Bodhisattva, whatever their rank in the celestial hierarchy. Once enlightened, the Buddha was emphatic that he was "the teacher of gods and men" and that he was the "conqueror" (jina) of birth and death and thus of the whole range of Samsara. All of the gods, without exception, despite their long lives extending in some cases over millennia, had to end their exalted existence when death finally over took them and they made way for another incumbent.

Even so, at times their assistance was critical, though as the great Bodhisattva moved beyond their reach towards the final achievement, it was of a more humble nature. They offered food to alleviate the ravages of fierce self-discipline and they prompted the girl Sujata to prepare and bring food when most needed and acceptable. Again they took care that the great Bodhisattva's family was not left in utter distress at Mara's deceitful news.

The case of Mara is quite otherwise. While the great Bodhisattva's progress took him out of reach of the gods, it also brought him into progressively severe confrontation with the great god of passion and death. From efforts at subtle temptation Mara was forced into attempts to destroy the great Bodhisattva under the Bodhi tree. This increasing hostility and opposition by Mara shouldn't really surprise us. From the moment of his Great Renunciation the Bodhisattva saw clearly that it was the interminable round of death and rebirth which had to be overcome. Any other achievement, even the highest states of meditation, was still a form of bondage. Thus it is entirely fitting that the last great confrontation and trial of strength should be against Mara just prior to the attainment of Enlightenment (Bodhi). And such is the nature of Mara and what he represents that even the great Bodhisattva had to call upon all the concentrated power amassed by his innumerable past lives to subdue Mara and his minions with a literally earth-shaking surge of fully ripened and purified energy. So the last enemy having been overcome, the gates of the immortal swung open once more and the great Bodhisattva passed through to the deathless and became the new Buddha of this age.

Significantly, no human eye witnessed this great event. Only the gods, among all living beings, knew and perceived what had taken place, and they all rejoiced.

Significantly, too, Mara, having failed to prevent this Enlightenment, continued his nefarious works by attacking the only traces of the new Buddha remaining to him, the anxious, waiting family.

We can now return to the new Buddha sitting quiet but resplendent under the Bodhi tree. He still had to fulfill his promise to bring relief to the world once he had found the Way. The various traditions tell us that it was to this that the newly enlightened mind was turned during the several weeks that elapsed before the Buddha left the shade of the tree of Enlightenment.

6. REESTABLISHING THE "ANCIENT PATH"

The ancient texts provide us with slightly varying accounts of what happened after Sakyamuni Buddha's Enlightenment. In outline they all agree, however, that there was a pause of from one to seven weeks immediately afterward. During that period the matter of teaching to others what was revealed by full and perfect Enlightenment was resolved.

First, the new Buddha remained seated under the tree, plunged into deep meditation on the true nature of things. In particular he is said to have reviewed the Chain of Causation or "Arising Due to Conditions" (pratityasamutpada), absorbing its full import and application to all beings and circumstances. It was clear to him that his newly won true knowledge was profound, subtle, transcendent—and hard to obtain. His direct perception of the capacities of ordinary people, and even extraordinary people, showed that they were enmeshed in so many attachments, ideas, and convictions that it would be difficult for them to gain access to the real and the ultimate state. This involved the deep penetration to underlying causes and conditions and the cessation of all passions. Both of these were beyond the reach of all but the most spiritually advanced of mankind. If the Buddha himself had only gained this full Enlightenment after eons of continuous striving and effort, how could men of the world, lacking his enormous endowment of merit and wisdom, be expected to understand, or even accept, a teaching of such profundity that it went "against the stream" of all worldly convictions and affairs?

Thus emerged a dilemma of far-reaching importance. The tradition in the Pali texts tells us that the Buddha hesitated over whether to teach his great wisdom at all; his first reaction was to remain silent because of the "weariness and vexation" of the inevitable misunderstandings. Other traditional versions from the Sanskrit confirm that the dilemma was there but that the great compassion for the world inherent in the Enlightenment experience itself overruled any hesitation. On surveying the world with his clear supernatural vision, the Buddha could see that there were some who were less immersed in the passions than others. His supernatural vision also allowed him to see and to know that all the Buddhas of the past and those yet to come had taught and would teach the profound wisdom. Thus the decision was made.

While these deliberations were going on, the gods were watching the quietly meditating figure, wondering whether or not he would decide to teach. As time went by they became anxious and then alarmed that perhaps after all this effort and their careful ministrations the great Teacher whom they had confidently expected and identified would, in the end, turn away from the task of making known to all men that the "Ancient Path" had at last been rediscovered. Toward the end of this post-Enlightenment pause, Brahma, king of the higher gods (in some accounts Indra or Sakra), descended from his heavenly realms, and taking suitable form, stood before the Buddha under the

Bodhi tree. With reverence and joined hands Brahma addressed the Buddha with the request that he have pity on the world and teach his newly won doctrine. Echoing some of the profound thoughts that had already occurred to the Buddha, Brahma said that there were beings of little impurity in the world who would relapse into the lower states if they did not hear and receive the Dharma.

In the Pali version it was just this request at the critical moment by the chief of the gods that overcame the Buddha's hesitation. In other versions, such as the *Buddhacarita* from mainland India, Brahma's request merely set the seal on a decision already made and gave the opportunity for the Buddha to avow his intention to teach. Whichever way it was, there followed the fervent utterance to Brahma that the gates of the immortal were now open and those who could hear and understand should attend to the Dharma about to be revealed. Some of the Pali accounts record that during the gestation period immediately after the Enlightenment the Buddha had devised the whole of the *Abhidharma*, which implies that the mode and method of teaching were prepared.

Before any teaching took place, however, there now appeared two travelling merchants who, together with their caravans, happened to be passing. This incident is mentioned in both sets of documents; in the Pali version these merchants are named Tapussa and Bhallika. The gods once more resumed their participation and prompted these merchants to approach the still-seated Buddha with offerings of food. After their proffered food was accepted, both merchants bowed, and as if moved by the splendor and assurance of that great presence, said to the Buddha that they took refuge in him and in his teachings, but omitted the third part of the Refuge formula, as there was as yet no Samgha. In fact these first "converts" received no teaching at all but were sent on their way with assurances of good fortune to come.

Now the Buddha turned his mind toward the practical problems of who could be the first to receive his teaching. Recalling first his two teachers, Alara Kalama and Uddaka Ramaputta, the Buddha soon perceived that they had died. His thoughts next turned to his erstwhile followers, who had abandoned him when he resumed taking food. Perceiving that they were now staying in the deer park of Isipatana at Benares, he resolved that they would be his first disciples. Accordingly, he then rose and left the seat of Enlightenment under the Bodhi tree and made his way along the road to Benares.

The interval between the attaining of full Enlightenment and the departure from the Bodhi tree perhaps contains some of the most profound implications of all the incidents in this traditional biography. In the first place it marks a boundary between the consummation of eons of struggle and the start of what that consummation could do for the world at large. From being focused on a single exalted being moving steadily and steadfastly toward an as yet unrealized goal, the story now begins to spread out to relate how that tremendous achievement was managed and released for others capable of responding to the direct testimony of one who had "gained the other shore." And here indeed, at the very threshold of the Buddha's first recorded teaching, the dilemma is intense.

What is involved in the great and unsurpassed wisdom of a Buddha's full Enlightenment was clearly beyond the grasp of even the most spiritually advanced of Sakyamuni Buddha's contemporaries. Had he not gained and abandoned the best that was available long before and was that not followed by six years of intensive search that took even one as greatly endowed as a Bodhisattva in last birth to the very limits of endurance? Evidently no other living being of the time could duplicate this singular attainment; an attainment, be it noted, which changed the whole being of the subject from a greatly endowed Bodhisattva Prince into a Buddha/Tathagata, a knower of all the worlds throughout time, a god of all gods, and a supreme teacher of men.

It is clear from the deep considerations that took place after the Enlightenment that the awesome depth and range of Buddha knowledge is just not transferable simply for the asking, nor can it be delivered as one might demonstrate a theorem. The situation is succinctly described in the early pages of the *Lotus* sutra, where Sakyamuni unequivocally states that only another Buddha can fully understand a Buddha. And yet to keep his own promise and to fulfill the task of every Buddha, he *had* somehow to teach and bring his rediscovery within reach of ordinary beings. No wonder the gods looked on in anxious concern while the dilemma was resolved.

So the choice of the first recipients and the substance of that first teaching are worthy of special note. As we shall see, the content of that exposition was embedded firmly in the world as it is, as normally experienced by everyone and particularly by those who already search for the real. Its general characteristic is of a mass of sustained suffering and turbulence. Nothing was said about the very essence of Enlightenment, the subtle chain of causal conditions that governs everything. Yet such was the skill of the Master that even that first teaching, addressed to the selected five, brought about their preliminary release and insight.

THE FIRST TURNING OF THE WHEEL OF THE
DOCTRINE AT BENARES

Walking along the road to Benares, the Buddha, now in his middle thirties, was seen and approached by another ascetic. This man is said to have been impressed by the serene appearance of the Buddha, and according to the custom and etiquette of the time, greeted him and asked what doctrine he followed and who was his teacher. At this, the Buddha, whose worldly appearance was that of a young man in the prime of life, must have astonished the inquirer, who probably expected an enthusiastic account of some local teacher to whom he could go and put questions. Instead, the Buddha pronounced himself the Victor and Conqueror of all the world, superior to gods and men alike, an All-Enlightened One endowed with omniscience and beholden to no teacher. This must have startled and disconcerted the ascetic, for there is no hint that he could see anything of the Buddha's true nature from his appearance. He muttered something like, "if only it were true," and took himself off rather sharply, leaving the Buddha to continue his journey.

According to some of the sources, this journey on foot from Bodh Gaya to Benares took eight days and followed the post-Enlightenment pause. Eventually the Deer Park was reached, and there the five past followers sat together under the shade of the trees. In one text they are named Kaundinya, Mahanaman, Vaspa, Asvajit, and Bhadrajit. They saw Sakyamuni coming toward them from a distance and conferred together as to how they should receive him. At this stage all five mendicants were completely unaware of the profound change that had taken place in the person they remembered. They still recalled him as the ascetic who had given up. When they saw him approach they therefore decided that he was not worthy of their respect, though the courtesies of the time required that he should be conversed with if he so wished.

As Sakyamuni came nearer, they found themselves unable to maintain such a condescending attitude. Some of them prepared a seat, some placed water for his feet, and others took from him his bowl and outer robe. While doing these things they addressed him by his family name of Gautama or as "friend." This drew a prompt rebuke. The Buddha told them it was not proper to address him by his family name, even less by the basic form of "friend." He said, "I am a fully enlightened Buddha, a Tathagata, and I now teach." Despite their reluctant respect, the five mendicants still were unable to accept this, and they asked the Buddha how, since he had given up striving, he could be believed when he now claimed to have achieved his goal.

The Buddha persisted, and after three such exchanges the five were convinced that here indeed was a teacher worthy of attention and reverence. Sakyamuni Buddha thereupon made the first exposition of the new Teaching or Doctrine (Dharma) now known to us as the first turning of the Wheel of the Law.

The five mendicants listened intently while the doctrine of the Middle Way was pronounced, a doctrine of avoiding the extremes of unrestrained passion and worldly indulgence on the one hand and the self-torture of severe austerities on the other. This Teaching was followed by the formula of the Four Noble Truths: 1) the universality of suffering; 2) its cause; 3) its termination; and 4) the eight parts of the Way to achieve the termination of suffering.

At the end of this exposition, one of the five, Kaundinya, gained a pure insight into the veracity of the teaching and was praised for it by the Buddha, who confirmed the attainment with the words, "Kaundinya has attained the knowledge. . . ." It is not said specifically that Kaundinya then attained Arhatship. Indeed the Sanskrit version maintains that he gained what was later to become known as "the Pure Eye of the Dharma."

Certainly a period of intense instruction followed for all five, because we are told that three of them went begging for food while the remaining two received instruction. All six shared the food received. Then the three were instructed while the two others went begging. In this way they fed themselves and received instruction until all five gained the fruit of Arhatship. All five were the first to be received into the Buddha's Order of Monks; Kaundinya first, followed by Vaspa and Bhadrajit, and finally Mahanaman and Asvajit. The gods, continuing to observe closely the progress of events, rejoiced and declared that the Wheel of the Dharma had indeed been set in motion once again.

The small group of disciples stayed with the Buddha at Benares for a while and soon the next recruit was gained. There lived in the city a son of a wealthy merchant called Yasa, and he, out walking at night in a disturbed state of mind, came upon the Buddha in the Deer Park. This young man listened to the same recital of the Four Noble Truths by the Buddha and very soon after attained Arhatship. Later, Sakyamuni accepted a meal at the family home of Yasa's mother and former wife, and they then became lay followers. Yasa's many friends and acquaintances, curious at the sudden conversions, came to see the Buddha, and more than fifty of them and their associates entered the Order and soon after became Arhats.

It was then, before leaving Benares, that Sakyamuni sent out sixty of the first Arhats in all directions to preach the Doctrine that they had heard and realized for themselves. This mass dispersal must have stripped the Buddha of almost his entire following of fulfilled disciples. Only Asvajit and Mahanaman and a few others seemed to have remained with him when he left Benares and turned his steps in the direction of Rajagrha, capital of Magadha.

Here we have seen a newly attained Buddha reaching out to find people suitably endowed to receive the news that the "gates of the immortal" were open. It was a commonplace of the time that disciples sought their own masters. Sakyamuni did just that when he first left home. Now, however, a unique being, a fully enlightened Buddha, does not wait for people to come to him; he seeks out his first disciples. This is partly the result of the dilemma previously discussed. People would certainly come to him, they already had. The two merchants were willing supporters, but they received no teaching. At this crucial beginning it seems to have been vital to select those who were capable of some understanding, willing or no.

At first we see the five "deserters" as unwilling even to receive the new Buddha advancing toward them. It is obvious that they could not see the majestic figure with the golden halo that many would see later on. But they evidently saw a different figure from the half-starved ascetic they had left in disgust. Some emanation reached them from the advancing figure that induced their deference, polite at first, compulsive soon after. And then there is the incident of the wandering ascetic who also perceived something remarkable about this young man striding out toward Benares. Again the "glorious body" was not in evidence, but something was, and the ascetic must have been taken aback to be told by such a young man that he was above all the gods. Notice, too, that no teaching was given here either.

The first recipients had been singled out and that was that.

Even with them there was to be no nonsense about calling a Buddha by the slightly condescending title of "friend." That response had called forth a stern rebuff. His titles were Buddha or Tathagata, and he was thereafter addressed either by them or as "Lord" (Bhagavan). A proper attitude toward him was clearly of some importance before his teaching could be dispensed.

As for the teaching itself, the first section of it consisted of the Middle Way between the two extremes. However we may interpret this teaching nowadays, it was certainly aimed then directly and specifically at those five who held the view that the practice of self-mortification was correct in its own right (they represented a large body of contemporary opinion) and that to abandon it spelled defeat and failure to achieve the goal of insight. One of the incidental discoveries along the great Bodhisattva's way to supreme Enlightenment was that body and mind had to be fit and healthy to sustain and support the enormous effort for Enlightenment. So here at the outset, wrong attitudes had first to be corrected and direct contact with where *they* stood was necessary. This Teaching also illustrates what was to be the hallmark of all Sakyamuni's teaching technique: that the exposition had to be fitted to the listener's capacity. This too flowed from those weeks of meditation under the Bodhi tree, when the dilemma of a message from beyond the world as generally known had to be conveyed intelligibly to those still in it.

Well might the gods rejoice and raise a commotion as the wheel of the doctrine started to turn again. And when the deceptively simple statement of the Four Noble Truths followed that of the Middle Way, they knew that the Dharma was well and truly launched. Especially so when, one after the other, the five disciples gained preliminary insight and release from the bonds. These five, and soon after them numerous others, gained the fruit of Arhatship, and one wonders at the relative speed of such attainments. In a way, these quick successes serve as a contrast to the immeasurably higher status of the Buddha himself as compared with his Arhats. And this has always been acknowledged: that while the release and higher knowledge of Arhatship is the same for the Buddha and his disciples, even so the Buddha stands out above them all in full and supreme Enlightenment.

GROWTH OF THE EARLY SAMGHA AND
CONVERSION OF SAKYAMUNI'S FAMILY

The journeying on foot from place to place over long distances was typical of the Buddha's habit throughout his long life. Now, on leaving Benares for Rajagrha, he would proceed by stages, stopping here and there so that the route was not always direct. As the crow flies, the distance from Benares to Rajagrha is little short of 200 miles, and with diversions rather longer. On just such a lengthy journey, walking the dusty track in the cool of the day, a Brahmin called Dona fell in with the Buddha's travelling party. It happened that Dona found himself walking directly behind the Buddha, and to his astonishment each of Sakyamuni's footprints left the clearly discernible mark of a wheel with 1,000 spokes. Under normal circumstances these special bodily marks, seen for the first time by the sage Asita on the child Siddhartha's body, are largely invisible to the human eye. The strong inference is that Sakyamuni wanted them to be seen by this man.

Later, when the party was resting and Sakyamuni was seated under a tree, Dona approached him and asked if he were a god or a spirit.

"Neither," was the reply.

"Then are you a human being?" asked Dona.

"Indeed not," Sakyamuni replied. "Just as a lotus is born and grows in the water and mud but is unsoiled by it, just so is a Buddha."

On the journey from Benares, along the banks of a river were several communities of religious ascetics led by the three Kasyapa brothers. Certain of the texts describe them as fire-worshippers with matted hair. In order to convert these men to the Dharma, Sakyamuni had recourse to a great array of supernatural powers. In particular he is said to have subdued local naga spirits who belched out smoke and flame at him. None of this stirred the elder Kasyapa from his beliefs. He merely acknowledged that Sakyamuni was a great master of magic. However, when Sakymuni denied that Kasyapa's path of practice led to full attainment, he began to have doubts and asked to join the Buddha's entourage.

Eventually all three brothers and their combined following of 1,000 entered the Order as disciples, and the Buddha preached to all of them the now famous Fire Sermon. This was to the effect that all the senses and their objects are on fire with the passions of greed, hatred, and delusion. Once this is known and understood, aversion and disengagement arise and with that release follows. On hearing this sermon many disciples became Arhats.

On arrival at Rajagrha, Sakyamuni and his now substantial following were met by the king, Bimbisara, and a host of citizenry. At first, because of the presence of the well-known Kasyapa brothers, the populace were not sure who was the leader of the monks. To clarify the position the elder Kasyapa acknowledged the Buddha as Lord and teacher and then Sakyamuni preached to all, including the king. Bimbisara was converted and gave to the Order the nearby Bamboo Grove.

It was near here, too, at Rajagrha, that the Buddha gained his two foremost disciples, Sariputra and Maudgalyayana (Moggallana in Pali). Both were wandering mendicants searching for "the immortal" and just then were followers of a local ascetic teacher. Each of them had assured the other that he would be the first to be told should one of them find what they looked for. While the Buddha and the Order stayed at Rajagrha, the Arhat Asvajit went out on his begging round. This was the same Asvajit who heard the first preaching at Benares. Sariputra saw Asvajit begging and was impressed by his demeanor. At a convenient pause Sariputra approached him and after the usual formal compliments asked who his teacher was and what was the teaching he followed.

Asvajit replied that he followed the Lord Buddha then staying in Rajagrha, that he himself was not a skilled teacher and could only give him the essence of the doctrine in brief. He then pronounced to Sariputra a four-line verse that became famous in later times. In translation it says:

> Dharmas which are born from a cause
> the Tathagata has proclaimed
> the cause as well as their stopping.
> Thus teaches the great ascetic.

Just as in the case of Kaundinya, on hearing this a sudden insight arose in Sariputra and he understood the universal application of arising and passing away—another case of inducement of "the Spotless Eye of the Doctrine." After expressing his thanks and taking his leave of Asvajit, Sariputra hurried off to tell his companion that their search was ended. Both now prepared to leave their teacher and go to the Buddha. Many of their companions who heard the news decided to go with them. Sakyamuni, who saw them coming from a distance, remarked to those nearby that the two who now approached would be his chief disciples.

Now the Buddha decided to return to Kapilavastu and visit his family. Journeying as usual on foot by gradual stages, he and his whole company of monks, now numbering many hundreds, left Rajagrha and headed northwest across the Ganges toward the Himalaya range. On arrival the whole party was lodged at a local park but no one offered the Buddha any particular respect.

As in the case of the first five disciples, the Buddha's status seemed to need acknowledgment before fruitful teaching could take place. Here, among the Sakya clan, a people notorious in their time for pride of race and of family, something more than persuasive explanation was required. So, there and then, in front of his father and all the nobles and retainers of his home town, Sakyamuni suddenly rose into the air and performed what became known as the Miracle of the Pairs or of Fire and Water.

Suspended high in the air above the astonished crowd, the Buddha caused fire to burst out from the upper part of his body while sheets of water cascaded down from the lower part. Then the fire appeared from his right side and water from the left. This was repeated in a number of variations, followed by the creation of a promenade of jewels in the sky along which he walked or appeared in various stances.

On completing this spectacular display he descended to earth, and his father and the assembled nobles bowed to him in awed respect. But no one invited him to a meal. The next day, therefore, Sakyamuni with his monks went begging for food in the city, as was normal. Everyone came out to watch the king's son, dressed in plain robes, beg from house to house like any other common mendicant. When they heard about this, the king and the family, as members of the warrior caste, were scandal-

The Pillar of Fire. *Detail drawing from a third century Amaravati stone relief*

ized and distressed. Suddhodana left the palace and sought out Sakyamuni on his round. With great respect but with firm disapproval Sakyamuni's father asked him why he was disgracing his family in public.

Surely no one of their royal lineage had ever begged in the streets before. At this reproof Sakyamuni replied that he was not now of that royal line. His lineage was that of the Buddha Dipamkara and others down to the Buddha Kasyapa, the last of the line before Sakyamuni. All these illustrious predecessors had begged for their sustenance, and so Sakyamuni rightly conformed to the practice. At this the king was finally convinced and he became a lay follower of his erstwhile son's Dharma.

Suddhodana soon became more familiar with the members of the Order and conceived the idea that a motley crowd of errant monks of uncertain origin was no fit entourage for his son, Buddha or not. He therefore decreed that a son from each of the noble Sakya families should join the Order to ensure that Sakyamuni should have "suitable" companions. In this way an element now entered the Order, not by desire and conviction, but by decree. Among these was Devadatta, whose later activities were to cause such dissension. Other "entrants by order" were a number of well-known relations and kinsmen, including Ananda, Nanda, Aniruddha, and the barber Upali.

A special mention has to be made of his wife Yasodhara and his young son Rahula. All the palace ladies, including Mahaprajapati, Sakyamuni's foster mother, came to see the Buddha and offer respect, except Yasodhara. She waited for Sakyamuni to go to see her, which he soon did, and in the presence of Suddhodana she paid him homage by touching his feet with her head. The king related how she had followed Sakyamuni's progress up to Enlightenment from the news brought by the messengers. Yasodhara had in fact copied Sakyamuni's mode of life to some extent by wearing yellow robes, taking only one meal a day, and abandoning perfumes and adornments.

Sakyamuni responded by telling of Yasodhara's devotion in previous lives as was the case for Suddhodana also. Yasodhara, however, had not entirely given up the idea that this was still her husband and that he might return to her. Some of the sources tell us that she prepared a love potion in a bowl of delicious food and oil and sent her seven-year-old son, Rahula, to the Buddha with it for him to eat. Sakyamuni, knowing this, created 500 look-alike Arhats and sat among them when the boy came. Rahula, despite this, came straight to the real Buddha without hesitation and offered him the bowl. Although the doctored food was not accepted, there was no doubt that here was a son who recognized his father.

On another occasion Yasodhara sent the boy to follow him to the park of residence, where Sariputra was told to admit Rahula as a novice to the Order. When news of this reached Suddhodana, he made complaint to Sakyamuni that it was painful for parents to lose their only sons to the Order, and it was especially so to him, for he had now lost both son and grandson. He asked that in future no one would be admitted to the Order without parental permission, and this was agreed and remains so.

According to one reconstructed chronology, several years of further wanderings were to elapse until in the sixth year after the Enlightenment the next major incident took place at Sravasti. During this interval King Suddhodhana died and Mahaprajapati, his principal widow, sought entry into the Order along with other Sakya women. The Buddha refused Ananda's pleading on their behalf, until at the third request he granted it, provided the ladies accepted extra strict rules, which had the effect of giving them lower status than the monks. These being accepted, the Order of Nuns came into being, but Sakyamuni told Ananda that the result would be a shortening of the life of the Dharma in the world.

Descent from Trayatrmsa. *Detail from a fourth century Gandhara stone relief*

While in Sravasti, the Buddha stayed at the Jetavana Park recently donated to the Order by the great benefactor Anathapindika. Here the Miracle of the Pairs was performed for the second time. On this occasion the whole Samgha was challenged by rival religious groups to a public display of magical prowess. Sakyamuni forbade any of his monks to perform for this purpose, but he evidently regarded the issue as sufficiently important for him to do so. Once again he entirely awed the crowd and his antagonists with the display of fire and water and by promenading in the sky. No one could improve on that.

It was also from Sravasti that Sakyamuni disappeared altogether from India for three months while he visited his mother in the Heaven of the Thirty-Three (Trayastrimsa). Maya had been reborn there after her early death, and Sakyamuni was aware that all the previous Buddhas had been at pains to convert their parents to the Dharma. The textual sources are agreed that the Buddha spent his time in the Trayastrimsa teaching his mother the *Abhidharma*. Although particular teachings are not specified, there is a certain significance in the fact that *Abhidharma* is mentioned at all at this juncture.

After converting his mother, Sakyamuni performed another of those spectacular demonstrations long remembered by generations of commentators and carefully carved in stone for the edification of countless pilgrims. Instead of returning to earth at Sravasti, he descended from the mountaintop heaven to Samkasya, on the upper reaches of the Ganges, 200 miles to the west. And contrary to his simple ascension to the heavens, his descent was full of splendor and grand display. On the night of the full moon in October the startled people of Samkasya would have seen a triple stairway slowly descending from the cloudy heights to touch earth firmly just outside their town. Soon, to the sounds of heavenly music, the Lord Buddha could be seen descending the grand stairway made of precious metals and jewels and accompanied by crowds of the gods. On his right the Buddha was escorted by Brahma, king of the gods, and on his left was Indra, or Sakra, ruler of the Trayastrimsa and the lower heavens.

By the time the Buddha had stepped off the stairway to earth, many of the leading Arhats in the Samgha, with Sariputra at their head, had hastened there to greet and receive this royal cavalcade. According to one group of texts, however, Subhuti, one of the principal Arhats, absented himself from this celestial levee. He remained in his cave retreat near Rajagrha, absorbed in meditation on sunyata (emptiness), which he considered the only true homage to the Tathagata. Far away at Samkasya, when Sariputra greeted the just-descended Buddha in the name of the Samgha, the Buddha said that Sariputra was not really the first to receive him. It was Subhuti who performed the true homage, not those who just saluted his perceived body. Much was made of this from the earliest times, when there was long pondering and discussion on the so-called Dharma-body. Such was the reverence with which this event was held that the site at Samkasya was marked with shrines, and it remained one of the cardinal sites on the pilgrim's circuit of the holy places in India until Hsuan-tsang's time and beyond.

If we had any doubt about the unique nature of Sakyamuni before his Enlightenment, we should have none afterward. On the occasions of contact with his early followers, and with casual meetings, there was something mysterious about his effect on people, and in his pronouncements on being superior to the gods. There was also the sensitivity about being addressed with too much familiarity.

But here in the exchange with Dona, when the imprint of the 1,000-spoked wheel was seen on his footprints, we have an unequivocal reply to a straight question. "Are you a human being?" Dona asked. "No," was the reply. Neither was he a god

Bodhi Tree Throne. *Detail drawing from a first century Sanchi stone relief*

nor any other category of being in Samsara. What then was (is) the Buddha? That is a prime question that emerges from the traditional biography, and it is one that exercised the minds and meditations of whole generations of Indian Buddhist masters. The answer to that question was a matter that divided whole sections of the early Samgha. The question nagged from the very beginning, and one of the sets of answers helped to lay the foundations for what we now know as the Mahayana. For us now, it is enough to perceive the question itself. Any answers we arrive at will to a large degree be determined by our individual tendencies and the extent of our understanding. At least we know what he was not. The ancient texts leave little doubt as to that.

The early sculptors of India who decorated the stupas of highest antiquity, such as those at Sanchi and Amaravati, portrayed this mysterious being with great subtlety and with striking originality. Where the Buddha was supposed to be present, they indicated his presence by an empty throne, or a Bodhi tree with a seat at its foot but no seated figure, or even by large footprints impressed with 1,000-spoked wheels. But never with a physical form. The first images of the Buddha in India were carved centuries after the establishment of the major divisions in the Samgha.

In the same category are several other incidents in this section. One is the distress and perplexity of Suddhodana on seeing his son begging in the streets and Sakyamuni's categorical rejection of the ties of worldly family. His lineage is that of the previous Buddhas, he insists, none other. Similar is his accounting for the present circumstances of Yasodhara and his father by the events of their past lives. This practice of explaining present situations by activities in the past was often resorted to by Sariputra, and others and later in this biography we shall see it again on a much larger scale. In the vast overview of the past eons of Samsara we seem to have a situation where certain "streams of development" ran parallel to each other for ages. So much so that the final ripening of certain actions in the past brought these parallel streams to a contemporaneous birth as the different characters of a dramatic climax—all the major characters being drawn around the central figure, all, in some way or another, dependent on him.

The descent to earth from the visit to Maya, on a jewelled stairway in majestic array, attended by the gods Brahma and Sakra, tells us in unmistakable terms that here is a being without equal in the entire world-system. Here at least is a positive ancient representation that should convey, by its royal trappings and its bringing together of the heavens and the earth, some indication of how the Buddha and his ministry were perceived by the ancients.

A LONG LIFE OF WANDERING AND TEACHING

Assuming that what is now widely accepted as the Enlightenment took place at the age of about thirty-five and death at about eighty, the Buddha spent forty-five years trudging the pathways and tracks of northern and eastern India. There is plenty of recorded detail about the first years of his ministry, and about the last year or so before his death, but little chronological narrative of the thirty-five years or so in between. Of course, all the scriptural texts give us quantities of anecdote and a mass of teaching topics, all of which must have originated during this long middle period. But the thread of the narrative seems to have been lost, or perhaps dropped, in favor of a great collection of unrelated stories and detailed expositions of doctrine and practice. This is not the place to recount all these incidents; nor is it possible without reproducing most of the canonical material.

Instead, this account will explore Sakyamuni's continuous wandering, his preaching, his conversions, and his instructions to the rapidly growing orders of monks and nuns. When we stop to consider what is known of Sakyamuni's daily routine, and of his extensive travels to spread the Teaching, it becomes clear that hardly a day went by during his long life when some instruction, exposition, or general preaching did not occur.

Consider first the area he travelled. All the towns and villages along the middle and lower Ganges basin saw him time and again. On the left bank, the northern boundary extended from Sravasti to Samkasya, covering about 300 miles. On the right bank, the southern boundary went from east of Rajagrha to the western limit of Kausambi, a distance of about 280 miles. The north-south axis of the territory was at least 250 miles wide.

This enormous area was traversed many times in the course of decades of peregrinations. It is recorded that, apart from the months of the rainy season, when the whole Order stayed put wherever it happened to be, the rest of the year was spent visiting one place after another, mostly on foot, but sometimes on the river. This perpetual movement during the larger part of every year must have taken up a substantial part of many a day's routine. It is clear, though, that stops were made of varying length at places of particular importance, such as the Kosalan capital at Sravasti, the Maghadan capital at Rajagrha, and the capital of the Vrjjian republic at Vaisali.

Regular features of Sakyamuni's daily routine other than travel were: the begging round; bathing and meals; the twice daily "survey of the world" with supernatural vision; preaching after being the invited guest at a meal; instructions to members of the Order on training; public preaching at any opportunity; long periods of meditation; rest and sleep, of course; taking individual questions from gods or men; dialogue with opponents or

Footprints of the Buddha. *Drawing from a second century Amaravati stone relief*

visiting dignitaries; and conversations with Ananda or other leading monks of the Order.

A lot of this took place every day, except when on the move. A daily routine of this kind, slightly variable according to where he was or whether he was on the road, could produce a minimum average of three expositions of teaching per day, not to mention incidental conversations. It is this constant flow of teaching and exposition that had to be remembered and collected together as the original Dharma. The sheer volume of it was enormous. A simple (perhaps over-simple) calculation will give us an idea of its magnitude. Assume three expositions per day. (During retreat periods the instruction was intensified, so a mean average of three per day is not untoward.) Continue that rate of output over forty-five years and we arrive at 49,275 expositions of varying length. Whether accurate or not, something of this order must have been the overall volume of the teaching. Of course, this takes no account of the type of teaching, whether in extended or condensed form, or with simple or complex content.

This essential dimension of the Teaching, its great volume, is important because one of the major traditions tells us that Ananda, when he was the Buddha's personal attendant, heard and remembered every word of teaching uttered and could recite it all, complete with detail of the place where it was given, to whom it was addressed, and in many instances the responses or the dialogue that accompanied it. This is the basic idea behind the opening phrase of every sutra or sutta text, "Thus have I heard, at one time . . . " For all the well-known memorizing skills of ancient (and some modern) Indian teachers, it stretches credulity that one man could recall every detail of such a vast body of verbal output at will. As we shall see later on, this is what is supposed to have happened at the first so-called Council at Rajagrha, shortly after Sakyamuni's death. Ananda recited it all, the other Arhats heard and remembered at first hearing, and they passed it on down over all the intervening generations without omission or mistake.

Well might we wonder at the feasibility of this. Indeed, some of the earliest matters of dispute within the Samgha concerned the possibility that the Ananda-line of recited recollections was incomplete in some respects. Again, this is not the place for critical appraisal. But it does lead us to select two of the stories to represent this vast "open" period of Sakyamuni's life, as they are of some purpose in this presentation.

The first story concerns Ananda himself. It appears that, on one occasion while at Sravasti, the Buddha declared that he was growing old and needed a permanent attendant. Up to this point the monks of the Samgha had taken turns attending him, carrying his bowl and robe, fetching him food and water, and on occasion regulating the press of visitors anxious to speak with him. This request for a permanent attendant seems to have happened in the twentieth year of his ministry, so he would have been about fifty-five years old. This is not an advanced age today, but is suggestive of the wear and tear that the incessant travel on foot must have produced.

There is perhaps another reason hinted at in the record. One of his attendants is supposed to have disputed the right path to take on a particular journey. When Sakyamuni insisted on one route, his monk attendant simply put down the Master's bowl and robe and left him! This may reflect a situation where the post of attendant in rotation was not popular with all the monks for some reason.

However it came about, the proposition was made. The first to volunteer was Sariputra. He was told that his work of teaching was too important, and his offer rejected. Likewise other principal Arhats were rebuffed. Eventually Ananda offered himself under certain conditions. There were eight of these, and they included the receipt of alms and invitations, the presentation of visitors, the right to approach the Buddha whenever he wished, and the repetition of any teaching given in his absence. The content of the conditions is not surprising, but the fact that he made any at all is. At least it indicates a wish to avoid foreseen difficulties. All the conditions were accepted, and Ananda thus became Sakyamuni's constant attendant for the remaining twenty-five years of his life. It was during this long period, over half the Buddha's teaching span, that Ananda performed the task of listening to and remembering all the Buddha's teaching. It is odd, however, that this was not one of the duties specified. Even so, what, we may ask, became of all the teaching given out in the first twenty years, before Ananda was in close attendance?

The second of our stories, which took place within the "open" period, occurred before Ananda took up his familiar post. The incident occurred among the monks of Kausambi, a city on the River Yamuna well to the west of the main Buddhist centers. Here a dispute arose over a monk who was accused of an offense that he denied. Nonetheless, he was expelled from the Samgha, and immediately the local Samgha took sides as to the justice of the sentence.

After three months of dispute and wrangling, the matter was still not settled, and the Buddha was asked to intervene. When he arrived Sakyamuni pointed out how unseemly it was for those who had left the world to engage in quarrels like ordinary householders, but to no avail. One of our sources records that the monks said to the Buddha that he, as the "Master of Law" could remain silent and above such matters, but they on their part could not refrain from replying when they were attacked. The Buddha was unable to reconcile the parties, and so he rose into the air and retreated to a forest, where he kept clear of the whole affair. Later, he went on to Sravasti, where representatives from Kausambi sought him out to confess their intransigence. We are left to wonder at a case where even the direct participation of the Buddha was insufficient to quell a relatively minor dispute splitting a local Samgha into opposing factions. But there was worse to come.

As considerable comment has already been given in the body of this section, the only matter for concluding remark is the schism at Kausambi. If nothing else, this incident indicates the growth of the Samgha to proportions where a location was self-governing, and by its very size, would come to include elements incompatible with one another in certain places and in certain mixtures of membership. The Order of monks led by the Buddha "in person" was still a body of people afflicted by passions of one sort or another. It has to be expected that then, as now, the "gates of the Immortal" were a long way off for the vast majority.

DEVADATTA'S SCHISM, THE ASSEMBLY AT ANAVATAPTA, AND THE DEATHS OF SARIPUTRA AND MAUDGALYAYANA

It will be recalled that Devadatta was a cousin of Sakyamuni and was of the Sakya nobility that joined the Order when Sakyamuni visited his family at Kapilavastu. It seems that by the time the Buddha was about seventy King Bimbisara of Magadha had been succeeded by his son, Ajatasatru. In the meantime, Devadatta had assiduously practiced asceticism and had acquired the so-called magical powers of reproducing himself under any guise and wherever he wished. By a show of these accomplishments to Ajatasatru, he won over his support and plotted to displace the Buddha, take the leadership of the Samgha and so, with Ajatasatru, gain spiritual and temporal control of the kingdom. Devadatta was ambitious and ruthless and had lost none of his Sakya pride of birth by his entry into the Samgha.

At first, Devadatta approached the Buddha and suggested that because of his advancing years Sakyamuni should relinquish the Order to him. On being refused, Devadatta persisted until Sakyamuni addressed him in very severe and harsh terms—a rare occasion. At this, Devadatta became angry and resolved to kill the Buddha.

His first attempt at murder involved the placing of archers along a path frequented by the Buddha. But on the approach of Sakyamuni, the archers found themselves unable to act, and so Devadatta resorted to direct action of his own. From a high cliff he threw down a large rock onto the Buddha walking below. Although the rock missed its mark, some splinters broke off, and one of these struck Sakyamuni's foot, drawing blood.

Undaunted, Devadatta let loose a fierce elephant along a road into the city where the daily begging round took place. At the sight of the enraged elephant thundering down upon them, Sakyamuni's accompanying monks fled, except for Ananda who placed himself in front of his Master to take the first shock of the animal's charge. The Buddha removed Ananda by his special powers and quietly proceeded on his way. As the elephant drew near, its rage evaporated and the animal stopped and knelt down submissively in front of Sakyamuni.

Devadatta then resorted to forming a rival Order by stirring up controversy among the monks. He advocated the obligatory acceptance of five extra rules of rigorous discipline by all monks. Although this was rejected as compulsory (though always allowed voluntarily), Devadatta deceived several hundred monks into following him, thus creating a major schism. The Buddha sent Sariputra to persuade the breakaway group to return, and they eventually did.

Thus all Devadatta's schemes came to naught, and he himself soon fell fatally ill. Feeling his end approaching, Devadatta asked to see the Buddha again, but Sakyamuni said that because of his deeds it would not be possible. Devadatta, borne upon a litter, came anyway to where the Buddha was. Before he got within view, however, the earth opened up and swallowed him, and he sank down to the lowest of the hells, Avici.

This story of Devadatta and the schism in the Order may indicate an actual breakaway party that continued to exist independently after his demise. One of our sources mentions an early record by the Chinese pilgrim Fa hien, who wrote of the existence of Devadatta's following, though whether we are to understand that such a group was still present in Fa hien's time, about 400 A.D., is problematical.

Now as we approach the latter years of Sayamuni's life we find one of our most venerable sources, part of the *Vinaya* of the Mulasarvastvadins of northern India, recounting the story of a strange gathering of the Buddha and 500 Arhats, including Sariputra, on Lake Anavatapta. This semi-mythical lake was located in the far north of India among the Himalayas. We are told that four great rivers emerge from the lake and flow down to the plains. Access to this lake for ordinary mortals is particularly difficult, and perhaps for this reason the gods made it a meeting place for their conventions.

We shall see that the assembling of the Arhats on Lake Anavatapta was for a specific purpose. Such an assembly at this place was one of the "Ten Indispensable Actions" that every Buddha has to perform during his life. It is a pattern of actions that was known to the Pali commentators, although the formal list of ten does not appear in the Pali texts. The ten items, which include several of the cardinal events of the Life after the Enlightenment, also contain other features on which some comment will follow at the end of this section. The list of ten necessary actions, as recorded in one of the north Indian *Vinayas* and preserved for us in Sanskrit, Chinese, and Tibetan, reads (in translation) as follows:

The Ten Indispensable Actions of Every Buddha (dasavasyakaraniyani)

The Bhagavat Buddhas do not enter Nirvana without remainder before they have:

1. Prophesied on the subject of the future Buddha.
2. Aroused in a living being a thought that does not turn away from the supreme state of a fully and perfectly accomplished Buddha.
3. Subdued all those who must be converted by him (sarvabuddhavineyah).
4. Designated a "pair of model disciples" (sravakayuga).
5. Instituted a body of moral rules (simabandha).
6. Fulfilled five-sixths of a normal existence.
7. Performed a great miracle at Sravasti (mahapratiharyam vidarsitam).
8. Been seen to descend from the heaven of the gods into the town of Samkasya.
9. Established in the Truths (satyesu pratisthitam) his father and mother.
10. On the great Lake of Anavatapta, accompanied by the Assembly of disciples, unravelled the web of past actions (purvika karmaploti).

Item ten of this list refers to the gathering on the Lake that concerns us now.

The account of this Assembly consists of the circumstances of the departure for the Lake. In the presence of the Buddha, thirty-six Arhats were invited in turn to explain to the whole gathering how his actions in previous lives had played a decisive part in his present state of emancipation. Some told how reprehensible behavior in previous existences will continue to fructify, even into the final phase of his last birth.

No indication is given of the period in Sakyamuni's life when this event took place, but as it certainly occurred before the deaths of Sariputra and Maudgalyayana, and as many of the best-known Arhats make an appearance, it can perhaps be placed in the latter half of the great "open" span of years mentioned above.

The event began after the Buddha preached to King Prasenajit of Kosala in his capital of Sravasti. Sakyamuni addressed his principal Arhats: "Let us leave now for the great Lake Anavatapta, where we shall unravel the web of our previous actions." The Arhats assented, and 500 of them accompanied the Buddha as they vanished from Sravasti and reappeared at the site of the lake. As they all approached, many great lotuses rose from the center of the lake, so that the Buddha was able to alight and sit cross-legged on one while the 500 Arhats alighted and sat similarly on others.

The first to open proceedings was Mahakasyapa, who told the Assembly of his conduct in the past, which had now produced a great fruit. He remembered in a long-past existence how he had seen an ascetic calm and dignified, and how he had a wish to emulate him. As he presented the holy man with a small measure of rough millet grains (all that he had), he also wished to meet more of such men in future. Mahakasyapa went on to explain that because of the power of that wish and gift he was reborn into the Heaven of the Thirty-Three (Trayastrimsa) 1,000 times over, and then into a family of Brahmins, from which he left the world to follow the ascetic path. Finally he had met Sakyamuni, joined the Order, and become an Arhat. He concluded by saying that all his wishes had been realized and that he had now gained his last birth.

After this first avowal, the most senior among the Arhats then invited Sariputra in this manner: "What action has the Venerable Sariputra accomplished in order to become, thanks to the retribution (vipaka) of this act, so wise and skillful?"

Sariputra responded with his story, which is similar to Mahakasyapa's. He was followed by his companion Maudgalyayana, but here there was a difference. In the latter case he started by telling how, in a previous birth, he had been so impressed by the demeanor of a local Pratyekabuddha that he formed a wish to become like him, like his predecessors. In consequence of the "good root," he gained mainly heavenly and happy human rebirths. But once, as a young son of a merchant of Rajagrha, he had annoyed his parents who had struck and reproached him. The boy had felt anger and conceived the notion that he would like to beat his parents to a pulp. Although he never actually carried out this youthful intention (some say he did), he nevertheless suffered torment in the Hell of the Black Chain (kalasutra) after that life expired. Even now, in his last birth as an Arhat renowned for his magical powers, he would suffer the final residue of that long-past mental act by being beaten to death. Only then, on the exhaustion of all traces of retribution, would he die and not be reborn again.

Others followed in turn, each invited to ". . . unfold the thread of his karman. . . ." In some cases relatively simple and mundane actions such as sweeping clean a stupa courtyard with thoughts of respect, or presenting a flower to a stupa similarly mindful, had resulted in repeated favorable births until the fateful meeting with Sakyamuni and subsequent final release. In one case, the Arhat Vagisa tells how he enjoyed ninety kalpas of an unbroken sequence without a bad destiny. And all this was produced because of his gift to a stupa of some perfume, garlands, and ointments, bought for the purpose with a few coins. Another case related how, when the Arhat lived a previous existence as a rich merchant, a Pratyekabuddha begged at his door for food during a period of famine. In a fit of anger and avarice the merchant had prepared poisoned food for the Pratyekabuddha, who died on the spot. For this, the merchant endured long periods in various hot hells until he finally regained human birth. Even then, after meeting Sakyamuni and destroying his passions, he was still sickly and would remain so to the end.

The Arhat Upasena told how when he'd been a hunter he had shot and transfixed a seated Pratyekabuddha, who had then died. Because of this he suffered thousands of years, both in the hells and as a wild animal roaming the mountains. Many times he was hunted and shot dead with arrows, but still he returned to animal birth, until one day his roaming brought him to a grove of penitent ascetics who, instead of chasing him away, sat and radiated light and calm. Thus confronted, the animal had experienced relief followed by feelings of respect and confidence in these humans. Because of the fruition arising from these thoughts, the animal had regained human birth, met the Buddha, and gained Arhatship. Even so, and despite his present purity, at the end of this his last life, he would enter a cave where a snake would bite him.

Our final example is unusual in another way. The Arhat Madhuvasistha related how in the distant past he had once been a king of the monkeys in the district of Vaisali. At that time there lived and preached in the area one of the previous Buddhas of the era. This monkey king used to squat at the top of a tree and listen to that Tathagata. Although he could not understand the words, he was drawn to that Buddha and presented him with a gift of meal. That produced a human birth and a meeting with the present Buddha from whom he heard the Dharma, clearly this time, and "gained the immortal."

Even the Buddha himself was not immune from the doleful effects of the ripening of past causes. Another of our north Indian sources describes nine mishaps or pains suffered by Sakyamuni that were direct results of past causes. These consist of false accusations, wounding in the foot by Devadatta, severe headache, poor or meager food, starvation and bodily torture during his years of austerity, an aching back, and an excess of cold and heat. This ripening of past causes formed the last section of the events at Anavatapta. Sakyamuni wound up the proceedings by describing how the occasions when these incidents arose had all issued from his past existences.

We now come to the last year of Sakyamuni's life. It is at roughly this point that both Sanskrit and Pali texts pick up the consecutive narrative and carry the story to its final scenes with a wealth of detail and background. Forming a kind of prologue to the last act of this monumental drama are the circumstances of the deaths of Sariputra and Maudgalyayana, who both died some months before Sakyamuni.

Sariputra took his leave of the Buddha knowing that his death would occur before that of his Master. Then he returned to his home village near Rajagrha to convert his mother and to die where he was born. Some monks went with him in attendance and lodged nearby. After establishing his mother in the first fruit of the Path, Stream-Entrant, Sariputra's sickness accelerated, and at dawn, soon after his mother's attainment, he expired into final Nirvana. His attendant monks arranged and performed the funeral rites and then returned to Sakyamuni and the rest of the Samgha at Sravasti.

For Maudgalyayana, however, the fructification of his past misdeed brought about a violent demise, quite unlike his friend's peaceful passing. Throughout his long life as an Arhat, Maudgalyayana's specialty had been in the wide-ranging use of his magical powers (rddhi). Often he is described as visiting the realms of the gods and of the various hells to seek out, by his magical prowess, the place of rebirth of this or that one according to his actions. On "returning," Maudgalyayana would relate to the Samgha just what had happened to this monk or to that heretic, and the Buddha would moralize on the reported destiny for the benefit of the listening monks. Of course, this kind of activity did not long remain an exercise in private within the Samgha. Some monks would relate Maudgalyayana's exploits to their lay donors. In most cases, of course, the stories contributed to the honor of the Buddha's following and to the discredit of his religious opponents.

At last some of the rival sectarians decided to remove this growing threat to their reputations. By a secret arrangement with local brigands, they agreed to kill Maudgalyayana. Several times thereafter the bandits waylaid him on his rounds, but each time he avoided them by rising into the air and removing to another place or by just vanishing. But as he himself knew and had recounted to his audience on Lake Anavatapta, nothing could prevent the retribution of his past acts, and so finally, as the bandits persisted and his magical evasions weakened, they caught him at last and beat him to the point of death. With bones and muscles crushed, Maudgalyayana was unable to move but he retained consciousness long enough to create a "mind-made" body, send it to where the Buddha was, and take his final leave. After this he expired and gained final Nirvana in just the manner he had himself foretold.

Thus departed the Buddha's two ablest and most eminent lieutenants. With their removal from the scene, we are prepared for the departure of the central figure. For now, with his advanced age, Sakyamuni knew, as all Buddhas and Arhats know, the place and manner of his final entry into Nirvana. In the case of the Buddha Sakyamuni, this closing episode of a long life is referred to as the Parinirvana.

We have already seen that a minor disruption had already taken place in the Samgha before Devadatta's more serious challenge. In the latter case there was an actual rupture, and some of the monks were drawn away to form a separate movement under Devadatta's leadership. In a mundane sense the story serves to illustrate that even such an otherworldly organization as a body of mendicant monks with the Buddha at its head was not immune to the effects of greed for power and prestige. On the other hand, the stories of a long-surviving following of Devadatta may give us pause to wonder whether we have inherited a rather "doctored" account by overzealous monks whose only concern was to present Devadatta as a devil incarnate.

However this may be, there is evidence for differing centers of gravity within the Samgha, with traces in the Buddha's lifetime, and certainly immediately after his death. The so-called "liberal" and "orthodox" groupings, which emerged in the first Councils, suggest that such divergent views on certain aspects of doctrine and practice were in existence long before but were largely held in check in deference to Sakyamuni's authority. In this light, it may be that Devadatta and others were simply impatient for change. Whatever the facts that underlie the ancient records, it should not be overlooked that, with such a large and widespread following, tensions were bound to be at work. That following, after all, had been drawn from all levels of contemporary society, from royal families to murderous brigands.

The account of the extraordinary convention at Lake Anavatapta and the list of "Ten Indispensable Actions" that justify that gathering take us into a different realm of concern altogether. This scenario returns our meditations to some of the inner significance of the sacred drama as a whole. In previous sections of this story we have seen that several of the principal characters (Sakyamuni's father and wife, for example) had prepared the way in previous existences for the last act of coming together to fulfill clearly defined roles.

The list of ten actions virtually sets out a series of obligations to be discharged by a Buddha before he passes into Parinirvana. They go some way in defining the "role" of the Buddha himself. A glance at the list of ten will show that they spread their concerns over the past, present, and future. The fourth and ninth, which concern the "model disciples" and the Buddha's mother and father, set the seal, so to speak, on past acts now brought to fruition. The seventh and eighth concern the present, in that the Buddha is established as the spiritual overlord of this world-system; notice that both of these incidents take place in public, for all to see. Also concerned with the present are the third and sixth actions, which ensure that everyone suitably endowed will have the opportunity to receive the Teaching and "subdue" the passions. They also set a minimum limit to the Buddha's human life span, though in the end

Sakyamuni rejected a portion of what life remained to him, as we shall see.

Actions one, two, and five are obligations concerning the future. These moral rules for the firm foundation of the Samgha and the Way are to be expected. In actions one and two, however, we seem to have a case of short- and long-term provision. For the (comparative) short term, the next Buddha to come is named and located, so that people are reassured that the immediate lineage is secure. But then the second action provides for a very long term indeed. The wording is very close to the idea of the Bodhicitta, the Thought of Enlightenment, which marks the commencement of the long career of the Bodhisattva. Certainly the intention appears to be the same; to launch at least one being on the Path, which will eventually lead to the full Enlightenment of a Buddha in the far distant future. And yet this is part of a text belonging to a sect that was firmly rooted in the community of the Elders (Sthaviras) and had nothing to do with Mahayana.

Finally, with the tenth action attention is directed toward the past, to trace out the manner in which Arhats can themselves see how they have arrived at where they are. In a manner of speaking, they are sacred dramas in miniature of the primary case of the Buddha himself. The same kind of distant chain of causes and conditions have been at work for them as for their Master and mentor. And not only do these "unravellings of past karman" show how small seeds grow into great oaks; they also show that bad as well as good actions ripen and deliver their results in long-distant future periods. And surely these examples are intended for later generations to emulate. Simple causes bringing forth great fruits, just as gifts of food and the sweeping out of stupa courtyards, are intended to encourage in the face of the dire results of violent crime. The biographies at the lake taken together with the list of ten actions can almost be seen as sketches or plans for a future re-run of the whole sacred drama, with major and minor parts.

7. THE LAST JOURNEY, AND AFTER

What was to be Sakyamuni's last earthly journey began at Rajagrha when, attended as usual by Ananda and a company of monks, he set out and headed north. His immediate destination was Vaisali, across the Ganges, and as was the custom the journey was made in several stages, with stops here and there on the way. Throughout this final journey, the Buddha made several important pronouncements, and he repeated and stressed to his monks some of the key features of the Doctrine. Sakyamuni also addressed the local people who gathered to greet and to listen to him at every stop.

Before crossing the Ganges River, he stopped on the south bank and observed building operations near a village. Sakyamuni foresaw the future greatness of that construction and told his listeners that one day what was then being built would become a great capital city called Pataliputra, as indeed did happen before Asoka's time.

After crossing the Ganges, the party moved on north towards Vaisali. Before reaching that city, two teaching statements were made. The first was to the monks in general about the need to attend to the Four Noble Truths. Now, as we have seen earlier, this was the subject of the first preaching at Benares, and here again the Buddha repeats it, as he must have done many times between. Here, however, he told the monks that rebirth will continue for those who do not perceive and understand this cardinal teaching. Those who do perceive it, he said, will cut off the causes of suffering, and for them there will be no more rebirth.

Further along the way Ananda asked about the destinies of those followers, monks and lay, who had died thereabouts. It seems that this had been a fairly frequent exercise, but now the Buddha told him that in the future he should use the formula called the Mirror of the Doctrine for this purpose. Anyone who maintained faith in the Three Jewels of the Buddha, the Dharma, and the Samgha, and who kept the moral rules unbroken, was assured of freedom from rebirth into any of the lower realms of hell, animals, or hungry spirits (pretas). The implied result in the contrary case was not explicit.

On arrival at Vaisali he stayed for a time and kept the seasonal retreat nearby. Here he fell seriously ill but used his special powers to restrain and suppress the sickness; he said it was not fitting for him to pass away before taking leave of the Order. Ananda, in close attendance, became very worried about Sakyamuni's condition and asked what was to be done about the Order after his Nirvana. The Buddha then told him that the whole of the Teaching had been given; what else was necessary for the Order? Using the title Tathagata, as he often did when referring to himself, the Buddha said that the Tathagata's body was old, and like a cart held together with straps and ties, what more was expected of him now? Then he said to Ananda that they all should live as islands unto themselves, having refuge in themselves, and continued by saying that after his departure they would not be left without a Master. The Teaching (Dharma) and the established discipline (Vinaya) should henceforth be their Master.

Later on, still near Vaisali, Sakyamuni told Ananda that a Buddha has it in his power to live on for an eon if he so wishes. In the Pali account Ananda did not grasp the implied invitation to request that he do so. After this, Sakyamuni moved away from Ananda and sat apart. Mara then made another appearance, his last to the Buddha, and invited him to enter Nirvana straight away, because all was accomplished. At this the Buddha said to Mara that indeed he would soon pass away into final Nirvana.

Mara then left him, jubilant. At the moment of the rejection of the remaining life span, the earth thundered and shook, firebrands lit up the sky and Ananda was petrified with fright. The point then dawned on Ananda, and he hurried over to ask the Buddha to stay for his full term. But it was too late. (The Sanskrit version of this incident makes no mention of Ananda's tardy request, or even of the Buddha's heavy hint beforehand. In it, Sakyamuni voluntarily renounces his remaining term immediately after the request by Mara. Ananda is simply shown terrified by the earthquake; on asking its cause he is told by the Buddha what he has just done.)

Then Ananda was sent to assemble all the monks, and the Buddha addressed them with the news that he would very shortly pass away into final Nirvana. He exhorted them: "Impermanent are all composites, strive earnestly."

After that the Buddha left Vaisali for the last time. As he reached the point on the northward road where the whole city could be seen, he turned his whole body around, as an elephant does, and gazed at Vaisali in farewell.

Continuing the journey, now ever more slowly, Sakyamuni and the monks passed through various localities, stopping frequently to rest, and at one of these the Buddha spoke of how, in the future, his followers could identify true teaching. This became known as the formula of the Four Great Authorities and consists of:

1. Teaching repeated by one who has heard it from the Buddha himself.
2. Teaching repeated by one who has heard it from the Elders of the established Samgha.
3. Teaching repeated by one who has heard it from several learned Elders.
4. Teaching repeated by one who has heard it from a single learned Elder.

In all four cases such teaching is to be checked with the sutras (Scriptures) and with the Vinaya (Discipline). If it is found there, it is true Dharma; if not found, it is not.

Journeying on further, the group came to the place of Cunda the Smith. Here the accompanying monks were served food by Cunda who, at the Buddha's request, served the "pigs' food" only to him. The other kinds of food were given to the monks. The exact nature of this "pigs' food" has been the subject of some debate, but whatever it was, the Buddha alone ate it, and it was the last meal he had. He seemed to be well aware of the effect that was to follow, for he insisted to Cunda that the remains of that dish should be buried.

Soon after this, Sakyamuni suffered a severe attack of pain and loss of blood. Despite this, the party proceeded on its way, but before long Sakyamuni had to rest near a stream. Ananda was sent to that stream for drinking water, and although it was at first muddy and turgid, the waters cleared and ran pure for Ananda to take to the Buddha.

At last they arrived at Kusinagara, and Ananda was asked

to prepare a couch with robes, its head facing north. The Buddha then lay down on his right side, with one foot on top of the other in the so-called lion attitude. Nearby, sal trees bloomed out of season, and their flowers fell to cover his body. One of the attending monks stood in front of the Buddha, fanning him, and was told rather peremptorily to stand aside.

This unusually brusque treatment prompted Ananda to ask why the monk should be spoken to so. The explanation was that myriads of gods were present all around them, wanting to see the Buddha for the last time. There was no vacant spot even the size of the tip of a hair for miles around that was not occupied by watching gods, and they complained that the monk blocked their view.

Ananda then asked for instructions regarding the funeral rites and was told that the ceremonies should be as for a "wheel-turning monarch" (Cakravartin), with a stupa accordingly. After this Ananda moved away to a quiet spot, and there gave way to tears, not only because he was about to lose his dear Master but also because he still had not gained Arhatship. The Buddha sent for him and encouraged him to exert himself to attain the goal. He also spoke to the monks on how well and faithfully Ananda had attended him through the years. This seemed to restore Ananda's composure for he then said that surely this place of Kusinagara was too insignificant for the final Nirvana of a Buddha. He was told that, though it was now small and unimportant, the place had once been the capital city of a wheel-turning king of a past age and so was entirely fitting.

Then Ananda was sent to the nearby clan of the Mallas to tell them the Buddha would pass away that very night so that they could come to pay their last respects. Soon they arrived en masse and were presented in groups. Among them was an ascetic of the locality called Subhadra, who asked if he could

115

question Sakyamuni on some troublesome doubts. Ananda tried to dissuade him, as time was limited, but the Buddha overheard the exchange and invited Subhadra to question him. The answers he received convinced Subhadra, and a short time he gained Arhatship. He was thus the last convert to be made by the Buddha himself.

After settling several minor matters, the Buddha addressed the assembled monks for the last time and ended his address with the exhortation he had used shortly before: "Impermanent are all composites, strive earnestly." These were his last words. Then, watched with rapt attention by the assembled multitude of gods, members of the Order, and local people, the Buddha, still lying on his side, entered the four absorptions (dhyana), one after the other. Ananda was moved to say to the Arhat Aniruddha standing nearby that the Lord had passed away. But Aniruddha corrected him by saying that the Lord had simply reached the stage of arrested consciousness.

The final stages were closely observed and reported by Aniruddha, who described how the Buddha passed back through the absorptions in reverse order and then, ascending them again, passed into final Nirvana from the fourth. Again the earth shuddered and roared with thunder while violent winds raged and darkness deepened because of the sudden waning of the moon. Brahma, king of the higher gods, watching with his retinue, uttered a farewell verse. Likewise Sakra, king of the lower gods, who was also present.

The whole multitude, except for the Arhats, gave themselves over to grievous weeping. Mara and his hordes, on the other hand, also watching the solemn event, were overjoyed. They danced and made a frightful din to celebrate the departure of their unconquerable opponent.

The Mallas took in hand the funeral ceremonies directed by the senior monks, and the body was placed on a bier, ready for cremation. When they attempted to light the fire, however, it refused to burn. Aniruddha was again on hand to explain that the cremation could only take place after the arrival of Mahakasyapa and his party who were hurrying to the scene even now.

While travelling in the direction of Kusinagara, Mahakasyapa had met a party of monks, who had told him of the Buddha's decease. One of these monks is said to have remarked that there was no cause for grief. They were freed from the restraints of the Master and could now do as they wished. Mahakasyapa's disgust can be imagined, but he hurried on to the funeral site, and as soon as he had paid reverence to the bier, it caught fire of itself and all was consumed. The rites were completed by a ceremonial distribution of the bone relics, which the Mallas conducted. The remains were divided into eight parts. Seven were shared among the rulers of nearby territories, and one they kept for themselves. All the recipients of relics erected royal stupas over them for perpetual honor.

The date of the Great Decease generally accepted by modern scholars is 483 B.C.

Sakyamuni's long life came to a peaceful end. The traditions tell us plainly that he became weaker in his last years and that he had bouts of illness that, restrained until the final onset, were brought to a climax by his last meal and finally carried him off at about his eightieth year.

Here, then, is a very complex being. Acknowledged as their superior by the gods, he is yet not of their number. This Buddha or Tathagata, as he called himself, is not human either and yet follows the normal pattern of human life. His span of years, his youthful appearance at the beginning of his ministry, his aching weary limbs in advanced age, his final passing and cremation are all normal characteristics of human existence. But then his special marks, his superhuman powers, and his own flat denial that he belonged to any of the levels of Samsara leave us with something of an enigma.

He has been seen as such from the very beginning. We are in excellent company in our uncertainty. Of all the major issues that occupied the entire Samgha in its early formative years, the nature of the Buddha was the most important. There were different, even contradictory, opinions. The largest contingent of the Indian Samgha, formed after the first major dissension less than one-and-a-half centuries after Sakyamuni's death, regarded the Buddha as an entirely supramundane being. All the events of his life from beginning to end were simply expedient means adopted to further the aims of the Teaching. His real existence was of infinite duration, and his powers of transformation and adaptation were proportionately immense. And these were the views held by Indian Buddhist masters three centuries before the word Mahayana was even coined.

For us now, reading and pondering the traditional elements of the story, it is fairly evident that we have a curious mixture of human characteristics, albeit of very high quality, and "supernatural" features, which dominate the record of how the Buddha referred to himself and that on special occasions were perceivable by others.

In short, the records taken as a whole reflect the current notions about what he was not, but are tantalizingly vague about what he really was. The extreme subtlety of the earliest carved monuments that only show traces of the presence can perhaps now be better appreciated. We are thus left to our own devices, and there is a strong case for consulting the doctrinal records of the earliest schools for their informed perceptions before any of us jump in with ill-considered ideas of our own. In this re-statement of the ancient traditions on the Life, we are content to let the case rest as something of a mystery.

Some of the Buddha's recorded pronouncements on his last journey are of importance, especially those concerning the future regulation of the Order and the Teaching. First it should be noted that all the Teaching had been given. That teaching and the established discipline were to be regarded as the sure guide after the Buddha's death. These statements, and others, are the basis for the age-old concerns over the preservation and proper transmission of the Dharma and Vinaya to future generations.

Much the same can be said about the authoritative criteria for what is and is not valid Dharma. In an age when nothing of this kind was written down, it was imperative to ensure that errors did not creep in. Indeed, this was another of the major issues of the earliest Samgha. Then, however, it was more a matter of what had been left out. Nowadays, although the written records of the Teaching are great in volume, we have a different version of this problem; the records we have are too little consulted, with the result that there is a great deal of personal opinion and not enough reference to the criteria we have been given.

A final comment concerns the monk who told Mahakasyapa that now that the Master had gone they could do as they liked. If we add this incident to those of Devadatta's schism and the earlier rumpus at Kausambi, we can see some sign of the internal tensions of the Buddhist community already remarked upon in these pages.

THE DHARMA RECITATIONS AT RAJAGRHAS

The canonical texts of northern India, preserved for us in Chinese, are now followed for the rest of the story. Elements of the same incidents are also preserved in Pali, but in the northern records we have a continuous narrative.

Many of the Arhats living in seclusion in the forests or mountains were well aware of their Master's demise. A large number of them decided there was nothing further to be done now that Sakyamuni had completed his ministry. They too, therefore, on their own volition, passed away into final Nirvana.

The gods, observing the mass exodus of the remaining Arhats, became disturbed and distressed. They thought and wondered who would be able to preserve and dispense the holy teaching so arduously gained by the Lord Buddha now that he was extinct and his leading disciples were also disappearing from the world.

In some agitation certain of the gods approached Mahakasyapa and asked him if he knew what was going on. Was he aware, they asked, that the lamp of the Dharma was going out in the world, that all the accomplished teachers and practitioners were abandoning the less fortunate? Before it was too late the Dharma must be firmly established for future generations.

Mahakasyapa, thus prodded, perceived with his Arhat's vision that the gods were right, and so he decided to gather the Teaching together. Accordingly he ascended to the top of Mount Meru and there struck the great gong. The sound reverberated widely throughout the world and carried with it Mahakasyapa's message to all the remaining Arhats: "Stay where you are! Do not pass into Nirvana! Remember the work of the compassionate Buddha! Beings yet to come will be lost and blind without the Eye of the Dharma! Wait until we have preserved his holy words and then pass into Nirvana if you will!"

The Arhats obeyed and soon hundreds of them gathered with Mahakasyapa at their head near Rajagrha. Ananda was excluded because he still had not attained Arhatship. Their deliberations were soon halted because no one in the gathering could recall enough of the Teaching (Dharma). All agreed that Upali, the Sakyan barber, was able to recite all the Vinaya regulations and the circumstances that gave rise to them. When they considered who might be capable of reciting the Dharma, they first decided to call upon an Arhat called Gavampati, who had been a close companion of Sariputra. All the assembly agreed that Gavampati knew and could recite both Dharma and Vinaya, but he remained in meditative retreat on the lower terrace of Mount Meru and had not responded to Mahakasyapa's call.

So Mahakasyapa sent a messenger to Gavampati asking him to attend the Council and recite for them. When the messenger arrived and put his request to Gavampati, the Arhat asked for confirmation that both the Buddha and Sariputra had passed away. On being told it was so, Gavampati said that as the Buddha and Sariputra had gone he would not leave his retreat but would follow them into Nirvana. Without further ado Gavampati rose into the air, performed the prodigy of fire and water, and disappeared into Nirvana. The messenger could only return to Rajagrha with the news of his failure.

So no Arhat could be found who was able and willing to perform the recollection and recitation of the Teachings. Ananda learned of the failure of the conference and put his mind to gaining the fruits of the Way so that he could be admitted to the august gathering. Throughout the whole night he sat in meditation, seeking fulfillment. At last he was exhausted. Without success he lay down to sleep. As soon as his head reclined for sleep he was suddenly awakened to the fruits of the Way and thus acquired the diamond-like concentration so lacking until now. He then rapidly progressed to the destruction of all the passions and gained Arhatship.

Quickly, he presented himself at the hall where the Arhats were gathered and banged on the door. When he learned it was Ananda at the door, Mahakasyapa told him to go away. Ananda protested that he was now an Arhat and qualified to attend. But Mahakasyapa, a hard man, replied that the door would remain closed and his only way of entry would be through the keyhole. Right! said Ananda, and exercising his newly won magical faculties he went in through the keyhole.

Then the whole gathering of Arhats, including Mahakasyapa, requested Ananda to recollect and recite the Teachings of the Buddha, which he did. Each incident and recitation was prefaced with the words, "Thus I have heard, at one time . . ." One of the Sanskrit texts records that Ananda was also called upon to recite the groups of Dharma topics and extended explanations that came to be known later as the *Abhidharma*. This he also did, and so, together with *Upali*, all three collections of the Dharma were brought together. This triple division of the whole Scriptural corpus came to be known as the Three Baskets (Tripitaka), and is so known today.

Another of the contemporary Arhats, Purana, lived with his following a great distance away in the south. He too responded to the call, but he did not arrive at Rajagrha until the proceedings were completed. He approached Mahakasyapa and asked if it were true that the Buddha had died and that the Elders of the Samgha had gathered to establish the Teaching. One of our sources tells how the Assembly asked Purana to accept the whole recitation as just collected. The other source recounts how the entire recitation was repeated for Purana's benefit. In both sources, however, Purana asserted that he would hold onto what he had himself heard from the lips of the Buddha. And there the matter rested.

Further consideration of how the enormous variety and volume of Sakyamuni's Teaching was recalled intact by one attendant and passed down to us word perfect and entire would lead us into the disturbed waters of controversy. But two of the incidents contained in this section are worthy of note.

First there is the question of Ananda's recitation. In the northern narrative the body of Arhats in assembly chose Gavampati for the Dharma recitation, and no doubt his close association with Sariputra had something to do with that. Had Gavampati agreed to recite the Dharma, one imagines that his memory of the Teachings would have covered the entire span and not just over half, as was the case with Ananda. Perhaps this was the reason why no one considered Ananda in the first place. The stated reason for his exclusion from the Assembly, not being an Arhat, could hardly have been decisive had he been the only one capable of the Dharma recollection and recitation. In this version of events, then, Ananda was clearly a second choice, very probably because his access to the full range of the Teachings was incomplete.

The other incident, Purana's late arrival and insistence on holding onto what he had himself heard from the Buddha, is remarkable in that it occurs in both the major traditions. Here we have a strong suggestion of some well-remembered teaching or instruction not contained in that first recitation at Rajagrha. Whether the omission was small or large is of no account compared to the significance of there being something missing, or felt to be so.

No wonder that there was anxiety and concern in those early years after the Buddha's death as to whether the recited canon at Rajagrha was complete in all respects. And this concern was to surface on several occasions when arguments and controversy about other matters led to a major division within the Samgha. When this happened, the two separate wings added to or amended the recited canon according to their views of what was right and proper. From then on, further fragmentation took place, and the several main Buddhist communities were free to incorporate into their own Dharma recitations those parts that had either been disputed by other groups or were unknown to them. Thus, to gain access to the whole range of remembered teaching in all its variety, one has to take account of the canonical records of all the earliest mainland Indian Buddhist schools and not just the one that has become the best known in the modern West. All that having been said, matters would have been far less difficult if only Gavampati had agreed to come down from his mountain and recite.

MAHAKASYAPA AWAITS THE NEXT BUDDHA: MAITREYA

With the Dharma teachings recited and consigned to the collective memory of the Arhats in attendance at the Rajagrha assembly, Mahakasyapa decided he could take his leave. No doubt some of his colleagues came to the same decision, especially if Mahakasyapa's order to convene at Rajagrha had prevented them from passing away into Nirvana beforehand. The northern Indian texts continue the story.

One morning, after completing his usual begging round in Rajagrha, Mahakasyapa retired to Vulture Peak, one of the city's encircling mountains, and told the other monks that he would that day pass away. Some of those monks quickly went into the city and informed the leading citizens. They were aghast at the news. As they said, first it was the Lord Buddha himself who departs, then large numbers of his Arhats are only restrained from doing the same by the example of Mahakasyapa. Now he is going too. They were very sad and downcast.

At dusk all the monks and the townspeople gathered on the slopes of Vulture Peak to pay their last respects, witness Mahakasyapa's departure, and perform the funeral rites of cremation. But they were about to witness the utterly unexpected.

In the cool evening, Mahakasyapa emerged from his customary meditations and sat down in front of the gathering. He then preached to them on the universality of impermanence, on the painful nature of all existence, and on the total lack of substance in anything (the formula of the Three Signs or Seals). On completing his homily he took up his cloak—given to him by Sakyamuni—his bowl, and his staff, and suddenly he rose into the air. There, high above the heads of the assembly, he performed the prodigy of fire and water, just as the Buddha had done before him. Fire and water poured out from his body in all directions. Afterwards he descended to the mountain-top and uttered a solemn promise that his body would not decay until the next Buddha, Maitreya, appeared. With that he turned and entered the rock of the summit ". . . as if he was going into soft mud. . . ."

After he had disappeared into the mountain, the summit closed over him with solid rock. Within the mountain

Mahakasyapa sank into the deep meditation of the "stopping of consciousness" and will remain thus, undisturbed, as if sleeping until the Buddha Maitreya shall come to awaken him.

In the distant future, when the next Buddha gains full Enlightenment in the world exactly as Sakyamuni did in the past, human beings will have a life span of thousands of years and will stand eighty feet high. The Buddha Maitreya himself will stand 160 feet high with limbs and features in proportion. He will convert and discipline innumerable beings, but, in general, the people of that time will be lazy and loath to exert themselves.

Perceiving this fault, Maitreya will come to Vulture Peak at Rajagrha. He will strike the summit a blow, and this will awaken Mahakasyapa, who will then emerge from the rock. His body will be whole and his faculties intact. Carrying his cloak, bowl, and staff, he will prostrate at Maitreya's feet and hand the cloak to him. He will say to Maitreya that this cloak was entrusted to him by Maitreya's predecessor. Once the cloak has been accepted, Mahakasyapa will again rise into the air and perform the prodigy of fire and water before Maitreya and the astonished eyes of his entourage and the people. This time, however, on completing the fire and water "pairs," he will destroy his body and disappear into Nirvana.

Maitreya's disciples and all the onlookers will then be curious. They will ask Maitreya, "Who is that miniature man dressed as a monk, and how is it he can perform such extraordinary feats?" They will then hear the story of how he was a premier disciple of the previous Buddha, how he ensured the precious Teaching was conserved after the Parinirvana, and how he has waited within the mountain for the next Buddha to appear.

And all this, says Maitreya, was accomplished by a man who lived in a difficult age when humans were tiny and had only a short time to live. Turning the story into an appropriate teaching device for his followers, Maitreya will tell them that the previous Buddha Sakyamuni had seen them all. It was he who set them on the path to deliverance but they have had to await the coming of Maitreya to attain it. Now they will have seen with their own eyes what such as Mahakasyapa had achieved. Even with a tiny body such great feats are possible, so why should not they with large bodies and correspondingly superior faculties do the same?

Thus the next Buddha, Maitreya, having released Mahakasyapa and induced shame in his assembly, will teach the Dharma and enable many to attain quickly the fruits of the Way. And those who quickly attain it will have been launched and guided onto that Path by Sakyamuni in a previous age. Others, on seeing such wonders and hearing the Teaching from the lips of Maitreya, will plant "good roots" for their advantage in future ages still.

Such is the story, in its full span of past, present, and future, of the appearance and the passing of the last Buddha Sakyamuni and the coming appearance of the next Buddha Maitreya. Although much has had to be omitted, the outline and major elements of the various traditions are here.

The story now completed, or rather left at a certain point, it can be seen that no end to the great drama is intended. Many strands of past events and past lives were drawn together around Sakyamuni's earthly life, and after his death many other ingredients were gathered and transmitted onward with care and concern. Even a direct individual continuity is preserved by

Mahakasyapa's wait to deliver the cloak to Maitreya. There is no doubt that Maitreya will follow the age-old precedents. How can there be an end to such a story? And how well these ancient traditions deserve their designation as sacred literature, to be treated accordingly.

8. The Buddha As Physician, the Dharma As Medicine

It has already been shown that the traditional biography of Sakyamuni contains strong elements of the Dharma or Teaching. In the biography those elements are intertwined within the story, though they can be unravelled, as the Arhats did their karman on Lake Anavatapta.

Now we turn our attention to the Teaching as such, the records of what the Buddha said, expounded, and explained as remembered and preserved by the Buddhist masters of India and Ceylon within the mainstream consensus previously described. That teaching is expressed at great length in the sutras and commentaries. Our concern here is to present the fundamentals of that teaching as plainly as possible. For that purpose the ancient technique of concentrating the main subjects into formulas is entirely suitable. The first and perhaps the primary formula of all is the one called the Four Noble Truths. It will be recalled that this was the subject of the first turning of the Wheel at Benares, and it was preceded by the pronouncement of the Middle Way.

Although this formula of the Four Noble Truths was the

first expressed teaching of Sakyamuni Buddha to the world, it should not be thought of as elementary, in the sense of easy or simple. It was the result of deep pondering under the Bodhi tree on how to express the inexpressible, how to convey the Buddha-knowledge to the worldly.

It should also be remembered that this particular teaching was delivered to a selected few to start with, those who were judged to be the most suitable to receive the new doctrine. So it represented something of a part-way stage between the full Buddha-knowledge of the Enlightenment and conventional wisdom. It was addressed not to "ordinary" people, but to experienced ascetics who had already left the worldly life but were deeply enmeshed in wrong views about the ultimate goal. In short, the formula itself is a veritable "Middle Way."

As we have seen, the gaining of full Enlightenment requires vast amounts of continuous development and favorable conditions. The Buddha saw that the unobstructed knowledge of "true nature" was beyond the capacities of unprepared beings. First of all, the hardened crust of impurity had to be at least partly removed and a new outlook adopted before the "deep, subtle, and transcendental knowledge" could be accessible.

In this connection a favorite simile of the Buddha was the example of the man pierced by an arrow. Such a man would be foolish to start a detailed inquiry into who fired it, from which direction, and so on. The immediate need is to remove it. Causes, reasons, and everything else can wait until the wound is treated; otherwise the patient will die, and both the questions and answers will be tragically irrelevant.

Such a supposed situation explains why the Buddha is sometimes called the Great Physician, who knows the nature of the disease or wound, who reassures the patient that a cure is possible, and who sets about the requirements of the cure first and foremost. This was just the position at the time of the first preaching, and it remains so. The formula of the Four Noble Truths presents us with the fact of the universal disease, that there are causes for it, and a cure. The cure requires a number of specific medicines, which should be applied at once.

THE BASIC FORMULA OF THE FOUR NOBLE TRUTHS (ARYASATYA)

Here then is the formula in its concise form:

1. All existence is suffering (duhkha).
2. The true origination of suffering has been discovered (samudaya).
3. The stopping of that suffering is possible (nirodha).
4. The Way leading to the stopping of suffering is eight-fold (marga).

Regarded in the light of the metaphor of the Great Physician, these Four Truths are described thus:

The first truth of suffering specifies the disease.
The second truth of the origination shows the cause of the disease.
The third truth of stopping is the cure.
The fourth truth of the Way or Path is the medicine that cures.

This basic formula summarizes the true situation as seen by an Enlightened Buddha and expressed with a view to convincing unenlightened people of the prevalent sickness while pointing out the means of restoring full health.

THE BRIEF MEANINGS

The pronouncement of the Four Noble Truths was actually made in rather more detail, though even here in a quotation from the texts there is much not readily grasped at first sight:

> "What, then, monks, is the Noble Truth of Suffering?"
>
> "Birth is suffering, decay is suffering, sickness is suffering, death is suffering; to be in situations one does not like is suffering, the separation from what one likes is suffering, not to get what one wants is suffering; in short, the five groups of the grasping/clinging personality (upadanaskandha) are suffering."
>
> "What, then, monks, is the Noble Truth of the origination of suffering?"
>
> "It is the craving/thirst (trsna) that gives rise to rebirth, together with the pleasure and greed that seeks delight here and there; the craving/thirst for sensual pleasure, the craving/thirst for further existence, the craving/ thirst for non-existence."
>
> "What, then, monks, is the Noble Truth of the stopping of suffering?"
>
> "It is the extinction of that craving/thirst,

renouncing it, forsaking it, liberation and detachment from it."

"What, then, monks, is the Noble Truth of the Way that leads to the stopping of suffering?"
"It is the Noble Path in eight parts, namely Right View, Right Intentions, Right Speech, Right Action, Right Livelihood, Right Effort, Right Mindfulness, Right Concentration."

It was in this form that Kaundinya heard it, becoming the first of the five disciples to realize the liberating truth of what it really meant. The other four took a little longer, and no doubt it was a further expansion of the formula that occupied them during the intensive period of instruction that followed.

EXPANDED MEANINGS

The necessary elaboration of this highly concentrated formula resulted in what came to be known as the Sixteen Aspects of the Four Noble Truths. Each of the Four Truths had four kinds of subsidiary meanings:

1. The Truth of Suffering (duhkha)
   because the very nature of existence is painful;
   because of the dependence of all things on causes;
   because of emptiness; nothing lasts;
   because impersonal; no real self can be found.
2. The Truth of Origination (samudaya)
   is the cause because seeds of past actions become causes;
   is the origin because manifestation is due to immediate causes;

is production because of a series of successive appearances;

is conditions because of the concurrence of a variety of conditions.

3. The Truth of Stopping (nirodha)

is cessation because the personality groups (skandhas) are extinguished;

is calm because greed, hatred, and delusion are extinguished;

is sublime because no calamity can occur;

is escape because there are no further causes of pain.

4. The Truth of the Path (marga)

is the Way because one travels it toward Nirvana;

is the correct method because it is effective and supplied with means;

is security because it leads to Nirvana;

is release because it produces a final exit into the beyond.

A definition was also given of each of the eight factors of the Path:

Right Speech is refraining from falsehood, from malicious, harsh, or frivolous speech.

Right Action is refraining from taking life, from stealing, and from sexual misconduct.

Right Livelihood is gaining a living by proper means.

Right Energy is stopping bad thoughts arising and dispelling those already present. It is production of good thoughts not yet arisen and sustaining those already present.

Right Mindfulness is mindful attention to the body, feelings, the mind and Dharmas.

Right Concentration is to attain and abide in the Four Absorptions (dhyana).

THE FORMULA AS FOCUS OF PRACTICE AND
THE FORMULA OF PRACTICAL TECHNIQUE

In all the early Indian Buddhist schools this basic formula (and others) was held to reveal more of its Enlightenment content as one progressed in the practice of its penetration. For the Way was always understood to be gradual. Understanding, revelation, and release were acquired in stages. One well-known text, the *Dhammapada*, puts it thus: "Let a wise man blow off his own impurities, as a smith blows off the impurities of silver, one by one, little by little, and from time to time."

The same theme occurs many times in the texts. It is just this way with the Four Noble Truths. The expanded meanings and the Sixteen Aspects illustrate the growth or depth derived from the original formula. At some point in the early Indian development the process was formalized into a five-stage passage leading to Nirvana. The detail of the five stages will be explained later.

Now, in connection with the Four Noble Truths, the middle stage of the five consists of a profound penetration of the formula similar to Kaundinya's experience, which conveys an absolute conviction of its verity and a direct perception of its operation. It is recorded that this experience was so moving that the meditator sometimes gave an involuntary cry: "Oh, what suffering."

This middle stage is known as the Way of Vision (darsanamarga), and its name suggests what is involved. The *Abhidharma* texts refer to this "visionary" perception as a "comprehension" (abhisamaya), and the whole process is surprisingly brief. It consists of only sixteen thought-moments, but each of these is very highly charged. The sixteen thoughts are directed upon the sixteen-aspect version of the formula in a particularly powerful manner. By means of eight pairs of moments, one a realization (ksanti) and one a knowledge (jnana), full comprehension of each aspect is gained and all doubt is destroyed. This is followed in series by the destruction of the gross passions of greed and hatred as well as the certain knowledge that one is released from them.

This stage of "vision" marks the entry into the Path proper. Final Nirvana can then be reached in a maximum of seven more births. Thus the stage of darsanamarga is also called "Entry into the Stream" (srota-apanna). The deep penetration to realization of the full meaning of the Four Noble Truths just described is a prime example of the conjunction of Teaching and Practice characteristic of the Dharma as a whole. In this case we have a visionary grasp of the content of doctrinal formulations that gives rise to positive, marked progress in the Way of extrication from the "fires" of greed, hatred, and delusion.

Another brief formula comes into play here. As all the major doctrinal formulas are examples of the interdependence of Teaching and Practice, they are meant to be opened out and explored as a means of obtaining insight (prajna) as well as that special comprehension (abhisamaya) of their essence that destroys doubts and certain categories of defilements (klesa). The brief formula this describes how that is to be done consists of just three Sanskrit words:

1. To listen to (or read) the Teaching attentively (sruta).
2. Then to ponder and consider what one has heard (cinta).
3. Then to apply to all that meditative concentration (bhavana).

This is the key practice technique that applies throughout the whole range of the Dharma, Mahayana, as well as Mainstream. The words of the discourse or of the formula have to be listened to (or read) with maximum attention and taken to heart. Their meaning and import then have to be mulled over, weighed, compared with experience, and carefully considered. Finally, the acute and sustained concentration (samadhi) developed by meditation practice has to be directed upon a distillation of all that until the inner meaning unfolds and the formula reveals its liberating insight. That revelation is what propels the practitioner along the Path.

Here we have one of the primary reasons for careful attention to the terminology and for the preservation and transmission of the Dharma texts. The words and phrases, especially in the formularies, are parcels and packages containing the real meaning of the Teaching. Part of the proper practice is to focus on these parcels until they open up. Thus dynamic cooperation between Teaching or Doctrine and the Practice produces progress in the Path.

TWO PHASES OF GRADUAL PROGRESS

Of course, the deep penetrative meditation of the Teaching and Entry into the Stream is an advanced stage. Yet it is open to all. Some may be fit to approach it because of their karmic inheritance, but intense and sustained application is required, and so efforts of this kind are usually reserved for the cloister. The Way is indeed gradual but there is a "fast gradual" and a "slow gradual."

The "fast gradual" is the rapid cure of the man wounded by the arrow. It consists of the removal of the arrow and the closing of the wound. The nature of the process can be painful, and it is best performed in the ideal circumstances of a sterilized operating theater. The "fast gradual" or rapid cure was regarded by all the Mainstream schools as the province of the monk or nun under close instruction. For such a candidate embarking on the approach to the Way proper, his instruction and mode of life centered upon three major elements—another formula:

1. Strict moral conduct (sila).
2. Developing skill in one-pointed concentration (samadhi).
3. Gaining access to insight-wisdom (prajna).

The first of these three, sila, is the foundation stone on which rests the whole structure of the teaching/practice combination. For the monk or nun actually beginning this "cure," strict moral conduct and detailed discipline are meant to detach the practitioner from superfluous involvements, cardinal passions, and defilements once and for all. By accepting this disciplines and regimen from the start, the monk or nun puts aside the natural turbulence and compromises of everyday worldly life so as to produce a degree of calm and mental clarity. This basis of strict sila acts becomes support and condition for the refinement of concentration, which can then be directed to the assembly of formulas or teaching "packages." The practioner thereby takes hold of the "packages" and begins to unravel them. This concentration in its turn becomes the initial element of the insight-wisdom (praina) that actually penetrates to the inner contents, and by probing the embedded arrow, enables it to be finally dislodged.

For the general majority, the less hardy, or those more closely circumscribed by their inherited circumstances, the "slow gradual" approach is prescribed by the Great Physician. For the wounded man of this kind, it is a case of alleviating pain, breaking off the arrow shaft to prevent aggravating the wound, and reducing the fever. This approach also involves finding shelter from exposure to further arrow wounds. The removal of the arrowhead has to be postponed until the fever abates and strength is restored. For them another formula applies:

1. Generosity and supporting activity (dana).
2. Basic moral conduct (sila).
3. Consolidating the conditions for a favorable rebirth (svarga).

This majority is the community of lay-followers, those who recognize and accept the Lord Buddha as their guide, his Dharma or Teaching as their torch to illuminate the Way, and those who help and support those "fast runners" who precede them.

These are the traditional Three Jewels of Buddha, Dharma, Samgha, which are the shelter within which all, monks and lay alike, take refuge. By generous giving and other good actions, the lay-follower sets in train the development of future happy and fruitful conditions for himself. By the practice of basic moral conduct they avoid falling into the lower destinies at death, and in the present they reduce their "fever" and prevent exposure to further arrow wounds. They look to a later opportunity for gaining full recovery when the ripening of conditions opens up the possibility of switching to the "fast track" of the rapid cure. A good example of this form of teaching to lay people, as employed by the Buddha himself, was presented earlier as the case of a gambler who makes a "lucky throw." The lay majority also looked to the "achievers" on the "fast track" to witness for them that the Path was indeed attainable and that it actually produced the results claimed for it.

These two groups of practitioners—the totally devoted candidate for the Path proper who has "gone forth" and the faithful householder supporters who keep them in the basic necessities and who observe their progress for encouragement and inspiration—these two groups formed the basis for the traditional mutually dependent wings of the Samgha. That is how it always was and how it remained in all the Samghas of Asia for many centuries.

THE THREE SIGNS OR SEALS OF THE DHARMA

The long vistas conjured up by the teaching of many successive Buddhas also emphasizes another crucial matter. Many times we find the statement that each Buddha re-discovers the ultimate truth, which is always there but unperceived and unreachable until a Buddha re-opens the Way. There are passages in the texts where the Buddha speaks to his monks concerning this and where he expresses something of the Enlightenment experience itself. These sections often contain enigmatic phrases, which should not now surprise us, given the nature of full Enlightenment and the difficulties involved in expressing, let alone teaching, what took place under the Bodhi tree. One such statement, whose few words belie its depth of meaning, is found repeated in the Pali canonical texts as well as in certain primary Mahayana sutras: "Whether Saints appear in the world or not, the true nature of things (dharmanam dharmata) is always present."

Even a casual reading of this brief quotation shows it to be very close to an absolute statement about "true nature." It also expresses in just two Sanskrit words what it is that Buddhas rediscover. No wonder these enigmatical remarks occupied the attention of Buddhist masters for ages. This "true nature" is the very stuff and essence of all the Teaching and the revealing of it for each one of us is the ultimate goal and purpose of all practice.

Such statements are not, like the Four Noble Truths, pitched to a particular level of listener. They are much closer to the heart of the matter and to things as they really are, and so they do not have a practical dimension at all. Therefore, when we find the same absolute style of expression being used for a statement on the "true nature" of things, which is also linked to the practical formula of the Four Noble Truths, we can be sure it is of more than usual importance.

Such a statement, also brief, is again to be found in the Pali canonical texts:

> Whether Perfect Ones appear in the world or
> whether Perfect Ones do not appear in the world,
> it still remains a firm condition, an immutable fact,
> and fixed law: that all formations are imperma-
> nent, subject to suffering, and impersonal.

It is obvious from a comparison of the two extracts that the opening phrases about Perfect Ones (or Saints) appearing in the world are variant translations of words which, in the original language, are the same in both cases. They are followed by the absolute mode, as in the words "always present" and "immutable fact." In the case of the latter extract, these immutable facts came to be regarded as the hallmark or special characteristics of the Dharma. As with so many of the main teachings this statement was later rendered as a formula and doing so emphasized the clarity and precision of the original. Here is the basic formula with the original Sanskrit added as it appeared in a variety of early texts:

All composites are impermanent.
 (sarve samskara anityah)
All composites are suffering/turbulent.
 (sarve samskara duhkha)
All the elements are without a Self.
 (sarve dharmah anatmanah)
Nirvana is peace.
 (santam nirvanam)

In the Sanskrit versions the fourth line on Nirvana is added, first to make this concise statement a complete representation of the Dharma as a whole, and second to complete the inner logic of the meaning. As in previous cases, the formula needs to be opened out. The difference here is that each line leads into the next, as we shall see.

INTERLINKED MEANINGS OF MAJOR FORMULAS

Everything and everyone changes incessantly (anityata). From the atom, up through mankind and the physical world to the stars and the nebula, all is in process of change. This is usually perceived or conceived of as happening slowly, and we sometimes call it development or evolution.

In fact, close analysis by instrumentation or by inward reflection shows that the change is actually brought about by moment-to-moment displacement or interaction of small constituents. For example, the shape of a cloud changes slowly, swelling or contracting and propelled en masse by the wind. What is really happening is that the constituents of the cloud, water particles, etc., are moving and combining rapidly, and it is their condensation and evaporation that determine the shape and the very existence of the cloud itself.

This brings us to a rather more precise perception. It is that everything and everyone is a composite (samskara), made up of a variety of basic elements. Because it is the nature of these basic elements to have a short life and give way to others, equally short-lived, the composite as a whole changes. But the change in fact takes place at the rate of its constituent elements, moment-to-moment. Thus the change involves the loss of one combination, to be replaced imperceptibly by another, ad infinitum.

Now for the second of the Signs or Seals. This incessant change, this replacing of certain things with others, with some dying and others being born, results in a general turbulence or commotion, described in the texts as the birth, growth, decline, and death of all phenomena.

We may very properly recall at this point the full meaning of the word Samsara, which includes just this. The birth, growth, decline, and death, the constant arc of existence, necessarily applies to everyone and everything. And it continues unabated into infinity. The arena and its performers are a non-stop show. Thus, the turbulence, the churning, the incessant change go on without a break and beyond any control. So, outwardly, "all composites are turbulent" (duhkha).

Inwardly too, the composites are turbulent, not only because our constituents describe the universal arc, but because the very condition of turbulence produces suffering (duhkha).

What we like disappears, and what we dislike reappears. What we like sometimes comes back again, but it soon goes, and the perpetual turmoil gives rise to constant loss and consequent instability. Here we are involved in an extended version of the first and second Noble Truths, and it is a clear example of how these main teaching formulas interlock with each other. The penetration of one leads into the others and we find ourselves moving through a highly integrated series of formulas, each of which contains insights of similar flavor.

With the third Sign or Seal the change of subject from composites (samskara) to elements (dharmas) is significant but is sometimes lost or obscured in an English translation. Under the third Sign, the formula treats the little wretches that actually cause the change, the turbulence and the suffering: the constituent elements (dharmas) themselves. Remember that the composite is what it is because of the combination of its elements. The composite is only how a conglomerate of elements appears to one's view. The cloud is simply the outward and visible shape that its constituent elements assume from moment to moment. In concentrated inward introspection, or in microscopic analysis of the physical organism, the elements are seen as in constant flux, no part ever at rest for a moment. Body and mind are alike in this; they are both in a perpetual state of modification. In this respect they only differ in the rate of change, in the speed at which the change takes place.

An inkling of what is going on can be gained if we stop and observe objectively what goes on in our own heads. But even here the intensity and quality of the observation change. If we want to sustain the observation, it soon has to be buttressed by other elements, such as the will. And here we reach the interrelated third Sign. Because the elements of the body and mind, as with all else, arise and pass away so remorselessly, there is no permanent, central, unchanging Self (anatman). There is no entity or inner core around which all the change revolves. There is no heartstuff or substance to which everything else happens or that possesses changing qualities, while it remains central, stable, and receptive.

In short, there is no soul or self that moves intact through life being affected by experience and eventually passing out of the body intact for more of the same somewhere else. There is, rather, an unstable mix of all the active elements changing or being displaced momentarily but preserving temporary forms and feelings. As long as the constituents (dharmas) repeat a certain pattern, form, or appearance, the composite (samskara) preserves a nominal identity. The shape of the cloud illustrates this well. The outward shape has a "character." There are storm clouds and summer clouds and clouds with silver linings. But the fundamental reality of their composition remains the same: total and constant flux.

All three Signs were brought together in a single teaching by the Buddha when he explained to his monks how this state of affairs should be dealt with:

> "What do you think, monks? Are bodily form and sense impressions (rupa) permanent or impermanent?"
>
> "Impermanent, Lord," they replied.
>
> "Are feeling (vedana), perception (samjna), mental composites (samskara), and consciousness (vijnana), permanent or impermanent?"
>
> "Impermanent, Lord," they replied.
>
> "But what is impermanent—is that pleasant or

the cause of suffering (duhkha)?"

"It is suffering, Lord," they replied.

"But of that which is impermanent—suffering and subject to change—when that is considered, could one rightly say; This belongs to me, this is me, this is my self?"

"No, Lord," they replied.

Therefore, whatever there is of bodily form, whether past, present, or future, internal or external, gross or subtle, far or near, one should understand it according to reality and true wisdom: this does not belong to me, this is not me, this is not my self.

Once again this is an extended formula meant to be penetrated so as to reveal its liberating insight. It is a formula that combines teaching and practice in high degree and so is a proper candidate for the exercise of that special technique of listening or reading that is considered a pondering prelude to meditative concentration.

It is hardly to be wondered that the formula of the Three (Four) Signs or Seals came to be regarded as a comprehensive summary of Mainstream Teaching as a whole. Entry into its underlying meanings and application lead into other formulas of teaching and practice, and, eventually, with the gaining of insight-wisdom, into proximity with the nature of things.

In the next section, we move somewhat closer to the great wisdom of the full Enlightenment. We shall consider some of the special formulas of advanced practice, including the king of all formulas, the Pratityasamutpada, or "Arising Due to Conditions." This formula summarizes, or tries to, the very essence of the Buddha's supreme insight into the world-process.

In addition, the next section will contain an exposition of the Buddhist doctrine of Karman. Once more the ancient texts will be called upon to explain a topic rarely treated in any detail in Western interpretations of the Dharma.

The Dharma:
Ends,
Means,
and Views

9. THE DHARMA OF PROGRESSIVE INVESTIGATION: DHATUS, SKANDHAS, DHARMAS

We have already seen that Sakyamuni Buddha's instructions and teaching often took the form of concise formulas that were capable of expansion and extension by way of explanation. These formulas are also interlocked with each other in a way that led from one doctrine to another. These interlocking, progressive formulas illustrate the underlying method and technique of the Buddha's teaching. The Buddha's teaching after his full Enlightenment showed that the awesome depth and range of full Enlightenment was just not within reach of ordinary people immersed in their worldly affairs. However, those with a degree of purity of conduct and of detachment were the likeliest candidates to hear and understand something. It was also clear that the first formulation of the Teaching to the five monks at Benares did not seek to express the inner content of Sakyamuni's Enlightenment.

The first major formula of the Four Noble Truths started from a position, a knowledge, and an experience familiar to the five monks—that ordinary worldly life is full of suffering. This basic point of contact was deepened and extended to include not only their experience but all experience and existence. From that initial linkage between the Enlightened and the unenlightened, the five were guided onward to perceive for themselves, first the illusory nature of their separate personalities, and finally the nature of the bonds preventing them from breaking free from all the defilements causing the suffering. If the Buddha had begun by describing his own Enlightenment experience the five would probably have listened but understood nothing, and they would doubtless have gone off shaking their heads in perplexity, like the ascetic who met Sakyamuni on the road to Benares from the Bodhi tree. In short, that kind of teaching would have served no purpose as far as the five disciples were concerned. In this, as in so many other cases, the events of the Buddha's life serve as a paradigm for us to read and to mark.

So there are certain essential features of the Teaching for us to bear in mind as we begin this series of expositions. Foremost among these is the fact that the various doctrines are set at different levels, beginning at points that are accessible to the many and which lead onward and inward toward the special insights and experience that form the necessary transit stages on a marked route carrying the practitioner to the ultimate goal. The whole length of this route is punctuated by further formulas or doctrinal expressions, which only deliver their full impact if and when the preceding stages have been realized by the prescribed interior practices. Of course, the doctrinal formulas have an intellectual content that has to be perceived as an essential ingredient in the assimilation process. But if separated from the experience, one is left outside the building, so to speak, admiring or criticizing to little purpose. Once again, then, it is necessary to emphasize the intimate connection between doctrine and practice.

It may not be superfluous, therefore, to remind the reader of the content of the prime formula of Mainstream Indian Buddhism, that of the Four Noble Truths. This formula makes a diagnosis of the disease, states the cure, the causes, and the means of achieving that cure. Contrary to modern medical practice, in this therapeutic system the patient himself has to arrive at a conviction of the validity of the diagnosis and the causes. Only then can the means produce the cure.

The detailed expositions of the Teaching or Dharma that follow should be seen in this light. All the formulas and explanations carry a degree of persuasion as they stand, but that is only part of the story. The intention is to arouse in the "traveller" a provisional acquiescence or confidence in a working hypothesis, which will then lead on to entry into the specific practices linked to the formulas. It is rather like an uncertain traveller who, shortly after beginning the journey into unknown territory, comes upon further signposts, which continue to point him in the right direction. Successful passage through the doctrinal practices is what provides the conviction, and the conviction in turn motivates the traveller to attempt the approach to the highway proper. Only then can a final arrival at the cure be anticipated.

THE FORMULA OF THE EIGHTEEN DHATUS

It is worth noting at once that the general thrust of the Buddha's teaching is inward, toward the root causes of every individual's response to events. Outward or external phenomena and worldly happenings are of secondary importance. The cure for the world's sickness is not to be found in the removal of the external factors that appear to give rise to the condition. Certainly removal of conditions provides temporary alleviation, but the nature of universal change and impermanence constantly replaces one set of sorrowful events with others of similar kind. Even a cursory study of history will show systems, dynasties, and empires imposing their weight on adherents and neighbors alike, giving way naturally or violently to others that proceed to do just the same, though perhaps in different ways. In the Buddhadharma the aim is to get at the inner workings of the world-process affecting each person and to disengage the linkage locking everyone into the constant and interminable repetition of trouble and distress. In brief, the cure is deliberately intended to be definitive and final for each person able and willing to fulfill what is required to that end.

Hence the distinction of the "fast gradual" and the "slow gradual." The fast gradual scheme is the means and method to be applied for the total cure of the third Noble Truth, that of stopping suffering forever. That is the only worthwhile therapy. The slow gradual is simply a partial application of the total cure with correspondingly partial results. Accordingly, the detailed formulas and practices described hereafter are those forming part of the total therapy and, as such, they are traditionally reserved for monks who have severed all ties of family and of worldly affairs for that express purpose.

The inward orientation of the Dharma is well illustrated by the next pair of formulas to be considered. The first of them, the Formula of the Eighteen Dhatus or Domains, deals with the world as such. But it immediately emphasizes that our connection or contact with the world in all its multifarious forms depends entirely on the reports of our senses and on the handling of those reports within the mind. In terms of our earlier metaphor of the man wounded by an arrow, this formula represents the probing of the wound and the incisions required to lay open the affected area to reveal the muscles, ligaments, nerves, and basic bone structure in which the arrowhead is embedded.

Such "probing" is an apt description of the process of inward examination and observation involved in these formulas for the purpose of gaining access to the working mechanism of our experience of the world, both inner and outer. The practice formulas also serve to concentrate the attention on root causes within and to check instinctive reactions which only sustain the mechanism.

Figure 1A is headed by a quotation from the Pali text of the *Samyutta* in which Sakyamuni instructs his monks on "the All." He says to them that the whole world in fact consists for us of the objects and relationships perceived by our five senses plus the mental phenomena or thoughts that arise in the mind. He then goes on to explain that contact with the world relies upon the linkage of each of the sense fields with its corresponding consciousness. The resulting general awareness of what is going on depends upon an amalgam of such groups of three, one triple group for each of the senses. The schematic grid diagrams this explanation together as a whole. In the text, the Buddha went on to say that nothing of the world is left out of this framework, all is spanned and contained within this series of six triads. Hence the opening statement about teaching the All.

An examination of Figures 1A and 1B will show how body and mind are analyzed and how the external and the internal are related. Notice in this formula that thoughts are treated as objects in just the same way as sense impressions of externals in that they are inwardly perceptible as factors or elements in our conscious life. What is not shown, but which forms part of the extended explanations of the *Abhidharma* treatises, is that each triad has to be complete before any actual experience takes place. If either the visual object or the eye faculty is missing no visual consciousness will arise. And if consciousness itself is in

The Eighteen Diatus

Bhikkhus, I will teach you the All. Now what is the All? It is just the eye and visible objects, the ear and sounds, the nose and odors, the tongue and tastes, the body and tangible objects, the mind and objects of mind. . . —Samyutta XXXV 23

Dependent upon the eye and visible objects, visual consciousness arises. Contact is the coming together of these three.
Dependent upon the ear and sounds: sound consciousness.
Dependent upon the nose and odors: smell consciousness.
Dependent upon the tongue and tastes: taste consciousness.
Dependent upon the body and tangible objects: touch consciousness.
Dependent upon the mind and objects of mind: mind consciousness. —Samyutta XXXV 60

Schematic Grid

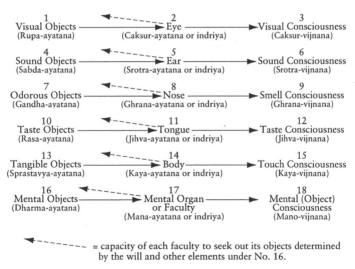

Figure 1A

155

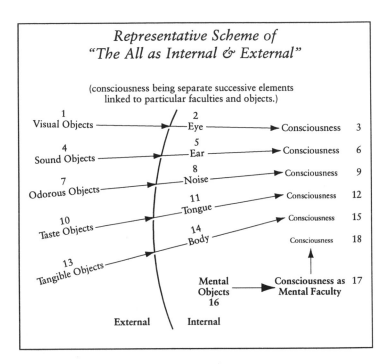

Representative Scheme of
"The All as Internal & External"

(consciousness being separate successive elements
linked to particular faculties and objects.)

1
Visual Objects ——————→ 2
Eye ——————→ Consciousness 3

4
Sound Objects ——————→ 5
Ear ——————→ Consciousness 6

7
Odorous Objects ——————→ 8
Noise ——————→ Consciousness 9

10
Taste Objects ——————→ 11
Tongue ——————→ Consciousness 12

13
Tangible Objects ——————→ 14
Body ——————→ Consciousness 15

Consciousness 18

Mental Objects ——————→ Consciousness as 17
16   Mental Faculty

External | Internal

Figure 1B

156

The Five Skandhas

Bhikkhus, I will teach you the things which should be fully understood and what is full understanding . . .

Now what, Bhikkhus, are the things which should be fully understood? The body [rupa] is a thing which should be fully understood. Feeling [vedana] is a thing which should be fully understood. Perception [samjña is a thing which should be fully understood. Mental activities [samskaras] is a thing which should be fully understood. Consciousness [vijnana] is a thing which should be fully understood.

And what, Bhikkhus, is full understanding? The extinction of greed, aversion, and delusion. —Samyutta XXII 23

The Scheme of the Five Groups (Skandhas) of Each Person

I →	II →	III →	IV →	V →
Rupa	Vedana	Samjña	Samskaras	Vijnana
(Bodily faculties and their objects.) Comprises: -all 5 senses and their fields.	(Feelings) A single element.	(Perception) A single element.	(Composites) Comprises:-7 groups of mental elements or energies. 1. Basics, including the will, memory and skandhas II & III. 2. Good elements 3. Defiled elements 4. Bad elements 5. "Outflows" from defilements 6. Indeterminate elements 7. "Special" elements	(Consciousness) A single element.

Figure 2A

157

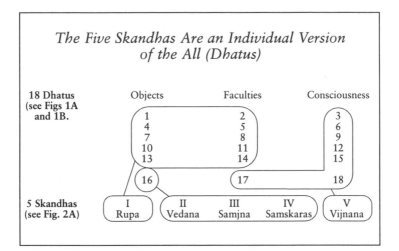

Figure 2B

abeyance—say we are "unconscious,"—then the linkage of the eye faculty with its visual object will not register. Each of the six sets of triads is thus interdependent.

All this is fairly straightforward, if rather simplistic, but for the monk practitioner this grid of "the All" had to be brought into direct view. He had to experience the fact of it for himself. Anyone who has attempted this mode of self-analysis will know that to maintain direct observation of the operation of this grid, the first requirement is to slow everything down. Our everyday awareness is normally a semi-chaotic mixture of sights, sounds, physical contacts, and surrounding thought processes, which defy observation in detail unless the volume and pace of the inflow of impressions is reduced.

This, too, is part of the therapy. The monk needs to withdraw from everyday activities; he needs seclusion and he needs to be still. Only then can the sensory ingredients be separated out. Of course, a monk practitioner of long standing can maintain this analytical observation while performing ordinary functions such as standing, walking, sitting, and eating. But he still needs to function with care and attention, with so-called mindfulness, a state of recollectedness that, once mastered, helps to produce that dignified, unhurried calm which marks the practicing recluse.

Needless to say, the self-disciplined inner awareness just described is not practiced for the sake of appearances. The purpose is mainly twofold. First, to penetrate to the actual workings of the psycho-physical "machine" so that the separate elements of its functioning are brought into direct view. Second, the very process of objective examination filters out the grosser forms of instinctive response or habitual reaction and thus establishes a degree of stability. Such an attitude is sometimes described in the texts as a state of "mindfulness and self-control." But this is only the beginning.

THE FORMULA OF THE FIVE SKANDHAS

The second of these initial practice formulas is called the Five Skandhas, meaning groups or aggregates. In the principal *Abhidharma* treatise, both dhatus and skandhas are combined because of the operation of the same elements making up the dhatus (see Figure 2B). Here, however, the skandhas are considered separately so as to show a different mode of operation as well as a vital function not displayed in the dhatu grid.

The quotation at the head of Figure 2A shows how the

Buddha presented this scheme to his monks. He first states that this is what has to be fully understood. Then he sets out the five groupings and concludes with the purpose of the exercise, which is the extinction of the three "fires" that attach to all five under normal circumstances.

As can be seen from Figure 2A itself, this is an analysis of each and every individual. Each person consists of these five groups of factors, and nothing more. The essential difference between this formula and that of the dhatus is that here a whole mass of mental impressions (groups II, III, IV) combine to produce ideas and colorings, which are interposed between the sense objects and consciousness. We rarely, if ever, perceive anything simply without it being surrounded and screened by mental responses. These responses interpret, assess, and color the perceived object in such a way that our everyday perception processes are bundles of sensory or mental composites tinged and qualified by emotional reactions plus images from memory.

An example of an everyday occurrence may help to show how the five skandhas represent our experience. Let us say that you see someone in the street whom you recognize. In very rapid sequence there occur:

Rupa: From the body, the eye sees an object, i.e., another person.

Vedana: Instantly there then arises a pleasant, unpleasant, or neutral feeling. This is not a like or a dislike, simply an instinctive reaction of harmful or not.

Samjna: Whether the object is male or female, whether it is it known or unknown, and its color combinations are then perceived.

Samskaras: Several bundles of states arise now. If known and liked, there is confidence and desire to meet again. Or if known and not liked, there is animosity and the desire to avoid.

Vijnana : All this is imprinted on consciousness, and one is aware of it all together. The whole composite experience can be recalled by memory later.

This illustration is highly simplified and is not a strictly accurate representation of what takes place. But it is generally correct both in the sequence of operation of each of the skandhas and in the picture produced by the slowing down of events. The exercise also brings into focus the cardinal doctrine of impermanence, in that it all lasts just a few moments and is immediately replaced by something else. And it also allows the formation of the "right view" of how the three "fires" of greed, aversion, and delusion are intimately involved in all our perceptions. The five-fold analysis, once mastered, shows in addition that because the separate groups of events come into view and then pass away, they are thus without an enduring substance. Despite their surface appearance of stability and identity, once slowed down and seen in their composite form there is nowhere to be found a lasting central entity corresponding in fact to our ingrained ideas of "me" and "mine." Of course, the inner and outer configuration of body and mind in contact with sense objects leads us to believe that "I" have seen someone, and "I" don't want to meet them, so "I" avoid them. That personal viewpoint is not denied. What is denied is that the "I" feeling is a real, separate, unchanging entity. The five-fold analysis reveals that idea to be deceptive. The actual sequence consists of elements of consciousness changing moment to moment under the impact of continuous sense impressions and responses. In fact, the feeling of "I" and "mine" actually encourages thoughts of like and dislike, wanting and rejecting, which in combination represent the second Noble Truth of craving, etc., which is defined as the root cause of all the suffering and disturbance.

Apart from the practical purpose of this formula it is worth noting that at least one of its special insights had significant results in the later Mahayana analysis of total subjectivity. In this present doctrine representing Mainstream Hinayana, the internal and the external are recognized as distinct categories. Thus the first group, Rupa (see Figure 2A), includes the external objects and the internal sense faculties. In this way the five-group combination comprising each personality extends to the objects perceived.

So, in a sense what we see, hear, touch, etc., is part of our make-up, although external to our physical organism. However, this merely serves to stress that what we experience as external has already been filtered and colored by the intervening mental processes, and so what we normally perceive as a result of sensory activity is not a true image of what is really out there.

The discipline of inward analysis is, in some respects, a means of transforming the Five-Skandha mode of experience into that of the eighteen dhatu. In the dhatu grid one arrives at what has been called "bare attention," or the experience of nothing but the sense impressions or nothing but the separate mental states. In this way the coloring and selectivity that arise from intermixing the feelings, emotions, and desires (Figure 2A, groups II, III, IV) with simple sense contact is removed. In the discipline of the eighteen dhatu, the contents of vedana, samjna, and samskara skandhas are confined to the grid section mental objects (Figure 2B, No. 16), where it can be neutralized.

None of the Mainstream consensus allows for total subjectivity, despite the Skandha system of including external objects in the personality combination.

All the Hinayana schools maintain that the external world is firmly "out there" and consists of elements of matter etc. What the Skandha scheme emphasizes is that each person's connection with the "out there" is constantly flawed in the same way that eyes with cataracts produce flawed vision: precisely because extraneous factors intervene between direct contact. Hence the need for rigorous discipline. Much later, when the Yogacara/Vijnanavada lineage was established, this intimate relationship between external objects and the perceiving personality was re-evaluated. The result for Yogacara was the doctrine that our perceptions of the external world are completely subjective, i.e., what we see outside is a projection of what is inside. But that is another story.

In earlier pages, mention has been made of the close interaction of doctrine and practice, as well as the interlinking of major doctrinal formulas. Now we have just seen something of the inward thrust of the analytical process designed to disentangle the filters and coloring agents from events as they are. To bring all this together into a schematic and practical whole, there now follows a *precis* of the prime textual handbook for this entire procedure.

The text occurs in both Pali and Sanskrit collections of scripture but is perhaps best known under its Pali title "satipatthana," which is usually rendered as "The Foundation of Mindfulness." In this text, which describes itself as "the only way" to release, the doctrines of the skandhas, dhatus, and the Noble Truths are linked together in a progressive system of meditational practice wherein the recluse detaches himself stage by stage from all the causes of grief and suffering. This text also tells us that the "very highest knowledge and release can be gained in just seven days of intensive practice following its detailed instructions." For us it demonstrates clearly the aim and the purpose of all the doctrines discussed here so far.

The sutta begins by telling us that the Buddha once addressed his monks while staying among the Kuru people. He said to them that there is only one way to stop suffering, to gain the right path and the attainment of Nibbana (Skt.: Nirvana), and that is the Four Foundations of Mindfulness. The four are: the body, feelings, thoughts (citta), and mental objects (dharmas). A monk should live by contemplating these four, being ardent, clearly comprehending, and mindful.

First, to contemplate the body the monk should go to the forest or an empty place, and there he should sit cross-legged, keeping his body erect and alert. Then he should attend closely to his breathing, knowing when he breathes in or out or whether he breathes short or long breaths. He trains in this practice to calm the body. Thus he arrives at awareness of the body both internally and externally.

After gaining that calm awareness of the body and breath, he proceeds to concentrated awareness of whatever bodily posture he adopts, whether standing, sitting, lying down, or moving. Mindfulness on all this is established, and he applies clear comprehension to all his activities, such as eating, speaking, natural functions, dressing, and undressing.

After that the monk reflects on the impurity of the body. He considers his body from the soles of his feet up to the crown of his head, thinking of all the organs, flesh, hair, bones, sinews, blood, and other liquids contained within his envelope of skin. He considers and becomes aware of all the various constituents.

He also considers how the body contains the four material elements of earth, water, fire, and wind.

Then he observes the corpses decomposing in the charnel ground, noticing all the stages of decay and disintegration, and he thinks that such a fate awaits his own body in due time and that there is no escape. In so doing he begins to detach from the world.

He then begins the contemplation of feelings (vedana) and distinguishes pleasant and unpleasant from neither. He comes to be mindful when such feelings exist.

After that he contemplates thoughts (citta) and distinguishes thoughts accompanied by lust, by hatred, and by ignorance. He gains awareness of thoughts that are distracted, developed, or concentrated. He notices those associated with higher mental states and with lower ones. He perceives when the impurities are present in him, impurities such as sense-desire, anger, sloth, agitation, and doubt. In this way he begins to identify specific mental states (dharmas); when they are present, when they arise, and when they pass away.

From this he goes on to consider the five grasping aggregates (upadanaskandhas). He brings into focus material form (rupa), feeling (vedana), perception (samjna), the composites (samskaras), and consciousness (vijnana). He gains awareness of how each arises and passes away.

He also brings into view inwardly the six internal and the six external sense bases. (These are the twelve objects and faculties, ayatana, of the dhatu grid, Figure 1A). He observes the eye and visual objects, the ear and sounds, the nose and smells, the tongue and tastes, the body and tangibles, the mind and mental objects. With each of these he perceives the hindrances that depend on each pair and how they arise and pass away also.

At this stage the monk also takes account of the special mental faculties that he acquires during the whole process. They are the seven factors of Enlightenment: mindfulness, investigation, energy, joy, tranquillity, concentration, and equanimity. He knows when they are present in him and when they are not.

Finally, the monk turns to the formula of the Four Noble Truths. He then knows according to reality "that this is suffering, this is its origin, this is its cessation, and this is the road to that cessation." He abides in that contemplation with mindfulness established.

The Buddha concludes this exposition by telling his monks that whosoever practices these Four Foundations of Mindfulness in this manner for seven years can expect two fruits of this practice. Either Highest Knowledge (the state of Arhat) here and now, or, if any traces of impurity remain, the state of Non-Returning (Anagamin, no more rebirth in the realm of all the passions, Kamadhatu). The Buddha goes on to declare that even seven days of such practice can produce the same result. This is the only way for purification, for the destruction of suffering, for attaining the right path, and for Nibbana. So the text concludes. The full translation together with introductory explanations can be found in several versions. The one used here is by Nyanaponika Thera.

For Mainstream Indian Buddhism or the Hinayana there is probably no better illustration of the intimate connection between doctrine and practice than the Satipatthana sutta just summarized. In it can be seen how the doctrinal formulations of the Skandhas, the Dhatus, and the Four Noble Truths are interlinked in a progressive meditational experience until the practitioner knows "according to reality" what it all means and what the words actually represent. The successful achievement of the whole sequence results in the ultimate goal of Nirvana (Pali: Nibbana) here and now and in the relatively short space of seven years practice. For the most ardent and determined and highly endowed, the goal can be gained in a mere seven days.

It should be clear to the reader that this method of inner contemplation by stages would be impossible without a preliminary knowledge of or guidance in the detailed formulas themselves. But at the same time, a study of the formulas, by itself, can never bring about the inner transformation aimed at by the meditational exercises, which actually carry the practitioner along the route marked out and specified by the formulas. In this manner the vital matter of the ends controlling the means can also be seen in action. The end purpose is Nirvana, and all the formulas and their related practices are oriented accordingly. Even the shortfall of result stated as a possibility provides for an existence out of the everyday world of ordinary experience.

Here the aims are uncompromising in their explicit intention. There is no question of using meditation as a pleasant form of relaxation or as an end in itself. This practice is arduous, it requires constant energy applied to continuous concentration, and it produces specific inner experiences, each of which contributes to a radical modification of the person engaged in the effort. Once again we should be reminded of the long and intense striving of Sakyamuni himself. Set against this yardstick some of the more popular, present day uses of "meditation" for relaxation, or for relief of stress and other ailments, whether real or imagined, can be seen as mere low-key imitations. Seen in the same light, some present day ideas about the need for meditation rather than study miss the point and mistake the purpose for which both are indispensably required. "Practice" is one thing, but the practice of the Path is very often something else entirely. The practice of the Path is what Mainstream Indian Buddhism was about. Indeed, all of the Buddhadharma, Mahayana included, was and is concerned with just that. And the practice of the Path, whether Hinayana or Mahayana, deals with specific, progressive stages leading to declared ends. The Dharma or the Doctrine maps out and details all this in a way that supports and directs the effort to achieve the aims. Thus any kind of practice without its related doctrinal support is unlikely to provide access to this Path.

PROGRESSIVE INVESTIGATION LEADS TO THE
SERIES OF BASIC ELEMENTS (DHARMA SAMTANA)

The text of the *Satipatthana* sutta, although it extends in translation over eighteen pages, is really an elongated formula. This formula contains the entire Holy Path, from the simple state of having "gone forth" up to the attainment of the ultimate goal of Nirvana, or just short of it. Because of the extent of its coverage, the component sections of the text are highly condensed, even stylized. Even so, the sections themselves are instructive as a summary in sequence of the major constituents of the radical cure. It represents an annotated chart-guide to what is actually involved in travelling this Path. We find in it the skandhas and a modified dhatu formula. The final section consists of the Four Noble Truths, and the practitioner who reaches this stage according to reality puts a stop to all further suffering and gains the safe refuge.

But for the purposes of this exposition, the *Satipatthana*

runs ahead of us. Our concern now is with the first four sections of this chart-guide. These opening sections comprise the "Foundation of Mindfulness," and they involve mindful attention to the body, feelings, thoughts, and mental objects or Dharmas, in that order.

The first thing to notice is how these four successive meditational practices follow the inward progress mentioned earlier. The body's breathing and postures come first, followed by feelings, thoughts, and Dharmas, the last being the most inward stage of all. And it is for the purpose of bringing into direct view these basic constituents of all existence that the four-fold practice is so constituted.

These basic elements or Dharmas are another of these key terms of profound significance that need to be understood in any attempt to gain an accurate picture of Mainstream Buddhist teaching. In all probability it is no coincidence that the name of the teaching as such (Dharma) is the same as that given to the elements of existence (dharma). For it is these basic elements that are the only true realities for all Indian Hinayana schools of thought.

The two major analytical schemes already discussed demonstrate this clearly (see Figures 1A and 2A), especially that of the skandhas (Figure 2A). Each of the five divisions of the skandhas scheme consists of a single or multiple of elements (dharmas). Such major formulas aim at describing, by various ways and approaches, the activity and means of dealing with the basic elements. This is the underlying intention of the constant inward thrust of both the practical and doctrinal formularies.

The formula of the Three Signs (or Seals) is another case in point. The first two Signs concern the composites (samskaras), which are again groups of Dharmas. The third Sign deals with the Dharmas themselves and states that among the Dharmas no Atman can be found.

The Atman, or what we normally conceive of as our "self" or "I," is in truth simply a name, a conventional mode of describing constantly changing Dharmas, which appear and disappear in groups or collections. This is true for every "person," event, or stage of practice. They are only names or descriptive means that refer to or designate Dharma activity. The Dharmas themselves are separate and distinct mental factors or perceived material elements. They really exist; that is, they have an independent and recognizable function, and their presence brings others into existence in their wake. Also, because they are momentary, they determine the actual process of change and development.

This underlying process of momentary change is what really comprises each individual, and as such is called the Dharma series or the Dharma stream (dharma-samtana). While it is conventionally acceptable to refer to a "person" or to "me," the true state to which those designations attach is the stream of interconnected and interrelated Dharmas that at a given time and place and in specific conditions appear and disappear in rapid succession, presenting the image of a moving, thinking, acting entity. That is the truth of the matter for all Indian Hinayana.

The most common present-day metaphor for this situation is the procession of visual and auditory images on a cinema or TV screen. The actors or personages all appear as real, separate, and autonomous personalities taking part in real events. But every image that we see consists of a rapid succession of single pictures, each one motionless but differing slightly from its predecessor. Without the innumerable single "stills," no moving talking image is possible. And all the characters and events portrayed have no independent existence other than the constantly changing, rapid sequence of single "frames," which link up in series to project a story or characters. By the same token, the development or activity of the projected images is quite unalterable and will repeat exactly as before unless and until the separate "stills" are understood and either manipulated or "cut."

Just so are the Dharmas in the Dharma-samtana. They are the fundamental entities that in combination-sequence produce the composites and the groupings that we perceive and experience. But because they link together to form various configurations, they are called the Dharma stream or Dharma series (dharma-samtana). Vasubandhu, the great Indian Abidharma master, describes and defines the Dharma-samtana like this:

> The Dharmas, being momentary, exist in series. . . . By series, samtana, we understand material and mental elements uninterruptedly succeeding one another in a procession that has action as originating cause.
>
> The successive moments of this procession are different therefore there is evolution (parinama), transformation of the series.

What are these Dharmas? A great deal of *Abhidharma* literature has been produced to answer that question. This should not surprise us once it is realized that a primary aim and intention of all the practices of the Hinayana Path is to gain access to the level at which they operate. We have seen that the *Satipatthana* sutta, which is nominated as "the only way," specifically leads the meditating practitioner to the Dharma realm in four successive stages of penetration. It has to be so, since every kind of experience, form, and perceived object is a conglomerate of Dharmas. And since it is Dharma activity that produces the suffering, they have to be "got at" in order to gain the third Noble Truth and stop the lot.

So it can be said that Dharmas are the real elements that make up the appearances of continuous change in every aspect of the inner and outer world we experience. While the skandha and dhatu schemes of analysis merely categorize all conscious and objective life into groups of operational factors, the Dharmas are the factors themselves, and as such they are irreducible further. Under normal, everyday conditions of life, the Dharmas are imperceptible, because, apart from their being submerged among our surface impressions and mental activities, they are also momentary. That means they emerge, function, and disappear within a minute space of time, and therefore our ordinary faculties of perception are too coarse to bring them into focus. For us, in ordinary circumstances, it is even difficult to isolate a single thought.

And Dharmas are not simply thoughts. Thoughts are themselves clusters of interrelated mental incidents; that is to say, they are multiples. The distinction is important because the special characteristic of a Dharma is its separate and unmixed nature. The meaning of the word in the etymological sense is as the bearer of a particular mark, quality, characteristic, or nature, not to be confused with any other. Thus the Dharmas are difficult to reach. Their momentary nature and their habit of intermingling in clusters of related entities effectively masks their identification from all but the most refined and acutely concentrated attention. And yet, small as they are, infinitesimal as their lifespan is, they in fact carry the causal impulses that ensure constant repetition and reproduction. It is at the dharmic level that Karman operates, that effects are produced, and that the past and the future make their fleeting contact, through the medium of an instantaneous present.

All the Mainstream Hinayana schools, and some Mahayana ones, subscribe to lists of Dharma-elements. The Sarvastivadins, for instance, have a list of seventy-five and the Yogacara/Vijnanavada a list of a hundred. In most cases they are grouped under the five skandha divisions, as in Figure 2A. Considerations of space and the inevitable onset of boredom in the reader preclude any attempt to deal adequately with the whole range of Dharmas (that too is an occupation of the *Abhidharma*), but a few examples are necessary. The most readily understandable, perhaps, are the Dharmas of the sense activities. The bare, single, exclusive instant of a visual object is a Dharma. That is, the actual moment that the sight object impresses itself on our consciousness and before any other idea of recognition, memory association, or any other factor appears in its wake. Similarly for sounds, tastes, smells, and tangibles. Each and every one is a Dharma.

These are "external" Dharmas, of course. A few of the important "internal" Dharmas are listed below, but remember that each of them is the single, unconnected instant characterized by the function only. Prolongation of the same characteristic over a period of time takes place when a series of single, separate instants repeat without interruption.

adhimoksa	factor of approval.
apramada	diligence or factor of application.
auddhatya	factor of disturbance or agitation.
cetana	the will, the directing or controlling factor.
chanda	factor of intention, tendency for action.
hri	factor of respect or modesty.
krodha	factor of anger or irritation.
pratigha	factor of hostility.
samadhi	factor of one-pointed concentration.
smrti	the memory, a factor repeated from the past.
sraddha	factor of confidence or faith.
upeksa	factor of equanimity or calm.
vihimsa	factor of active harmfulness.
virya	factor of energy or effort.

Two hypothetical examples now follow to show how a succession of related Dharmas can arise and continue in series.

Imagine a temple or shrine in which there is a statue of the Buddha with flowers, candles, and incense placed before it. The hall or room is quiet, and there are devotees seated in silent meditation. A Buddhist visitor enters and looks attentively at the Buddha-rupa. At the moment of that look Dharmas of the visual object arise in continuous succession. That particular visual object is sustained by the Dharma of the will (cetana) and is accompanied by Dharmas of memory (smrti). As soon as that combination is established, other Dharmas are drawn in such as approval (adhimoksa), respect (hri), and faith (sraddha). All of these in continuous succession are amalgamated with and sustained by the long look at the rupa, until together they induce the appearance of equanimity or calm (upeksa). That combination prompts the visitor to sit down, thereby opening the way for the Dharmas of application (apramada) and concentration (samadhi) to operate. All this takes no more than a few moments.

Imagine the same temple or shrine with seated devotees. Say the time and place are the eleventh century in Buddhist Kashmir. A Muslim warrior dismounts outside and strides in through the door. He, too, looks at the Buddha image. The same visual object Dharma activates and is also joined by Dharmas of memory, but of an entirely different kind. That look and the associated memories give rise in him to Dharmas of agitation (auddhatya) and anger (krodha) at the sight of an idol and its infidel worshippers. The anger prompts hostility (pratigha), which is rapidly joined by intention for action (chanda) and then active harmfulness (vihimsa) as he calls in his companions and draws his sword. There follows an orgy of destruction and slaughter, which in their turn give rise to more visual and sensory images and their associated streams of Dharmas. All this takes no more than a few moments.

These two examples are based upon the same external environment, the temple and the rupa. Yet the sequence of mental and active responses to the initial visual object are diametrically opposed in the two individuals who perceived it. But they are exactly similar in the manner of the Dharma-activity that ensues. These two examples are cross sections of two distinct Dharma streams (dharma samtana) and of course are picked out for our purposes from the unbroken Dharma series of each individual concerned. We would ordinarily see those occurrences as persons doing this or that, and in a sense that is correct. But at the Dharma level of existence, at the level of the talkie-film reel, what is really happening is the rapid succession of basic elements forming into clusters and prompting other similar or derived elements to surface and form new clusters, which dissolve and give way to yet more. This is the level at which cause and effect operate, because it is the Dharma elements of any particular moment that determine what immediately follows and what will follow later. The Dharma sequence of anger and hostility cannot give rise to equanimity and calm, and vice versa.

Thus, for mainstream Hinayana the reality of any given event or person is the activity of one or several or innumerable Dharma samtanas, or chains of successive and related sensory and mental factors, which perpetuate themselves by past and present inner motivation or Karman. The idea of "I," "mine," "you," and "yours" is simply a nomenclature we habitually attach to temporary combinations of the unfolding series, the Dharma samtana. As one writer put it recently with striking originality: one is born as the self of today, a self that has transcended yesterday, as a result of one's own acts up to and including yesterday, and in the same way one will change into the self of tomorrow.

In terms of the Dharma samtana the lineal succession of factors from yesterday through today, and on to tomorrow, is real and has a reproductive identity. But nothing remains of yesterday other than its results, and nothing will survive to tomorrow other than an extension of the momentary series of Dharmas. That is the intended meaning of the third Sign or Seal: "All Dharmas are without a Self." Only now could that meaning be stated precisely.

For all of Indian Buddhist doctrine and practice, the understanding of the Dharma samtana is crucial. Not only is it the actual level at which effective practice of the Path takes place, but the understanding itself is an essential ingredient of the "Right Views" without which little of consequence is possible.

It has to be added that all shades of Indian Mahayana took over the doctrine of the Dharma samtana, and no accurate comprehension of their teachings is likely without some acquaintance with both the concept and the reality of the Dharma series.

10. KARMAN

Sakyamuni's own Enlightenment experience, as described in the texts, began with the clear knowledge and direct perception of his own Dharma-series (dharma samtana) stretching back into the past. That direct perception then spread out to include the totality of the Dharma series of all other beings, back into the past and then forward in unbroken succession into the future.

In just the same way, the doctrinal route-markers confine their attention first, to the inner realms of the individual, until a point is reached where the real entities (dharma) come into view at last. Then the operational behavior of these entities is spread out from the coordinated stream of the practitioner to all other "persons" and "events." Thus the individual Dharma samtana is an example in miniature of the whole causal, reproductive process known under its general name of Karman. (Here it is necessary to digress briefly on a matter of terminological usage. In the Sanskrit language, which became the main scriptural language of mainland India, Karman is the correct noun form while the more common Western usage of Karma is only strictly accurate when used as an adjective as in Karma-formations.)

It has been said before in these pages that Karman actually functions at the level of the Dharma samtana, the stream of

Dharmas which in configurations and groupings presents the appearance of an acting, moving individual. Within the limits of the individual stream clusters of Dharmas arise and propagate similar or developed clusters before passing away. Our hypothetical examples in the previous section illustrated how one thing leads to another and how the mix varies according to past impulses present or inherent in a particular stream.

In addition to the Dharma sequence produced in a single stream, it has to be remembered that no stream flows in isolation. The responses prompted into action in one stream are, in their turn, points of departure or prompters of responses in other streams that may also be present. The other streams may then transmit reactions onward to other streams several times removed. For example, the cries of the victims of the slaughter in the Buddha-hall could reach other devotees outside, giving rise to feelings of fear and panic followed by headlong flight.

In this way, moment by moment, the flow of Dharmas links and reacts inwardly and outwardly from any given point. From the point of view of Samsara, the flow or the stream of a given individual takes place within the flood of the entire interconnected mass of all the streams of all beings. Of course, the single-stream individual is not aware of the whole unless he makes the effort required to become a Buddha. But he is certainly aware of and constrained by his immediate surroundings, which determine in large degree what is possible and impossible at any given time, place, and circumstance.

This brings into view another feature of Karman, which is conditions. Not only is it a matter of what is produced directly from previous causes, but those causes will produce results or not depending upon the conditions then in existence. To return to our example of the Buddha-hall. That image and its attendant devotees in the Buddha-hall were the conditions that provided the necessary framework within which the separate and opposite activities of reverence/repose or anger/violence could come into play. Without those particular surroundings, neither of the sequences of response would have surfaced at that time. Later, perhaps, but not then.

We thus have two factors involved in Karman, causes and conditions. But there is more to it than that. In a carefully composed and concise statement that appears in a number of Sanskrit and Pali texts, as well as commentaries, we are given the full picture:

> Acts do not perish, even after hundreds of
> millions of cosmic periods. On meeting the
> right combination of conditions and time they
> bear fruit.

Notice in the quotation that it is "acts" that project results and "bear fruit." Both the acts and the long interval before fruition summarize detailed doctrine on causal action (hetu) and ripening (vipaka). The other ingredients are "the right combination of conditions" and the fruition. These summarize further related doctrines on conditions (pratyaya) and fruits (phala). It is at this point that we must definitely cross the threshold of *Abhidharma,* for it is here that Sakyamuni's brief recorded words are supplemented by explanatory material supplied by named authors, the ancient masters of India, Ceylon, or wherever.

At this point also—where the doctrinal guide lines begin to open out from matters of gradual "personal" practice like the Satipatthana scheme to matters of general or universal application like the quotation above—we begin to approach the content of Enlightenment itself. And it will be remembered that

Sakyamuni selected with care what he should at first teach. Only later, when speaking to Sariputra, Ananda, or other monks, did he broach such subjects as the causal laws governing all phenomena, the future destinies of beings, and the nature of reality. In many cases, even then his words were brief, concise, and full of inner meaning. Such brevity was capable of—indeed, needed—proper expansion. Often Sariputra would do just that. When the Buddha had retired to rest he would pick out such a part of a discourse and elaborate on it for the benefit of the monks.

The exception to this characteristic of brevity is the case of the king of formulas, "Arising Due to Conditions" (pratityasamutpada), which was, at various times, delivered by Sakyamuni in extended form and which we shall discuss below. Apart from that, we are confronted with brief utterances by the Buddha expanded by others like Sariputra, who is credited with composing an *Abhidharma* of his own. Several such short pronouncements now follow, all from the Pali texts, although they could be matched by others from the Sanskrit.

First from the *Anguttara*:

> It is impossible, monks, it cannot come to pass, that the fruit of a deed well-done by the body, speech, and thought should have for result that which is unpleasant, hateful, distasteful.
>
> But that it should be otherwise is quite possible.

Also from the *Anguttara*:

> When a person is reborn, his act ripens and, when this act is ripe, he undergoes the retribution of it in this life or elsewhere.

Now it is surely clear that if those statements were made to us here and now we should want to know a lot more before we could understand the intended meaning with confidence. That situation illustrates the place and purpose of the *Abhidharma* commentaries. And on a related topic of terminology, consider once again an earlier quotation, taken from the *Samyutta* and the *Anguttara:*

> Whether Saints appear in the world or not, the true nature of things (dharmanam Dharmata) is always present.

In this case, only too frequently met with, our right understanding of the meaning absolutely depends on our seeing the original terms, Dharmanam Dharmata. The phrase "the true nature of things" by itself only conveys the intended meaning if one knows that "things" is a translation of "dharmas." Having reached the level of the Dharma samtana, we now know that because of these two Sanskrit words the meaning is located in a specific direction and no other.

There is no question here of any general "nature of things"—the way things are or what always happens. What is referred to is the fact that, whatever the external circumstances or appearances, the only really existing entities, the elements that underlie and produce the world and all its beings, are the Dharmas. And in this quotation we are told something more; Dharmas have a specific character, all their own, that "true nature" in the Hinayana system never changes. It is always there, come what may. Alternative readings are also possible, hence the *Abhidharma* literature. Indeed, the Mahayana read this text much more deeply and subtly, but whatever the interpretation, it is Dharmas that have to be interpreted. Without those terms misinterpretation is inevitable.

But let us return to our first quotation and the root matters we extracted from it: causal actions (hetu), ripening (vipaka), conditions (pratyaya), and fruits (phala). These four technical terms contain the actual meaning and import of the word Karman. For the Karman doctrine to be properly used, these four terms and their meanings that should be involved. Thus the word Karman is another of those key terms that have to be unlocked, unravelled, and unwrapped.

Just for the moment we shall proceed in true *Abhidharma* style and present some important definitions from Indian commentaries. Concerning the acts themselves we can start with a general definition by Asvaghosa:

> The Karman (act) that bears a fruit, either
> pure or impure, can be clearly stated in these
> terms: by the purity of actions happiness is
> gained; suffering arises from their impurity.

Notice two things in particular about this extract. First that the word "Karman" is actually used where we would expect the word "act." Then the division of acts into pure and impure. In a very real sense, as we shall see, the whole extent of the Path in Indian Hinayana can be described as a progress from impurity to purity.

Vasubandhu, in keeping with his great reputation as the *Abhidharma* master par excellence, goes further and is more exact:

> What is the act? . . . The sutra says that
> there are two acts, volition (cetana) and the act
> after having willed. . . . These two acts form
> into three, bodily act, vocal act, and mental act.

Here again we have a clear example of the *Abhidharma* process. The quotation refers to what the sutra says, what the Buddha is recorded as having said, and it goes on to explain that. As to content, this is one of the prime definitions of karmic actions, i.e., those having outflows as a result. Such actions are preceded by the will. In other words they are intentional, premeditated in the strict sense of the word. Thoughtless actions or mere habitual reflexes have no karmic outflow; they are themselves the results of past actions that, when they fructify, have no further impetus other than as a part of the surrounding conditions. This will be discussed later. Staying with definitions of the causal actions, Vasubandhu goes further and brings in two other ingredients: the moral dimension and the degree of intensity:

> One distinguishes the act "done" and the act "accumulated" (upacita). What are the characteristics and conditions of the accumulated act? The act is called "accumulated" because of its intentional characteristic, its completion, the absence of regret and counteraction, the escort. . . . The act done voluntarily or intentionally is accumulated, not the contrary case and not the act done in haste, though voluntarily.
> Because of the completion of the act
> Because of the absence of regret.
> Because of the absence of confession
> Because if the act is bad and has a bad escort, i.e., when one is pleased at having committed it.

Accumulated actions, then, are actions of special intensity, especially if they are bad in addition to being willful and are not followed by regret but by approval and satisfaction. Such actions produce outflows of retribution in the bad destinies after death, or more immediately, dire results in the present life.

And if such bad acts involve all three modes of action, body, speech, and thoughts, then the heaped up intensity is all the more potent. If it be thought that Vasubandhu has introduced unwarranted morality into his definitions, the Buddha-quotations above should remove that objection.

Willed or intentional actions, therefore, produce an ongoing outflow of resultants, which will give rise in the near or the distant future to directly related occurrences within the same Dharma-stream. Our second and third sutra quotations say as much with less detail. But another Buddha statement on the results of actions that lead to a particular category of future birth is explicit.

From the *Anguttara:*

> Monks, a certain person accumulates acts of body, speech, and thought that are discordant. As a result of so doing he is reborn in a world that is discordant. So reborn, contacts and feelings that are discordant affect him, [some] utterly painful as, for instance, dwellers in the lower destinies feel.
>
> Another person accumulates [threefold acts] that are harmonies. He is reborn in a world that is harmonious. So reborn, he experiences the utterly blissful, such as the gods feel.

> Yet another person accumulates [threefold
> acts] that are both discordant and harmonious.
> So reborn, he experiences a mixture of pleasure
> and pain such as some humans, some gods, and
> some dwellers in the lower destinies feel.

This unusual case of a rather extended explanation by
Sakyamuni himself is included to show that, for all their careful
definitions and precise terminology, the *Adhidharma* masters
remain firmly within the bounds of the sutra records.

And with the last quotation, we find a clear statement that
karmically potent actions produce effects in a future birth,
meaning in a distantly projected extension of the Dharma samtana. This distant extension, as we have seen earlier, consists of
an infinite number of Dharmas appearing and disappearing in
succession without any permanent substance or fundamental
support underlying them. The succession itself, governed by
strict laws, can never be broken or interrupted, but it can be
gradually changed, even stopped altogether by the successful
completion of the Holy Path. As Vasubandhu says: ". . . if something appears, such and such a result will follow. . . ."

And because something else always appears from one
moment to the next, the Dharma series continues to infinity
unless it is progressively reduced and finally stopped by the total
therapy of the third and fourth Noble Truths.

It is not possible at this point to grasp how it is that a particular Dharma follows any particular Dharma. That may
emerge after we have discussed the other three parts of Karman:
vipaka, pratyaya, and phala. On the other hand, it may not. It
has to be remembered that we are here dealing with matters that
were only fully revealed to an enlightened Buddha. Explanations
can go so far (and in the *Abhidharma* they go some way), but

however refined and acute the descriptive system may be, it will always recoil or wither at certain depths.

Perhaps it is thought that because of this the attempt should not be made at all. Not so. It is just because Sakyamuni himself pronounced on these topics that effort was made to understand him. After all, his words were preserved and recorded for future generations to listen to and learn from. But this is where formulas and statements can be recognized as belonging to an advanced state of progress. Such teachings presume an already acquired preparation in the earlier practice formulas. Nevertheless, as already remarked, all the formularies have an intellectual content that has to be assimilated in conjunction with all the other necessaries. So with those reservations we shall proceed in the knowledge that at the very least an understanding of the "markers" in the map-guides prevents the grosser forms of wrong view.

To help us see one aspect of this strictly regulated succession of Dharma activity we can use some of the Dharmas listed in the previous section. Consider again the example of the Muslim warrior about to spring into a flurry of sword-wielding fury. In the example the successive Dharmas that arose and developed in his series after he saw the interior of the Buddha-hall went something like this:

agitation (auddhatya)
anger or irritation (krodha)
hostility (pratigha)
intention for action (chanda)
active harmfulness (vihimsa)

This is an over-simplified sequence, of course, because each Dharma appears together with its satellites or related cluster, and so the moment-to-moment succession would consist of a host of Dharma factors. But the thread of the development would still be true of the case.

Now it should be clear from the elements of the sequence that once this progression moves from the first two, the rest are very nearly inevitable. The Dharma of agitation cannot produce as its immediate successor the Dharma of calm (upeksa); neither can the Dharma of anger/irritation immediately produce the Dharma of respect (hri). And nowhere in the series can the Dharma of regret (kaukrtya) appear. There is much more likely to be approval or satisfaction (adhimoksa).

For the same reasons, the last Dharma, active harmfulness, will not appear on its own without an appropriate preliminary sequence. The Dharma stream of the Buddhist devotee pacified by what he saw in the Buddha-hall can be treated similarly. The fact is that successive Dharmas can only produce those of their own kind or similar and they cannot immediately produce their opposites.

However, even the warrior could have been pacified, given time. Even the devotee could have been roused to hostility, given time. But the time allowance would have to consist of an entirely different series of Dharmas. So causal actions (hetu) such as these are those Dharmas dominated by the will and intention, those expressed and completed by acts of body, speech, and mind, or a combination of any of these. They are also karmically intensified if accompanied by satisfaction or approval of what is done.

Such actions launch a rapidly developed sequence in the Dharma stream that is so interlocked that it precludes the appearance of any but elements of a similar kind. Such a sequence can be "short-circuited" or countered, but this requires either time for a gradual changeover or an even more intensive act of will that itself needs certain conditions to function.

In the family of Indian Mainstream Hinayana schools, each one specified different kinds of causal actions (hetu). Vasubandhu, in expounding the system of the Sarvastivadins listed and explained six kinds. Here we shall mention three only:

Sahabhuhetu: cause as co-existent.
   i) the candle flame and its light; one causes the other but always together.
   ii) the shoot of a plant, growing in the light, and its shadow.

So he defines this kind of cause as Dharmas that are effect, one from the other.

Samprayuktakahetu: cause by association.
   i) thought and the mentals (citta/caitta), as when in the moment of seeing, the eye is the point of support of a visual consciousness.
   ii) the journey of a caravan of merchants is assured by their associating together and by the mutual support they provide for each other.

Sabhagahetu: similar cause.
   This is the category that applies to our examples above, or, as Vasubandhu says, ". . . like things are the sabhagahetu of like things. . . ." The other three kinds of hetu are, Karanahetu (controlling factors), Sarvatragahetu (defiling influence), and Vipakahetu (cause of ripening). The latter will be discussed below.

Having already mentioned how conditions play a decisive part in what particular Dharmas are likely to arise, we can proceed with some definitions. Our example was the Buddha-hall itself containing the image and the devotee. In the Sarvastivadin system there are four conditions (pratyayas), but we shall confine ourselves to two of them.

Samanantara Pratyaya: all the thoughts and mentals present.

In other words, all the accompanying thoughts and mentals that act as a surrounding, conditioning influence. We might say the prevailing mental climate, outlook, or attitude at a given moment. An example might be one's suspicions of a speaker's motives, which render him unbelievable, whatever he says. Political speeches are very prone to fall into this category.

Adhipati Pratyaya: predominating conditions.

In other words, the most active and potent surrounding conditions of the moment. An example might be crowd hysteria at football matches, where powerful emotions engendered by mass reactions affect those present. The other two pratyayas are, hetupratvaya (causal conditions) and alambanapratyaya (all other Dharmas present as conditioning factor).

As a general definition of pratyaya or conditions we can include:

i) secondary causes, which are distinct from the primary causes, the hetus.
ii) they can be seen as environmental causes.
iii) if hetu is the seed, then pratyava is the soil, rain and sun shine.

Thus the pratyayas are the pre-existing conditions that allow primary causes to function. Conversely, the absence of such conditions prevents such causes from functioning. Or to resort to metaphor: in a high wind and in the open one cannot light a candle even though matches, candle, and intention are all present.

Here we can recall that part of the first quotation of this

section that says " . . . on meeting the right combination of conditions. . . ." So much for the hetu and pratyaya constituents of Karman.

We now turn to the vipaka (ripening, retribution) aspect of Karman. Although it is listed among the six hetus of the Sarvastivadin system, its characteristics are special in that, despite its being a direct causal action, its resultant is delayed, sometimes for ages. Because of that, it is much more difficult to explain. Indeed, another of the Hinayana schools, the Theravada, produced a distinct doctrine to supplement the teaching of vipaka, and this will be mentioned in due course. For this writer at least, the vipaka doctrine so firmly and frequently expressed in the sutra texts by Sakyamuni, was one of the several major matters that the Hinayana schools failed to explain satisfactorily. As time went on some of them began to unravel the inner meaning, but it fell to Indian Mahayana to fully decipher and uncover the detailed matter of vipaka. The *Yogacara-Vijnavada* achieved this deeper level of understanding and explanation, but that is not our concern here. This book is an exposition of Mainstream Hinayana, and so it is their teaching and their views that must be presented, warts and all.

The delay in the appearance of the resultant is clearly expressed in the first quotation of this section, and in the opening lines: "Acts do not perish, even after hundreds of millions of cosmic periods." It comes again in our third quotation: ". . . when this act is ripe, he undergoes the retribution of it . . ." Also in our eighth quotation: "As a result of so doing, he is reborn in a world."

Stated simply, it is a case of act now, pay later. Whereas all the other causes and conditions function and react to each other within the Dharma stream of a given moment or short series of moments, vipaka is a cause whose impetus into the future is not immediately apparent. In its case the impulse launched by the action with a future result immediately disappears from sight and only prompts the eventual result within the Dharma stream much later, when particular conditions and lapse of time coincide exactly. That is the intended meaning of our first quotation; it is a description of the vipaka process.

Of course, the major difficulty is that all Mainstream Hinayana schools hold firmly to the idea of momentary Dharma elements, which have no underlying, supporting substance. What there is from moment to moment and throughout time is a constantly changing kaleidoscope of cooperating, reproductive Dharmas that disappear as soon as their function has been completed. In such a mix of ever-changing factors how is anything as closely related as a cause and its effect separated by ages? By what means is the transmission of the causal impetus sustained unresolved from one age to another? In the first place there are two kinds of vipaka. Vasubandhu describes them as Vipakahetu, the outflowing impulse from a karmically potent act, and Vipakaphala, that impulse having arrived at the moment when it bears fruit. The answer to the question as to how these take place is again given by Vasubandhu:

> The retribution is not simultaneous to the act that produces it, for the fruit of retribution is not tasted at the moment when the act is accomplished . . . the cause of retribution depends for realizing its fruit on the development of the series.

And further:

> The Dharmas, being momentary, exist in series. When they appear in a place far from where they are situated, it is because they are produced without discontinuity in the intermediate place.

In a later work, the Karmasiddhiprakarana, Vasubandhu addresses the problem with more precision and introduces a special term that was later to unlock the whole deep, hidden process and to figure predominantly in the Mahayana re-evaluations of ancient teachings. That term is vasana, meaning, perfume, residue, impregnation, pervasion, deposit, or trace. Vasubandhu wrote:

> "... a special volition exercises a perfuming (vasana) on the mental series (cittasamtana) and creates a potentiality there. By a special evolution (parinamavisesa) of this potentiality, a particular fruit will later be born ..."

So for the Mainstream Indian Hinaya, vipaka as retribution or ripening had two phases: the causal act, particularly when "accumulated" or reinforced, deposited an impulse in the Dharma stream that carried a delayed action result. That impulse remained latent in the stream, developing as a potentiality, until its required conditions for fructification came together in an exact conjunction of time and surroundings. That conjunction triggered the delayed response, and the effects, the fruits, surfaced in a new cluster of Dharma activity. Such an extended resultant could also be achieved by straightforward, uninterrupted development, as is the case in the more advanced stages of the practice of the Path.

Vasubandhu again, as quoted in the earlier section on the Dharma-samtana:

> By series, samtana, we understand material and mental elements uninterruptedly succeeding one another in a procession that has action as originating cause.

193

> The successive moments of this procession
> are different; therefore there is evolution (pari-
> nama), transformation of the series.

In case it is thought that this explanation results in a rigid determination, i.e., because actions produce certain categories of results everything is fixed and unalterable, the system denies this and explains. All the manifestations of vipakaphala, that is to say, those Dharmas that arise later from causes in the distant past, are karmically spent when they finally appear. Technically they are called "undefined" (avyakrta), meaning that those Dharmas cannot of themselves produce any further karmically charged responses. On appearance they act only as conditions bearing upon the stream. But of course even as conditions they are powerful in the circumstances they impose. Such conditions or fruitings could be a rebirth in a lower or higher destiny, and they would certainly be powerful circumstances.

But results of this kind need not be so conclusive. An example might be someone in times gone by who was caught at night crossing the windswept moors. That situation and those conditions would be vipakaphala. The traveller has a candle in a lantern, and with his flint box and striker he tries to light the candle. These are all Dharma elements in the "personality" stream, including the will, the intentions, and the means of lighting the candle. Yet for all that, the surrounding conditions prevent it, the wind is too strong, and there is no shelter where he is. Here then, the fruits of past actions determine what can and cannot be done.

However, the traveller searches for and finds a gully with some bushes for shelter so that he does eventually light his lantern. But to do so he had to move away from the influence of the unfavorable conditions, and this he could do with a successful realization of his original intention, lighting the lantern. The constant difficulty in all this is, as we have said, the question of sustaining a particular causal impulse without modification through the medium of momentary Dharmas with specific characteristics.

The Sarvastivadin system, which dominated Indian Mainstream doctrines for centuries, relied on two other Dharma-entities to provide the function of carriers. One was the Dharma called life-force (jivita), which by constantly repeating served as a continuity base. The other was the Dharma of cohesion or possession (prapti), which served as a binding agent keeping all the Dharmas of a particular stream together so that causes and conditions could not dissipate. The latter raises problems of its own, of course, but no matter.

The Theravadins, on the other hand, being confined to Ceylon and thus not so responsive to mainland solutions, were nevertheless aware of the problem and came up with their own solution. They called it Bhavanga. One explanation of this term tells us that it is the "foundation of existence" and a process, flux, or stream in which all impressions and experiences are stored up but concealed from ordinary consciousness. One is led to wonder at what time this special teaching made its appearance, because on the surface at least, it bears a resemblance to certain Mahayana doctrines in evidence among texts of the third and fourth centuries A.D.

On the other hand, Bhavanga does seem to be similar also to the contents of our above quotation, where the Dharma samtana is acted upon by a process of deposits (vasana). However this may be, its purpose is clearly to provide a vehicle of transmission. And in providing this necessary means of conveyance, the ancient masters had to balance precariously between the demands of the no-substance, no-unchanging-self doctrines of

Sakyamuni, which are incontrovertibly and frequently stated in the sutras. On the other hand, there is also the equally incontrovertible doctrine of Karman/vipaka, which spread causes and effects over many lives. As in numerous other cases, the awesome range and depth of Sakyamuni's full Enlightenment eludes precise and satisfactory explanations in rational terms.

We can now see, probably dimly, what the Buddhist doctrine of Karman amounts to. Its four main ingredients of hetu, pratyaya, vipaka, and phala reveal to us several important matters of a general nature. First and foremost: that intentional and "accumulated" actions have outflows of results which necessarily and unavoidably follow either sooner or later. The results of such actions cannot be avoided; once the vipaka process is set in action, no control is possible. However, the pratyaya or conditions can be minimized, augmented, or replaced by others to precipitate or delay results "in the pipeline." Thus one can provide bread crumbs for the birds to come to your garden, or scarecrows to drive them away, but the birds will be around whatever you do.

The other side of this vipaka coin is that our actions, both mental and physical, actually create our own future. The flow of the stream from the present to the future can be taken in hand. This involves a mode of operation usually conveyed in one word, bhavana, or cultivation. Once the Dharma realm is gained and recognized, our actions and propensities can be channelled, even manipulated, to achieve a propitious "mix" of Dharma elements. This is the meaning of gaining "good roots"; a mix can be deliberately brought together to produce an outflow of wholesome, pleasant, or desirable outcomes. The operative tool for this is the "Four Great Efforts."

Our conditions can also be utilized to some extent. For instance, knowing the deleterious impressions and reactions that take place at certain soccer matches, we just don't go to them. And knowing the beneficial and calming effects of being in the presence of Buddha-rupas and their attendant devotees, whether monks or laymen, we try to attend such gatherings whenever possible. The use of the Four Great Efforts and the care over surrounding conditions is part of what is involved in the cultivation (bhavana). But really effective cultivation, in this system, requires a knowledge and some understanding of the inner process of the Dharma stream as well as the sphere of actual causes. We have to know what makes us tick, or tock, as the case may be.

The inner processes that have to be penetrated if cultivation is to be effective are not easy of access. The difficulty of gaining contact with the realm of causes was one of the prime reasons why this Path is always characterized as gradual, whether "fast gradual" or "slow gradual." The arrowhead of the wounded man is buried deep and requires delicate but decisive surgery to remove it. In fact, the sharp point is enmeshed in the blood vessels, nerve tissue, and muscle, and these are the supporting elements of the whole organism. In just the same way, the Dharmas and their karmic characteristics are the supporting elements of the whole organism and it is they that fester and molder away, poisoning the whole development.

The Dharmas and their characteristics constitute the sphere of real events, where the bacteria and the corpuscles engage in the continual struggle for dominance. They are no mere figment of philosophical analysis. They are, moment by moment, the actual constituents of our makeup and of everything around us. The Dharmas and their operation were one of Sakyamuni's real discoveries; their activities and the possibility of controlling them showed that the Dharmas are the means of salvation, or damnation, as you will.

Prior to Sakyamuni's time, Karman was seen as the creator and destroyer of all the worlds, in the hands of the gods. Some even denied that the gods had any hand in it. The Ajivikas, who were roughly contemporary with the Buddha, taught a rigid pre-destination. For them, Samsara and all its denizens were like a ball of string whose loose end was held in the hand while the ball was flung high in the air. Only when the ball was totally unwound by the velocity of its flight would its progress be brought to a halt. For them, nothing had any effect on the "natural" unrolling of the ball. Similarly, humans had to endure all the births and all the suffering willy nilly, until they came to an end of their own accord.

The teaching of the Buddha contradicted that flatly. The Great Game, the Great Enterprise, was to take these momentous matters in hand. It could be, it must be done. The Buddha's unmatched and universally ranging insight resulted in a re-evaluation of Karman as Dharma-activity with a moral/ethical dimension. Vasubandhu once again has a succinct turn of phrase at the beginning of his monumental work, the *Abhidharmakosa:*

> Since, outside of the discernment of Dharmas, there is no means of extinguishing the passions (klesa)—and it is by reason of the passions that the world drifts in this ocean of existence—in view of this discernment, the *Abhidharma* has been pronounced by the Master, they say.

This discernment and this extinguishing is the very essence of the cultivation (bhavana). For this, practice and perseverance are needed, but it has to be practice of a particular kind to qualify for the description, "the practice of the Path."

11. PRATITYASAMUTPADA: ARISING DUE TO CONDITIONS

Those hardy readers who have stayed with us up to this point could be forgiven for thinking that they have now arrived at more familiar ground. The teaching of the Pratityasamutpada is certainly likely to be better known than the analyses and the Dharma samtana that we have presented in the previous sections. Even here, though, the original language of the title has produced a bewildering variety of alternative renderings.

Indeed, it is surprising that this principal formula of the Dharma is recognizable at all in English due to the many variant forms given to its name. Pratityasamutpada has been represented by "the Chain of Causation" (E.J. Thomas), "*Production en dépendence*" (E. Lamotte), "Dependent Origination" (Bhikkhu Nyanatiloka), "Conditioned Co-Production" (E. Conze), and several others. Not to be outdone, this author has come up with another version, given in the heading of this chapter: "Arising Due to Conditions." The interesting thing is that each and every one of the variants mentioned is valid in that it describes the twelve-linked process of the formula with some accuracy, though none conveys more than a fraction of what the formula itself involves. Another case, perhaps, for keeping to the original term once the meaning has been laid out and understood.

Here, however, the understanding part is something of a pious hope, for we are now confronted with one of the major pillars of Buddhist doctrine, one that figures prominently in Mahayana no less than in Hinayana. A little attention to the progressive nature of the twelve links of the formula (Figure 3) conveys the general idea without too much difficulty. But we are warned about too facile a view of what is meant. Ananda was once reproved by the Buddha for thinking he fully understood the formula. Sakyamuni said to him:

> Profound Ananda, this is Pratityasamutpada and profound does it appear. It is through not understanding, not penetrating this law, that this world resembles a tangled ball of thread . . . and that a man does not escape . . . suffering from the round of rebirth.

At another time Sakyamuni was even more emphatic:

> Who so understands the Pratityasamutpada understands the Dharma, and who so understands the Dharma understands the Pratityasamutpada.

It is that warning and emphasis that has persuaded this author to reserve any discussion of this great formula until after the associated subjects of Karman and the Dharma samtana have been dealt with. For it is the causal acts in conjunction with the necessary conditions operating within the Dharma streams that are the inner content and actual functioning level of the twelve-linked chain. As we shall see, each of the links represents a particular phase of Dharma activity under the impulsion or thrust of karmic forces. Karman, with its four-fold components described in the previous section, provides the threads, which are woven into a skein with twelve knots then stretched out to cross the gulf after death and prior to rebirth. As is the case so often, the Buddha's terse statement that whoever understands the Pratityasamutpada understands the Dharma, is nothing but the literal truth.

Thus it seems entirely fitting that this chapter should be devoted to the Pratityasamutpada and, calling upon much that has gone before, to a survey of the specifically Buddhist doctrines of Rebirth.

Before we turn our attention to the substance of this king of formulas, we must first consider a few preliminaries. We are told in certain of the commentaries that the whole extended formula is based upon the simple axiom that:

> This being present, that arises;
> Without this, that does not occur.

One of the examples frequently employed to illustrate this axiom is fire and its fuel. We can state the example thus:

> If fuel, air, and ignition conjoin,
> fire comes into existence.
> Without any or all of those prerequisites,
> no fire.

This is another way of describing indispensable conditions, and there is nothing very esoteric about that, you might say. But again, we need to be on our guard against too simplistic a view of this teaching. The straightforward axiom is a prelude to much that is far from straightforward.

In case it has been forgotten, let it be repeated that this great matter was part of the final stage of insight that the Great Bodhisattva reached under the Bodhi tree and that set the seal on the metamorphosis into a fully enlightened Buddha. When he surveyed the twelve-staged progression forward and backward the newly enlightened Buddha was seeing the constant arising and subsiding of all beings endlessly repeated. The unique, penetrating insight not only brought "true nature" into view, but the whole causal structure of it was laid bare to him. What is perhaps more important and which lends even further credence to the brief statement in our last quotation is that, by reversing the process and dislocating the linkage, he perceived and understood that there was a Path out of the bondage of the forward thrust. Thus he finally discovered the Way Out, the solution he had long sought.

We have presented the preliminaries and the warnings, so now we can consider the manner in which Sakyamuni presented this formula to his monks.

This extract is from the *Nidana Vagga* of the *Samyutta:*

> The Lord said: "Bhikkhus, I will teach you Dependent Arising. Listen, attend carefully, and I will speak."
>
> "Yes, Sir," those Bhikkhus replied to the Lord.
>
> The Lord said: "Now what, Bhikkhus, is Dependent Arising? With Ignorance as condition, Bhikkhus, the Composites come to be; with the Composites as condition, Mind and Body come to be; with Mind and Body as condition, the Six Faculties come to be; with the Six Faculties as condition, Contact comes to be; with Contact as condition, Feeling comes to be; with Feeling as condition, Craving comes to

be; with Craving as condition, Grasping comes to be; with Grasping as condition; Becoming comes to be; with Becoming as condition, Birth comes to be; with Birth as condition, aging and death, sorrow, lamentation, pain, grief, and despair come to be. That is how there is an origin to this whole mass of suffering. And this, Bhikkhus, is called Dependent Arising.

But from the complete disappearance and cessation of Ignorance, the Composites cease; from the cessation of the Composites, Consciousness ceases; from the cessation of Consciousness, Mind and Body ceases [and so on for each of the successive links until we come to]; from the cessation of Birth, aging and death, sorrow, lamentation, pain, grief, and despair cease. That is how there is a ceasing of this whole mass of suffering."

It will have been noted, no doubt, that in this translated extract we have yet another version of Pratityasamutpada; this time it is "Dependent Arising."

It can also be seen quite readily that this formula is firmly connected to that of the Four Noble Truths. Indeed, in a very real sense the Pratityasamutpada is a restatement of the Four. First, the universal state of suffering is posited, having to be explained. Then we have the second and third Truths embedded in the narrative: Craving as the origin of suffering is expanded so as to show how the Craving comes about. Then the Stopping, which consists in discontinuing the links one after the other. And finally, the Path; it is clear from the first quotation of this chapter that the Path consists in "understanding and penetrating," followed by the actual exercise in dislocation from one to the other until all are stopped and ". . . there is a ceasing of this whole mass of suffering. . . ."

Another thing to be noted before we pass on to the formula itself is the fact that each of the twelve links overlaps the next. That is to say, the preceding item is repeated in each line as in ". . . with Craving as condition, Grasping comes to be. . . ." This is of some significance because it indicates that we are here dealing with "conditions" in its technical meaning embodied in the word "pratyaya." Again it will not have escaped the sharp-eyed that "pratyaya" is very close to the "Pratitya" of the title, and indeed they are derivatives. Thus we straight away have an important indicator pointing back to one of the ingredients of Karman. Remember it. It will help to unlock some of the meanings of this grand doctrinal statement.

We can now examine the formula in detail (at Figure 3). To emphasise the fact of consensus our diagram presents the links of the formula as given in both of the main scriptural languages of India, Sanskrit and Pali. The two versions are matched side by side from items one to twelve and the short descriptions of each of the links are drawn from the two principal commentaries: Vasubandhu's *Abhidharmakosa* and Buddhaghosa's *Visuddhimagga*. The nuances of interpretation, in this writer's opinion, add something to our understanding of the whole.

The first thing to take in from this diagrammatic formula is the forward thrust, illustrated by the hollow arrows down the center of the diagram. That thrust, from the past through the present and on into the future is punctuated by schematic divisions into three groups of links. Numbers one and two take place in the past, in the past life of the being in question.

Numbers three through ten take place in the present, in the present life of that being. Numbers eleven and twelve will follow in the future, in a future resurgence or rebirth.

That is not to say that the three groupings are separate and distinct in any but an explanatory sense. Each link serves as a condition or prerequisite for the next to appear and because of this overlaps and precedes the next in the chain. This overlapping is not shown in the diagram (it is already overfull) but is clear in the textual extract in the preceding quotation of Sakyamuni's presentation of it to his monks.

Thus we have a continuous, unbroken, overlapping chain, a Dharma samtana in another form, in fact. This continuity is often given special emphasis by joining numbers twelve and one at the twelve o'clock position, thereby forming a complete wheel, a continuous circle. This is the basic form of the celebrated "Wheel of Life" that figures in Tibetan art. An example of such a "wheel" appears in Part One of this book. In that illustration the twelve successive links are pictorially represented around the outer rim of the wheel.

Let us start at the top of the diagram, link number one (remember to examine both left and right sides of the arrows as we go down the chart).

Avidya, Ignorance

This is the primary condition underlying all others. It is that psychological condition in the past that lacked a knowledge of the moment-to-moment succession and the causal process. Not only is it ignorance, but it is also wrong knowledge and false perceptions, such as that "I" exists. Lacking right knowledge, specifically knowledge of the Four Noble Truths, this ignorant state is sustained and supported by the unrestrained activity of all the previous defilements of body, speech, and mind. Because of this basic condition of ignorance and defilement, the karmic flow of action and result continues unhindered and by so doing presents the conditions that allow number two to arise.

"With Ignorance as condition . . . the Composites come to be . . ."

Samskara: Composites or Formations

These are the clusters of karmically potent Dharmas of past circumstances (that is, in a previous existence), which deposited their seed or "perfume" into the series and which have to produce results in a later stage of the same Dharma stream. In other words, we are here dealing with the "vipaka" or ripening of results from past willed and voluntary actions, as described in the previous chapter on Karman. In this case the willed acts are those performed in a past section of the "personality" stream back beyond the birth of the present being. Those actions were part of a stream that lacked any knowledge of Dharma-activity sufficient to prevent the natural "outflow." That outflow of seeds from the past with the potential for germination is the prompter which, by presenting the required conditions, allows number three to arise.

". . . with the Composites as condition, Consciousness comes to be . . ."

Vijnana: Consciousness

This is the cognizing function that arises at conception.

Such a renewed awareness is one of the fruits of retribution (vipakaphala) of the past acts. The particular "imprint" or latency of that retributive fruit also locates the renewal in the appropriate destiny (gati) or level of Samsara. This consciousness comes into existence as the direct but delayed result of

Arising Due To Conditions

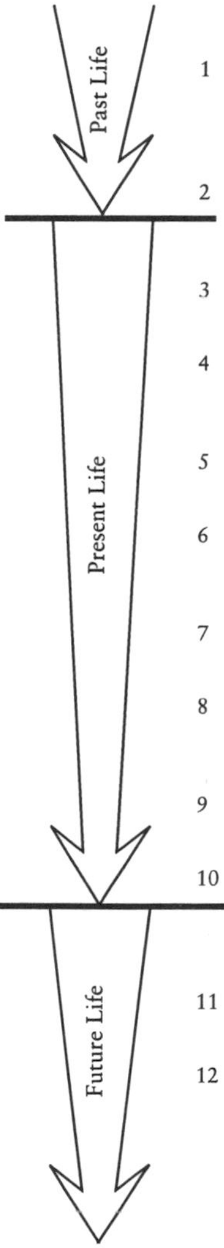

Sanskrit Version

1 *Avidya* = Unknowing, ignorance. The 5 skandhas of the former life immersed in all the defilements.
2 *Samskara* = Composites. Activities of the former series which produce results.
3 *Vijnana* = Consciousness. The renewed 5 skandhas at the moment of conception/rebirth.
4 *Nama-Rupa* = Mental-physical. Development of the 5 skandhas in the womb.
5 *Sadayatana* = Six Faculties. Establishment of the 6 faculties in the embryo.
6 *Sparsa* = Contact. The encounter of the faculties with their respective objects.

7 *Vedana* = Feeling. Feelings of pleasure, pain, and neither.
8 *Trsna* = Craving or thirst. The desire for pleasant experience including sexual union.
9 *Upadana* = Grasping. The active search for pleasure and passion.
10 *Bhava* = Becoming. Actions performed and accumulated in the search for pleasure. These actions produce results.
11 *Jati* = Birth or reappearance. The future rebirth. Same as No. 3.
12 *Jaramarana* = Decline and death. Repetition of development and decline specifically Nos. 4, 5, 6, 7 in future life.

Pali Version

1 *Avijja* = Unknowing and wrong theory. Ignorance of the Four Noble Truths and conditioned arising.
2 *Samkhara* = Formations. States with the nature of result either meritorious or demeritorious
3 *Vinnana* = Consciousness. Cognizing function manifested as rebirth-linking
4 *Nama-Rupa* = Mentality and materiality. Functions of association and dispersal.
5 *Salayatana* = Six base. Activation of the sense doors.
6 *Phassa* = Contact. The coincidence of the internal and external bases and consciousness.
7 *Vedana* = Feeling. Experiencing pleasure and pain.
8 *Tanha* = Craving. Insatiability for sensory and mental things.
9 *Upadana* = Clinging. Seizing and not releasing.
10 *Bhava* = Process of becoming. The generative karma-process volitional activity producing results.
11 *Jati* = Rebirth process. Karma-resultants in the next birth.
12 *Jaramarana* = Old age and death. Old age and death decisively conditioned by birth.

Past Life

Present Life

Future Life

Figure 3

unresolved Dharma-activity in the past. Thus we have the Samskaras of link number two representing the vipakahetu, cause of ripening, and here at number three, Consciousness represents the vipakaphala of those earlier actions. This consciousness also carries the "coding" or inherent pattern of the Five Skandhas that will develop later.

The dissolution of the previous mind and body complex at death is simply the exhaustion of a particular combination of active skandhas under the universal law of "all composites are impermanent." At the dissolution its reservoir of unripened "seeds" is propelled into a new cluster about to develop.

". . . with Consciousness as condition, Mind and Body come to be. . . ."

Nama-Rupa: The Mental and Physical Constituents of the Embryo

The presence of consciousness activates all the other ingredients of the psycho-physical organism. These are divided into the immaterial (naman) and the material (rupa). The inherent "coded" pattern of the Five Skandhas begins to operate. All the parts of the embryo begin to position themselves appropriately for further development. Thus the embryo, once activated by consciousness, becomes a rudimentary mental and physical organism forming the basis for the next decisive phase.

". . . with Mind and Body as condition, the Six Faculties come to be . . ."

Sadayatana: The Six Faculties or Six-fold Base

Once activated, the embryo continues to develop. With the proper distribution of the mental and physical parts the organism produces the six sense faculties of sight, hearing, smelling, tasting, touch, and coordinating brain. As soon as all these faculties are established and functioning, the conditions are present for number six to arise.

". . . with the Six Faculties as condition, Contact comes to be. . . ."

Sparsa: Contact

Now that the sense faculties are active, contact can be made with their respective objects, visibles, audibles, smells, tastes, tangibles, and mentals. The fundamental experience of internal and external is stabilized as consciousness receives and records the various sense impressions. Physical birth takes place at this stage. All Five Skandhas are now established, and the newborn child, being fully equipped, provides the conditions for the next link to take its place.

". . . with Contact as condition, Feeling comes to be. . . ."

Vedana: Feeling

The activity of the senses now focuses the already inherent capacity of feeling into responses of pleasant, painful, or neutral. Each of the six sensory activities provokes its own alternative among the three-fold feelings. At this point, also, conditions are present for further fruits of past acts to ripen and exert influence within the expanding stream of Dharmas. The distinction between the pleasant and the otherwise forms the basis for the next phase.

". . . with Feeling as condition, Craving comes to be. . . ."

Trsna: Craving or Thirst

Under the impact of sensory and mental impressions distinguished as pleasant or otherwise, delight and desire arise. This is the insatiable craving for repetition of pleasant sensations. And with this desire for more of the pleasant and aversion for the unpleasant all the latent passions are re-activated. More and more fruits of past actions are encouraged to emerge, and the Dharma samtana is once again in full flood. Full potential being reached, the will, intentions, and choices are now the order of the day, and innumerable new seeds and deposits are crowding into the Dharma stream. All this brings about another link in the chain.

". . . with Craving as condition, Grasping comes to be . . ."

Upadana: Grasping and Clinging

The craving for pleasure combined with an active will produces the deliberate searching out of desirable objects, including sexual activity. Once found and experienced, the grasping and clinging resist the irresistible impermanence, and a further dimension of suffering is added to the basic commotion of the clamoring passions. The desire and the seizing create patterns of activity that are self-propagating and thus produce suitable conditions for what follows.

". . . with Grasping as condition, Becoming comes to be. . . ."

Bhava: The Process of Becoming

Deliberate and accumulated actions are now performed in abundance under the impulsion of desire, aversion, and all the obscuring passions. The combination of all these conditions open up possibilities galore for past acts to deliver their results. Already, previous acts in the present existence with immediate or proximate results are also sending up their crop. Consequently, the desire and the passions increase, which in turn augment both the ripening and the depositing. The thrust forward into further desirable situations is overpowering. All kinds of activity patterns form up, designed to bring about what one likes or to avoid what is disliked. The "ship" is in full sail, all canvas spread and plunging forward from moment to moment and year to year. Under these pressing conditions of Becoming, life in general unfolds its arc of arising, functioning, and decline until the final disintegration takes place. But not only are there more ripening actions from the distant past waiting for resolution, there are yet more freshly deposited in the present existence that must inevitably fructify. All these seeds and their characteristic of forward propulsion create the conditions for the next link to appear.

". . . with Becoming as condition, Birth comes to be. . . ."

Jati: Birth, or the Process of Re-Appearance

As in the connection between links two and three, the sum of action-resultants of this and of past lives produces a rebirth process. This means that the Dharma samtana, released by the dissolution of the skandhas at death, concentrates and gravitates toward an appropriate level of new existence. The mental acts and the traces of physical acts that can only ripen later preserve a continuity within the Dharma stream, which projects, under its own momentum, toward a newly impregnated womb. A new birth is then launched and the process resumes as at link number three.

". . . with Birth as condition, aging and death, sorrow . . . and despair come to be. That is how there is an origin to this whole mass of suffering."

Jaramarana: Decline and Death.

Because of the back pressure of unresolved actions that require results to manifest, the whole cycle of development starts again, and each link of the chain extends, one by one, into the next. Thereafter in the future existence, which will be brought about by the happenings and residues of this and of previous lives, the same explosion of the passions will take place and will then decline to dissolution and to further rebirth, on and on without end.

As previously pointed out link number twelve is sometimes joined to link number one to produce the unbroken circle of never-ending revolution. In that sense, the flow or flood of actions and their results, of the passions and their retribution, of the natural growth of this from that, all combine as the overriding all-pervasive condition in which ignorance thrives. The slavery to the passions, the unwitting or indifferent conforming with the "ways of the world," but above all the deep and invisible causal chain that grinds on keeps us unaware, mercifully ignorant perhaps. This situation adds up to that special form of ignorance and impotent knowledge that lubricates the causal chain so that it continues smoothly, silently, and unmolested to infinity.

Thus the Pratityasamutpada and its presentation as the Wheel.

The Buddha, however, armed with his great penetrating wisdom, has seen it for what it is and has explained to us how the whole monstrous affair works. The whole mass of suffering (first Noble Truth) that is thrown up by the constant revolution of this Wheel is caused by thirst or craving (second Noble Truth). But it can all be stopped (third Noble Truth), and the means of stopping it has been declared (fourth Noble Truth).

In the original formula of the fourth Noble Truth, eight factors were given as the means. In truth, however, all the eight mentioned there are themselves preliminaries or conditions for the actual stopping procedure contained in the reverse order of the Pratityasmutpada. Even a cursory examination of the elements of the fourth Noble Truth will show a certain imprecision, a lack of conclusive explanation as to how the "stopping" is to be brought about by these means. Some of that uncertainty can be dispelled by the realization of the close relationship between these two prime formulas of the Hinayana. For in the Pratityasamutpada there is no such imprecision, no uncertainty as to how the stopping is achieved.

The key to the operation is latent in the simple axiom on which the whole chain is based:

> This being present, that arises.
> Without this, that does not occur.

If the prior condition is removed or de-activated, then its successor cannot come into being. That is the key to the stopping process known as the breaking of the links, or, the formula put into reverse.

And that was one of the great secrets that the Buddha discovered on his Enlightenment. He set out from home, it will be recalled, to find the state in which there was no old age, sickness, or death. He discovered that such a state there was, but it was a state that absolutely precluded birth of any kind. For birth, of whatever kind, set in motion its locked-in arc of decline and death. When birth occurred, death followed, inevitably. But the second part of the axiom is equally true: without birth, no death. Therefore, stop birth and all the rest is stopped for good.

The matter of the stopping of birth is the essence of the reverse application of the Pratityasamutpada formula, and in this, as distinct from the content of the fourth Noble Truth, there is no imprecision. The final paragraph in Sakyamuni's presentation of this formula to his monks describes the step-by-step procedure. Each of the twelve links in turn is eliminated until,

213

with the elimination of the Birth link, ". . . there is a ceasing of this whole mass of suffering. . . ." We, in our turn, can retrace the negative process with the aid of our Figure 3 by proceeding thus:

>Without avidya, no samskaras.
>Without samskaras, no vijnana.
>Without vijnana, no nama-rupa.
>Without nama-rupa, no sadayatana.
>Without sadayatana, no sparsa.
>Without sparsa, no vedana.
>Without vedana, no trsna.
>Without trsna, no upadana.
>Without upadana, no bhava.
>Without bhava, no jati.
>Without jati, no jaramarana.

Certainly this is as precise as one could wish, and the full impact of that destructive precision is felt all the more if one takes the trouble to carry the meanings of those terms through the sequence. But precision must not be confused with simplicity. Unfortunately, the actuality is not so simple as the mere statement of a retrogressive formula. As is to be expected, the retrogression starts at link number one, avidya, but as we know, avidya was operative in the past life and the lives before that, as well as the present. So, in practical terms, the process cannot start with avidya and eliminate it directly. Avidya, in this context, is only to be approached obliquely, through intermediaries. Such a "sideways" approach was part of the ancient practice by ardent monks that comprised a form of link breaking. The *Satipatthana* sutta, mentioned and summarized earlier in the last chapter, tells us how the normal, unrestrained progression from one thing to another can be short-circuited. And the key feature here, as in much of the Hinayana Path, is the encouragement of disgust, leading to detachment and eventually the extinction of craving—back to the elements of the Four Noble Truths, in fact. The meditation on the body, and on the sights, sounds, and smells of the charnel ground are cases in point.

The "sideways" approach is similar to the evocation of detachment, and in terms of the twelve-fold linkage can be described as the method of driving in the wedge. As an example, turn again to our Figure 3 and look at link seven, vedana. At this point there are three possible alternatives. If feelings of pleasure or pain arise, then craving or aversion will follow and grasping will follow that, and so on. But what if, by an act of will preceded by special training (as specified in the *Satipatthana*), only the neutral feeling was allowed to arise from contact? And further, what if neutral feelings were only ever to arise under whatever circumstances of contact of the senses with their objects? In that case, the seventh link would be neutralized, de-activated as a positive, generative condition.

That being so, the next link, number eight, could not arise, because its necessary condition had disappeared. In effect, number eight would be blocked off. And if number eight, craving, failed to materialize, what about number nine, grasping? That too would fail to appear because its antecedent condition was not there. Proceed onward until number eleven, birth, the crucial one, is reached, and if that is stopped in the same manner the whole mass follows into oblivion, as stated in our earlier quotation.

That process, the breaking of the links (starting midway, or the "sideways" approach), if and when successful, becomes itself a condition allowing the opposite of avidya to arise, i.e., the knowledge of the causal process demonstrated decisively by its piecemeal destruction. And having disposed of avidya by an oblique approach that supplants it by its opposite, none of the links from one to twelve can ever arise again. In fact, that brief summary describes the highest levels of the practice of this Path, and it equates with the skillful demolition of the "house" referred to in the Introduction.

Yet again we have the most pregnant of all the doctrinal formulas revealing its practical dimension—way out of reach of most, but practical for the few nonetheless. We are shown, unmistakably, how the doctrine and the practice are integrally connected. One without the other just won't do. It also shows how the operation of doctrine and practice in combination can produce what is sometimes called the "higher knowledge" or prajna (wisdom). Such higher knowledge, at full strength, coincides with release or liberation from all the bonds, as in the case of the higher knowledge engendered by breaking the links and stopping rebirth forever.

There are some, however, who would maintain that this king of formulas applies, in full, to the present. That avidva, samskaras, and all the rest up to jaramarana have equal force in explaining the ebb and flow of the Dharma samtana in its day-to-day aspect. Quite so. Immersed as we all are in the primeval ignorance, the field is clear for forces from the past to color consciousness together with mental and physical faculties, in such a way that sense impressions and responses to them develop into passionate desires or dislikes propelling us into actions that then inexplicably lose their motivating power and decline into forgetfulness.

All true. And the Pratityasamutpada can be quite properly applied in this way. But not exclusively. Its primary purpose, revealed in the manner of its delivery by the Buddha to his monks, and by the authoritative commentaries on the text by the ancient masters, not to mention the circumstances of that supreme revelation during the night of Bodhi—its primary purpose is to describe the "mechanics" of the infinite onward flow of becoming, wherein a single "life" is incomprehensible if looked at in isolation.

The more universal application of this formula is also strongly signalled by its intimate connection with that other "universal" formula, which also stemmed from the night of Bodhi, the Four Noble Truths. It may be that, because of a too exclusive application of the Pratityasamutpada to present circumstances and to immediate causal processes, the past existences and the future rebirth elements of the formula have been overshadowed and lost sight of. If that is indeed the case, then the discussion of rebirth in Buddhist terms that follows in the next chapter should not come amiss.

12. PRATISAMDHI: REBIRTH

In the Introduction, mention was made of the intrinsic strangeness to Westerners of much of the Indian and other Asian forms of the Dharma. There is perhaps no better example of this than the teaching of rebirth.

For most of us brought up and educated in a Western society, such an idea has had no place. Indeed, for any society rooted in Christian culture, the idea of rebirth into successive terrestrial forms of life must be at worst anathema, or at best a highly dubious notion. To begin with, then, the teaching of rebirth in any guise, whether it be reincarnation, transmigration, or metempsychosis is quite foreign to our cultural heritage and to the norms of traditional Western theology.

Thus we have little or no common ground on which to meet and assimilate these Oriental notions. Nevertheless, as many of us know, there have been ideas of reincarnation floating around in popular literature and in Theosophical circles for many decades. An unusually large number of people harbor half-formed, semi-wishful notions of having "been here before" and of "coming back again." One popular national newspaper, now defunct, in 1960 published a survey of its readers on the subject with extracts from correspondence and from interviews with both clerical and lay contributors. Nearly all the examples concerned the survival of the soul or the so-called "astral body" after death. Then there are the Spiritualists of various kinds, who, with the aid of specially endowed "mediums," claim the ability to contact those who have "passed over" and to produce messages from the departed. Little of this has much credence in orthodox Christian theology. For Westerners, then, our only yardstick of comparison consists of what might be called extramural theories intermixed with much that can only be called folklore, all of it highly amorphous and indistinct bits of this and that.

Another difficulty, already mentioned previously in these pages, is that the specifically Buddhist doctrines of rebirth have not been spelled out for Westerners in anything like a sufficient degree. What is worse, where any consideration at all is given to the subject, the ideas presented have been all too often intertwined with some of the folklore and extramural theories mentioned above.

For example, there is still a body of opinion among some followers of Buddhism that having achieved a human birth one can no longer descend to the lower realms after death, such as those of animals or disembodied spirits (preta). Now while this may well be the teaching of certain Theosophical schools, it is not part of the Buddhadharma. Some of the scriptural evidence against this misconception has already been presented. The textual authorities against such an idea could easily be doubled. Certainly, as a human being one can behave in such a way and think in such a way that the lower destinies are thereby blocked. But that is a different matter and is agreed and approved by all Mainstream schools of Buddhist thought.

On the other hand, automatic establishment among humankind in future births simply by virtue of being human now is no part of any Indian Mainstream teaching and so was not taught in the original Dharma. Here, then, the Dharma as given stands in need of close attention if we are not to be unwittingly misled by versions that sometimes masquerade in an appearance of the outward signs of authenticity. Such versions are more likely to be Western subcultural themes in Oriental disguise. To accept such concoctions unquestioningly would be rather like regarding Gilbert and Sullivan's superb comic opera, *The Mikado*, as a presentation of actual Japanese custom and practice. This veritable mine of wit and wisdom has the appearance of what the Edwardians thought Japanese life was like, but underneath the grease paint and costume it was the same old d'Oyly Carte Company (and no disrespect is meant to that excellent Company or to that magical composer partnership).

Yet another difficulty for us that surfaces from time to time among serious and devoted practitioners is the present day relevance of the historical dimension and records of the Dharma. And here, of course, it is not only the rebirth doctrine of the original teaching but the present-day evaluation of Dharma historicity itself. The traditions about Sakyamuni's life are frequent victims of this uncertainty.

At this point it may be helpful to posit a distinction between "Buddhism" and "the Dharma." To this writer's mind the word Buddhism can be properly applied to any historical or present-day body of practitioners who consider themselves to be followers of the Buddha and who subscribe to a body of teaching that they believe has descended from or has connections with the Great Teacher himself.

The Dharma, however, *is* the Teaching itself, especially when enshrined in the hearts and minds of its followers, but particularly as recorded and preserved for us in the great corpus of Dharma literature which has been transmitted and exemplified by the masters of the established Asian lineages. The Dharma is what is, or should be, constant in all the various and culturally modified Buddhisms that have appeared in all parts of the world. Certain of these Buddhisms are, very likely, approximations to the original. And the reasons for their divergences are very often sound without distorting the essence of the original message.

But there can also be interpretations that damage or even invalidate the original purpose of the teaching. Cases of this kind occurred in China's long Buddhist history and no doubt elsewhere. Thus, to be genuine, to be capable of producing the end results aimed at by the original or by its lineal descendants, each and every "Buddhism" has to be matched up to the Dharma at frequent intervals. The case can be likened to the manufacture or construction of a piece of reproduction "period" furniture. The material, the construction, and the accessories have to be matched minutely against the original design. If not, you may end up with a piece of beautiful furniture, but it will not be Louis XIV, or whatever. In the same manner, unless we have access to the "original design" and make use of it conscientiously, our inherent propensities, our cultural inheritance—which is something other than the true Dharma and is a kind of baggage we carry around with us willy nilly—all that lumber will interpose itself, don new togs, and produce a Mikado charade without our being aware of it.

Of course, this is not to say that we must become pseudo-Orientals and imitate them and their methods while discarding our own. On the contrary, it is only if we absorb the Dharma, thoroughly digest it, then act upon it firmly supported by completely assimilated material, that our form of Buddhism will truly reflect the Great Teacher's intentions. If that is done then the Dharma will perform its special "magic" and our version will preserve the effective essentials yet have characteristics and strengths of its own. Such was the case in China, where it took nearly 400 years of effort and dedication by countless thousands of unnamed and unremembered devotees to deliver a superb model of the Dharma specially adapted to Chinese ways. For all its adaptations and modifications, Chinese Buddhism preserved the essentials of the original to such an extent that the highest fruits of all the Paths were produced in abundance. Similarly in Tibet and in Japan. And for this great fruition these different cultural families had to "go back to the drawing board" again and again to re-assert or re-formulate the original message in their own languages, idioms, or forms. There can be hardly any doubt that we, who approach the Dharma from outside, so to speak, shall find the need to do no less than they.

On a rather different level of concern one is obliged to look ahead from the present context of Indian Mainstream Hinayana to that of the Mahayana. The so-called second turning of the Wheel of the Dharma falls within the field of Indian Buddhism but is beyond our present interest, except in one vital respect. Although it may be felt in the West that Mahayana can be approached and indeed followed independently (there is much to recommend that view) it is clear from a study of the early Mahayana sutras and of the works of Nagarjuna that Indian Mahayana is a direct development from certain of the Hinayana lineages which preceded it.

Yet there is considerable partisan polemic directed against Hinayana convictions, and the context of that argument reveals a thoroughgoing mastery of the Hinayanan doctrines. And that mastery was a major factor in the radical re-evaluation of certain doctrines that emerged. On our part, therefore, the majority of the characteristic Mahayana themes, including that of sun-yata, cannot be understood in terms of their original meanings without some familiarity with such Mainstream Hinayana features as we are outlining here as anatman, Dharma activity, Dharma samtana, and the detail of the Path. Mahayana, in a very real sense, rides upon major Hinayana themes and heads them in different directions. Much of what Mahayana texts set out to present and explain assumes such prior knowledge on the part of its readers and partisans. In the more profound sections of Indian Mahayana sutras it is as if the Hinayana themes, particularly the *Abhidharma*, are used as a stepladder to carry the inquirer up to a certain level, from which another kind of doctrine and practice amalgam opens out. Then, and quite suddenly, the stepladder is kicked away, and if you've understood anything, you may begin to move along the new level. If you have not, then you fall to the ground among the debris of the Hinayana, and you have to pick up pieces all over again. In any case, without the stepladder of Mainstream Hinayana the Mahayana level is out of reach to all but those with special endowments. At least, it is out of reach in its own terms. Approximations abound, of course, but here one is exposed to what we may now call the Mikado syndrome.

For all these reasons the Dharma in its original form has to be contacted, investigated, and retained. In addition to this it has to be used as the master design that regulates and shapes all its subsequent models so as to maintain reliability, credibility, and effectiveness for its own purposes. Modification and adjustments have to be limited by those criteria or else the model will turn into something else entirely.

Now there is a very obvious drawback in all this. Expressed plainly, it is that everyone who approaches Buddhist doctrine and practice cannot be expected to make all these investigations and evaluations for himself. But one would expect those who present the Dharma to the public to have a care of this kind. The minimum necessity is the ability to distinguish between individual opinions, even practice experience, and the Teaching itself as preserved in sutra and sastra. If both presenters and audiences can be made aware of such distinctive criteria, the Dharma will be safeguarded and the seekers after it well served.

After that long but necessary prologue we can get down to business. We have postulated the subject of rebirth as an example where the majority of Westerners enter a terra incognita and there is a need for some map making. Although the subject of rebirth was brought into view in the chapter on Samsara, we could then only refer to it in the most general terms. Now, having gained some background of what is involved in the principal doctrinal formulas, it is possible to discuss the subject in rather more detail and with a degree of doctrinal accuracy.

To begin with, it has to be understood that rebirth forms part of the earliest strata of Mainstream Dharma. There is no possible doubt about that. The only doubt of any value is, what kind of rebirth was it? What did this early teaching consist of? Let us start by establishing that rebirth is part of the earliest Mainstream teaching. We can do this without difficulty from the material we have so far presented as the Mainstream consensus of Indian Buddhism. The fact of rebirth was never a matter of dispute in any of the first Buddhist schools. The manner of rebirth was disputed, as we shall see, but never rebirth itself. We can therefore say that rebirth is an integral part of the Original Dharma because:

1: Rebirth is implicit in the expanded teaching of Samsara
and it is explicit in the descriptions of the passage through
the Five (or Six) Destinies comprising Samsara.

2: Rebirth is explicitly stated as being directly perceived by
Sakyamuni's crowning insight on the night of Bodhi.

3: Rebirth is explicit in the Second Noble Truth.

4: Rebirth is explicit in the final part of the Satipatthana sutta.

5: Rebirth is elaborated in the doctrine of the Dharma sam
tana, particularly in the vipaka or ripening process.

6: Rebirth is explicit in the major formula of the
Pratityasamutpada.

7: Rebirth is the target of the final stages of the Path, at the
completion of which it is stopped forever.

For all these general assertions many Buddha-quotations
have already been given in these pages and more will follow as
we proceed. The textual evidence for it is so overwhelming that
one can only wonder at the selectivity at work where little or no
mention is made of the topic in present day expositions.

The question remains: what kind of rebirth? The cardinal
doctrine of anatman precludes any form of reincarnation as generally understood. Having come so far in this book, the reader
will recognize that the answer lies in the teaching of the sub-surface activity of Dharma elements collected together in a continuous series of disparate factors.

Another way of arriving at the Buddha's teaching on this
subject is to consider what the Indian systems contemporaneous
with Sakyamuni's lifetime taught and that he consistently denied
were valid. The spiritual and philosophical milieu of the
Buddha's time has already been remarked upon, we saw then

that there were several ancient systems already well established by the time the Great Bodhisattva approached the Bodhi tree. The important ones and their rebirth doctrines were:

1. The Brahmanical System Based Upon the Vedas.

The *Brhadaranyaka Upanishad* describes the death-rebirth process in some detail. At death, the senses and thought cease in turn. Then the Self (Atman) residing in the heart leaves the body through one or other of the apertures of the head. When the Self leaves, the body is dead. Then, under the propulsion of his knowledge and deeds, the Self of the dead person enters another body according to what his past actions allow.

This Self is unborn, undying, immortal and is Brahman.

This Self and its reincarnation Sakyamuni denied.

2. The Jaina System As Taught by Mahavira.

For the Jainas every being possesses an enduring substance (jiva) that is impregnated by foreign substances, contaminating its original purity. At death-rebirth the jiva, stained by karmic influences, leaves the body and proceeds to the place of rebirth.

Jivas are described as immaterial, indestructible, independent, innately perfect, and with a tendency to rise to the summit of the universe in their pure state.

This too Sakyamuni denied.

3. The Samkhya System Based Upon the Yoga Tradition and on the Upanishads.

Here, every living being comprised three major parts: matter (prakrti), life-monad (purusa), and subtle body (linga). The life-monad transmigrates by means of the subtle body that retains all the traces of our experience as well as the whole psychic apparatus. This subtle body containing the life-monad is impelled from one birth to the next by the effect of the defilements. The life-monad (purusa) is described as eternal, without parts, existing in all beings as pure Spirit. Sakyamuni denied this also.

The denial of these and other known systems is contained in the long opening sutta of the *Digha Nikaya*, called the Brahmajala suttanta. In this text, one of the oldest in the Pali collection, the Buddha describes and condemns sixty-two kinds of false views that are mere speculations.

Each of the three main rival systems taught an unchanging "soul" (atman, jiva, or purusa) that reincarnates from one body to another at death. It is this soul aspect that is denied and that led directly to the Anatman or no-Soul teaching now enshrined in the formula of the Three Signs (or Seals).

At this point, then, we know that rebirth is an integral part of the Dharma, and we also know what it was that Sakyamuni disapproved of in the other systems and that he relegated to "false views." Now we need to have some specific statements from the Buddha on the rebirth that he had discovered and which he taught to his followers.

To provide these we shall again have recourse to the Pali texts, though it should be understood that the extracts that follow could be paralleled by similar ones from the Sanskrit Canon. It is perhaps worth noting, in passing, that most of the Sanskrit Canon was largely destroyed in India by successive invasions between 100 A.D. and 1,100 A.D. Fortunately, a large proportion of Sanskrit texts of every description was exported to China and Tibet, translated into Chinese and Tibetan with careful annotation as to where each came from, when it arrived, and who translated it. A huge body of this literature exists to this day, but apart from catalogues and selections, it remains for the most part untranslated into any Western language.

The first category of rebirth statements we can call "general," that is to say, affirmative that rebirth takes place but saying little about how it occurs.

In the *Sutta Nipata* we find this:

> [Those who are] deprived of the emancipation of thought and the emancipation of knowledge are unable to put an end to Samsara; they will verily continue to undergo birth and death. Those who again and again go to Samsara with birth and death, to existence in this way or that, that is the state of avijja [Sanskrit: avidya]. For this avijja is the great folly by which this existence has been long traversed, but those beings who resort to knowledge do not go to rebirth.

In the Dhammapada, we find:

> If a man becomes fat and a great eater, if he is sleepy and rolls himself about, that fool, like a hog fed on grains, is born again and again.

In the *Anguttara* we find:

> Sariputta, any white-frocked home-man. . . who acts controlled in these five steps of training (the Five Precepts) may . . . declare: "Destroyed is hell for me, destroyed is animal

birth, destroyed is the realm of ghosts,
destroyed is the ill-way, the abyss . . ."

Again from the *Sutta Nipata*:

Seeing men caught in craving Pingiya, you
should be heedful and renounce craving so as
not to come to birth again.

The next category of statements conveys rather more in the
way of explanation. Once more we turn to the *Anguttara
Nikaya* for the next extracts. Mention may be made in passing,
especially for those readers who may want to look up some texts
themselves, that this author counted over forty separate quotations concerning the results of actions to be expected in future
lives, in just two volumes of this translated text. The *Anguttara*
is crammed with statements on rebirth. However, now, we are
looking for something more specific, and we find:

Ananda asked the Lord, ". . . to what
extent is there becoming?"
". . . Ananda, action is the field, consciousness the seed, craving the moisture. For
beings that are fettered by craving, consciousness is established in the lower worlds. Thus in
the future there is repeated rebirth. In this way
there is becoming, Ananda."

Again from *Anguttara*:

Volition [cetana], O monks, is what I call
action, for through volition one is performing
the action by body, speech, and mind. There is
Karman, O monks, that ripens in hell . . . that

> ripens in the animal world . . . in the world of
> men . . . in the heaven worlds. Threefold is the
> fruit of Karman, ripening at lifetime, the next
> birth, in successive births.

None of these general or particular statements on rebirth addresses the problem of what is reborn. To all such questions, and they were asked many times, Sakyamuni usually replied with a version of the formula of "Arising Due to Conditions" (Pratityasamutpada). One instance from the *Samyutta* must suffice:

> When a noble disciple has well seen this
> dependent arising and those dependently
> arisen phenomena according to reality and
> with perfect wisdom, it does not occur to him
> that he should run back to the past, saying,
> Did I exist in the past? Did I not exist in the
> past? . . .
> Nor that he should run ahead to the
> future saying; Shall I exist in the future? Shall
> I not exist in the future? . . .
> Nor that he should now, in the present,
> have doubts, saying, What am I? This being,
> where did it come from, where will it go?
> What is the reason? It is because the noble
> disciple has well seen this dependent arising and
> these dependently arising phenomena according
> to actuality and with perfect wisdom.

In this last question we have the clearly intended meaning that the question of rebirth is only to be answered rightly by reference to the great formula of "Arising Due to Conditions," or as this translation has it, "Dependent Arising." Thus we have to attend carefully to links two and three for the arising in the present existence and to links ten and eleven for projections into a future existence (see Figure 3). Link number eleven is simply a re-run of number three, but transferred to the future.

So the rebirth doctrine largely concentrates on the process described in links one, two, and three, which we have discussed in some detail. In brief, that doctrine involves others, such as vipaka or ripening, which in turn involves the Dharma samtana or Dharma series, which in turn involve Dharma elements and Dharma activity. All this we have discussed and described.

In the light of those earlier discussions it is possible to formulate a statement of the Buddhist doctrine of rebirth. At this stage, however, that statement has to be taken as provisional, first, because it will be incomplete and other elements will have to be added later. And second because it presumes all that has gone before in these pages on the associated doctrines of vipaka, Dharma samtana, and Dharma clusters. We are now fortunate in being able to presume so much. Without such presumptions straight answers to questions of this kind are impossible.

A brief, provisional statement then, on rebirth, Buddhist style. The rebirth doctrine involves the activity of sub-surface elements (Dharmas), which appear and disappear momentarily but in sequence or series, controlled by certain causal laws. Those causal laws are of two kinds: direct and linear such as those producing given conditions such as soil and weather in relation to seeds. The second kind is indirect, in the sense that the result of causes can be separated by ages, certainly by lifetimes, from the original impulse. Because that original causal impulse is deposited within the continuous stream of separate, momentary elements for later effects to arise, it is improper and incorrect to speak of "beings" or "life-monads" or "souls" moving onward through time to receive their rewards or punishments. And in a similar manner the seemingly definitive break at death is an apparent rather than real dislocation, having to do with our inveterate insistence on perceiving beings or persons where only streams of successive elements exist in clusters of temporary formation.

The crux of the doctrine is that the stream or series (samtana) is never broken, it simply continues beyond our perception into new forms or clusters directly or indirectly connected with past conditions and causes. To be brief in this matter is, as you see, a rather relative notion.

This improper and incorrect manner of speaking, thinking, or understanding leading to wrong views on cardinal matters, often drew a correction from the Buddha to his questioner. Because of this, and because of a heightened sensitivity over the inadequacies of language to convey the subtle experience of reality, Sakyamuni himself and his early followers were sometimes referred to as "Vibhajyavadins," meaning, those who make distinctions. In terms of getting a correct answer to a question it means that if the question is wrongly phrased or wrongly worded (indicating an underlying wrong or confused view), the words themselves preclude a true answer.

Two favorite examples of this from Indian texts, not only Buddhist, are: what is the name of the son of a barren woman? And: How long are the horns of a hare? Both are linguistically, grammatically, and terminologically correct. But neither can be answered in their own terms because they ask about something that does not exist in any real sense. Not that that would prevent some from postulating, even inventing, anecdotes about the one and characteristics of the other. One is reminded of the musical piece about that Lieutenant Kizhe of Russian legend. It is just so with questions about the rebirth of me, you, him or whosoever. Once the question is reformulated in conformity with real events or with actuality, then an answer can be given that also conforms with real events. Of course, the questioner may have to abandon his question altogether and investigate some more before he can reformulate the question. In this case on the subject of rebirth, questions and answers, to be accurate and truthful, have to be couched in terms of ". . . this dependent arising and these dependently arisen phenomena. . . ."

Now to recall our brief statement on rebirth above, no mention of the Pratityasamutpada was made in it—yet another reason for describing it as provisional. Let us be clear: that statement is not incorrect, it is provisional. This lapse into pedantic hair-splitting has been made to indicate how much care is needed if one is to speak or write on such doctrines both clearly and accurately. To be a Vibhajyavadin often means being called other less complimentary names, but there is a real necessity for clarity and precision on such matters. Some of the Buddha's dialogues with his questioners show this with some force. Perhaps the best and clearest example occurs in the *Samyutta*. The Buddha replies to a wandering mendicant:

> What then, Venerable one, is aging-dying and to whom does the aging-dying belong?
>
> This question is not correct, replied Bhagavat.
>
> If one asked, O monk, "What is aging and dying and to whom does the aging and dying belong?" Or if one said, "Aging-dying is one

thing and the one to whom aging-dying belongs is another," these two phrases would have the same meaning [although] with different words.

If one is of the opinion, O monk, that the vital principle is identified with the body, the religious life is not possible; but if one is of the opinion that the vital principle is different from the body, the religious life is not possible either.

Avoiding these two extremes, O monk, the Tathagata teaches, by a middle way, the true Law [by simply saying], that aging and dying have birth for condition.

Regardless of the meaning and purpose of the exchange, the need for proper formulation of questions so as to get true answers is plain. And this very discipline leads one into the belief that short, brief answers to questions of substance are likely to be misleading at the very best. "Firecracker" answers have their place, but not in doctrinal expositions. An example of this might be: Question. What is reborn? Answer. Nothing. While the answer is strictly correct in the precise terms of the question, what does it tell you? Nothing. Precisely.

We have said above that something had to be added to our brief statement of the rebirth doctrine. One of those additions we can now bring into view. From the very earliest times the major Indian Mainstream schools were unable to come to a consensus view on the actual process of death-rebirth. All agreed without demur that the correct doctrine was enshrined in the formula of "Arising Due to Conditions" and had to do with the re-assembling of the Five Skandhas at rebirth.

But serious differences arose over the nature of that reassembly. One may presume, with justification, that much formulation and reformulation of questions and answers went on at this time. It is not our purpose to enter into matters of controversy in a work which describes itself as a presentation of the consensus view, but in the case of rebirth the controversy brings to light three different doctrines to explain this crucial event. As these doctrines were Buddhist they must have a place in our discussion of the characteristics of rebirth in the Buddhadharma.

One group of early schools, the Pudgalavadin/Sammatiyas, taught that the Five Skandhas, or the Dharma stream operating as a five-group configuration called "the personality," actually transmigrated in its five-fold form from the death state to the reborn state. An examination of the Sanskrit version of link number three may suggest how this interpretation was made. Although this teaching was hotly disputed by the remaining majority as being too close to the wrong view of a "personality" being reborn, the majority on its part, divided into two groups of orthodox opinion.

On the one hand there was a body of schools, today represented by the Theravadin doctrine, which maintained that rebirth is instantaneous, that there is no interval between the last moment of the death-state and the first moment of the reborn state. Everyone agreed that the stream of Dharmas between links two and three is unbroken, but this view had it that these two links follow each other immediately. The Mainstream schools who upheld this version were the Mahasanghikas, the Mahisasakas, and the Theravadins.

On the other hand, another very important group, equal, even senior, to the other group in age of establishment, maintained that the Dharma samtana continued after death in a form called the "intermediate existence" (antarabhava), which is an attenuated series linking the death-state with the reborn state. This antarabhava consisted of mental and non-material Dharmas that preserved the unbroken linkage of momentary elements for a certain duration. This attenuated Dharma stream was propelled toward its appropriate level of renewed conception by its inherent karmic impulses. Partisans of this doctrine included the Sarvastivadins, Darstantikas, and the Purvasailas. It is highly likely that Tibetan teachings on the Bardo owe something to the antarabhava doctrines of the Sarvastivadins.

Much explanatory material exists on both these main variants of the theme. Pages of quotation and discussion are to be found in Vasubandhu's *Abhidharmakosa* supporting the antarabhava thesis. Likewise, the contrary view of immediate death-rebirth linkage is explained and textually supported in the Pali Abhidhamma and in Buddhaghosa's commentaries. All this goes far beyond the scheme of this book, which is concerned to set out the major doctrines as plainly as possible. But having brought these rebirth themes into view, we must call a halt. The topics of *Abhidharma* proper are impossible to condense satisfactorily without falling into the trap of mis-wording and mis-phrasing, which produces wrong notions. The arguments on both sides about this matter are clear but complex. They have to be studied as they are.

For the purpose of this exposition of the Buddhist rebirth doctrine we can summarize certain matters that have been established either in this or in some other parts of this book:

1: Rebirth is an integral part of the Dharma, as demonstrated in its major doctrinal formulas and some key-terms.
2: Rebirth in the Buddhadharma is different and distinct from other teachings of the reincarnation of "souls."

3: The Pali texts abound with general and particular state ments about the fact of rebirth.

4: The formula of "Arising Due to Conditions" (Pratityasamutpada) contains the crux of the rebirth doc trine, but it requires the supplementary doctrines of vipaka and Dharma samtana to render that formula intelligible.

5: All the Mainstream Indian Hinayana schools taught this particular rebirth doctrine, although there were three fur ther variants on which there was no consensus.

Some readers may now be expecting this author to revise his earlier brief statement on rebirth and present a definitive formula or description. If that is so then those readers will be disappointed. In the first place, a definitive formula is impossible, only the existing formulas can be explained and expanded. And, of course, for rebirth, the prime formula is the Pratityasamutpada. What can be done is to explain that the rebirth doctrine in the Buddhadharma is an amalgam of the special teachings on the Dharmas, and the component teachings of Karman, both combined and threaded into the skein of the Pratityasamutpada. Add to that the variant teachings on the death-rebirth progression among the Indian schools and then remember the need for careful distinctions in handling the language used to convey these special meanings. If all that is done and digested, then one is certainly on the right path to an understanding of the rebirth doctrine. But if one insists on a recipe, then here's one:

Take the Pratityasamutpada formula, add the discussion of the links which follows.

Add to that the provisional statement on page 231 and expand as necessary by the expositions of the various features in the relevant parts of this book. Select one of the three alternative theses of the Indian Hinayana on death-rebirth, or use all three. The resulting doctrinal amalgam should then be read back into the Pratityasamutpada formula. That resultant should be a close approximation to the teaching of rebirth in the Buddhadharma.

We can now bring Part Three to a close without apology for the difficult and compact nature of its contents. It should be evident by now to those determined readers who remain with us that the Dharma is indeed subtle and against the stream of worldly thought and opinion, especially the Western variety. And yet if one comes to grips with the textual expositions and with the primary formulas and their special terms, then the meaning and import is capable of penetration. Naturally patience, application, and care are required, but above all one has to get things in the right order. Whether, all that being said and done, the original meaning can be adequately conveyed by relatively straightforward English language is a matter about which there must always remain some doubt.

What cannot be open to doubt is that the Dharma itself, as preserved and transmitted to us in the shape of the sutras and commentaries, is a miracle of precision combined with multivalent meanings. This is especially so when one has taken the trouble to unlock the terminology. But always, within and beyond the terms and their meanings, beckons the Path itself. That Path is the consolidation of the teaching with the particular experience related to each and every doctrine. That consolidation activates those special Dharmas associated with wisdom (prajna). Once prajna is activated and developed, the whole Dharma stream becomes suffused with insight, realization, and release from bonds of defilements. That is an altogether different dimension from any understanding conveyed or gained by means of the written word. It is just that Path, in its ascending stages and final consummation, that the next and final section sets out to explore and describe.

The Path
and
The Three
Ways

PART FOUR

13. THE FIRST TWO PATHS: SAMBHARAMARGA AND PRAYOGAMARGA

The Path (marga), whose route and stages we shall shortly begin to trace, has already been discussed in these pages. In fact, much of its general direction and many of its requirements have emerged from our earlier expositions. Those expositions already contain specific details of the Path, especially the fourth Noble Truth, which contains the eight factors of the Path; the method of final stopping (nirodha) contained in the reverse process of the formula of Arising Due to Conditions; and the graduated sequence of practices described as "the only way" in the *Satipatthana* sutta.

All these different explanations point in the same direction, from impurity to purity, from suffering to a total absence of suffering, from repeated births to no birth, from Samsara to Nirvana. For many, this matter of the Path is the only subject worthy of attention in all of Sakyamuni's teaching, and those who have this idea are likely to regard the doctrinal topics with something less than enthusiasm.

Yet those readers who have followed this presentation so far should be aware that in certain key areas doctrine and practice are so closely interwoven that they are almost inextricable. In fact, it would not be overstating the case to say that without a thorough familiarity with the formulas of the Four Noble Truths and the Arising Due to Conditions, this Path is virtually impossible to complete successfully. Even if that be accepted, as it needs to be, the difficulties involved remain formidable.

There is however, another, larger scale of difficulty. This concerns the length of the Path and the problem of where one starts. Or, more precisely, what are our inherent capacities when we first approach this Path? Despite the promise of the Satipatthana that the ultimate goal could be attained in seven years or less, it was always understood that the final attainment could be a long and arduous process. To begin such an enterprise without a substantial inheritance of good works and a natural bias toward detachment lengthens the Path so that it extends over a number of lives. In terms of the Dharma-samtana, with which we are now familiar, if the "mix" or content of an individual stream is greatly contaminated with worldly desires and if it also has a heavy "accrued balance" of past defilements to work off, then the Path of Purification will take that much longer and be that much more onerous.

Even the apparent rapid attainment of the goal by the first Arhats is deceptive. The revelations by each of those Arhats of Sakyamuni's time assembled at Lake Anavatapta show clearly that many lives of various kinds had intervened between the first wish to emulate and the final achievement. The conclusion is inescapable. Those Arhats were fully matured and receptive when they first encountered Sakyamuni.

If such considerations apply to the modern Western student or seeker—who is almost certainly a layman, and who possibly has family dependents and responsibilities in addition to his own intrinsic deficiencies—then the likelihood of his making much progress on this Path while remaining a layman is very limited. Indeed, as we shall soon see, certain eminent laymen of the Buddha's time complained that Dharma matters were being withheld from them because they were laymen. And so the fully elaborated Path came to provide for lay activities and preparations at the early stages. But to approach the Path proper, to gain the states required for the rarefied air of the heights and summits, entry into the monk-Samgha, though not obligatory, was and is prudent and sensible.

The Samgha of Buddhist monks (Skt.: bhiksu, Pali: bhikkhu) was created for this purpose, to allow a definitive break with all worldly ties prior to embarking upon the approach to the Holy Path. For such a monk, even if his deficiencies are dire, the mild or stringent asceticism open to him within the Samgha will begin the purification process and shorten the eventual journey. The layman, on the other hand, unless he is capable of abandoning all ties and involvements without joining the Samgha, is very distantly placed. If he remains within the family he has to seek protection in the Three Refuges and fulfill his worldly obligations with patience. Above all, he must gain access to Dharma teaching and support those who precede him on the Path. His primary concern must be to avoid worsening his condition and to ensure a "good rebirth" by ethical behavior and generosity. In so doing he plants "good roots," which help to clear away obstructions and allow his Dharma-stream to develop and flow on into more favorable circumstances.

All this detail, of preparatory measures and of the actual journey, is documented in the fully elaborated doctrines, known in Indian Mainstream as the Five Paths. The first of those five is the Path of Acquiring Equipment.

THE PATH OF ACQUIRING EQUIPMENT
(SAMBHARAMARGA)

The Path, which was outlined by Sakyamuni in the fourth of the Four Noble Truths, and which was given more depth and direction in the formula of the Arising Due to Conditions, was further elaborated by the Arhats and teaching masters of early Indian Buddhism. In its developed form, the Path consists of five graduated stages:

1. The Path of Acquiring Equipment (Sambharamarga)
2. The Path of Preparatory Practices (Prayogamarga)
3. The Path of Vision (Darsanamarga)
4. The Path of Repeated Meditative Cultivation (Bhavanamarga)
5. The Path of No Further Training (Asaiksamarga)

The whole scheme is shown in diagrammatic form in the sequence of figures 4 and 5. In this section on the Two Preparatory Stages we shall examine the background and content of the first two Paths, represented by our Figure 4.

Although the graduated system presumes entrance at the first of the Paths, followed by passage through each of the successive stages in due order, in life and in fact things are not that simple. As mentioned earlier, it is not easy to know where we are when we start. Some may have accumulated the necessary equipment in a previous life, enabling them to embark on the ascetic career at once. Such a person will find no insuperable obstacle to joining the Samgha if he or she so desires and so will be able to engage in the special practices without much ado. This would be the entry and rapid passage through Sambharamarga.

Others may have been monks or nuns previously and now find themselves drawn powerfully back to the Samgha again, where their past experience will surface in a rapid adjustment to the spartan life and where their previous skills will enable them to cross into the second stage. For our purposes, such cases will be regarded as exceptional and we shall assume entrance is to be made right at the beginning, and from a worldly mode of life. This, after all, is the norm even for the most advanced.

Our starting point is therefore ordinary people of the world, homeowners with families, unattached young people, men and women of all kinds and conditions. All are immersed in the everyday affairs of time and place and all are either struggling to preserve what they have or are trying to gain what they do not yet have. In short, they are ordinary people doing what comes naturally. Certain of these will meet with disappointment or disillusionment. Others will discover an appetite for a more satisfying philosophy of life. Others again will tire of the ways of the world altogether and will want another mode of meaningful living, though of what kind they know not. Yet others will have some idea of what they are looking for and will almost certainly know what they want to avoid.

Sooner or later some of these people will begin a deliberate search, and by searching they will be drawn in the direction of the Dharma by various means, seemingly coincidental or accidental. If their ripening factors and surrounding conditions are favorable, they will eventually make contact with the Dharma, perhaps through hearsay, through books, or through other people. If and when that happens, it is likely that they will have the experience that certain things seem to "click into place" and a kind of unknowing recognition occurs. Whatever form of the Dharma is encountered, this way it will appear to be "right" and powerfully attractive. In this way, and in other ways, one can be drawn into contact, and provided that contact is consolidated, a distant sighting of the Path can be gained.

Of course, in the countries of the East, where Buddhism has been long established, ordinary people of both low and high estate need have no such inclinations. Yet for them the Samgha is an institution of distinction, venerable, worthy, and meriting their support. They are well aware of its purpose, and it fills a clearly understood role in the society, due to the influence of Buddhism on their culture. For those of us in the West, however, such things are far from clear, and the Order of Buddhist monks remains, by and large, rather exotic and without a role that is generally understood.

For the ordinary man or woman of the world in Western society who gains contact with the Dharma, the monk Samgha is unlikely to be part of the initial attraction. The first "pull" is much more likely to come from some particular part of the teaching, heard or read. The place and purpose of the monk or nun Samgha is a matter that only becomes clear after certain parts of the teaching take on meaning for the newcomer.

Assume, then, that contact has been made. From then on learning about another kind of life can begin, learning of noble and ignoble forms of activity and of the substance of the teaching itself.

In our day and place most aspects of Dharma teaching are wide open to investigation, though not entirely to realization. Many of the sutra texts are available in translation, and there are Buddhist centers of all kinds that welcome inquirers. Although rather thin on the ground, the Samgha of monks and nuns is also present in this green and pleasant land. Clerics of various Buddhist persuasions are engaged in teaching, and public lectures and study courses on the Dharma are taking place at frequent intervals. For us, then, the outer doors are wide open to all and sundry. For people of Sakyamuni's time in India, it was not quite so open and easy.

According to the early sutra records, Sakyamuni himself was not always totally forthcoming to lay people who showed interest in his teaching. Much seemed to depend on his direct perception of their receptivity and their inherent capacities. Rarely, if ever, were teachings about the Pratityasamutpada or about Nirvana given to laymen. Sometimes the Four Noble Truths would be spoken of, but the main doctrines offered to laymen concerned the need for generosity (dana), moral conduct (sila), and the opening of the Way to a heaven rebirth (svarga). The heaven rebirth largely depended upon the first two. If the layperson subsequently professed faith in the Buddha, as so often occurs at the end of many of the suttas of the Pali texts, then more in the way of teaching might follow.

But, generally speaking, the heart of the teaching-practice combination was reserved for those who left the world altogether and joined the ranks of monk Samgha. One or two examples may serve to illustrate the point. One case already referred to in these pages was that of Yasas, the young man who wandered into the Buddha's presence at Benares soon after the conversion of the first five disciples. He was the recipient of a virtual re-run of the discourse of the First Turning of the Wheel. Because of this he heard about the Four Noble Truths right away, without any preamble. He promptly entered the Order and shortly gained Arhatship. Similarly, in the meetings with the Magadhan king Bimbisara and with the Vaisali courtesan, Amrapali, the Buddha first expounded the lay credo on giving, morality, and heaven-birth and then, as the text says, "when the Lord saw that their minds were prepared, softened, free from bias, elated, and well disposed," he went on to tell them about the Four Noble Truths.

It was quite otherwise for the lay people of Patali village. To them, the Buddha simply stressed the five misfortunes and the five blessings of lay activity. Again it was a question of the necessity of moral conduct requiring vigilance, which results in a heaven rebirth after death. Also included was the prospect of renown and wealth that accrues to vigilant and morally endowed people.

One of the most generous benefactors of the early Samgha, Anathapindika, was likewise excluded from the substantial teaching. It was he who secured the Jeta Park at Sravasti for the Order by covering the entire area with gold to meet the purchase price. Even so, only low-key teaching was given to him for a long time.

After many years as a lay follower he happened to fall ill, and he sent to ask Sariputra to visit him. Sariputra, perceiving the gravity of his illness, preached to him an appropriate discourse on the subject of disgust for and detachment from all sense objects. Anathapindika was greatly impressed and sustained, but he reproved Sariputra because he said that never before had he heard teaching on this subject, although he had long revered the Buddha and served the Order. Sariputra replied bluntly that such doctrine is normally reserved for monks. Thereupon, Anathapindika, evidently not a man to mince his words, complained with feeling that the Dharma should be available to lay people unreservedly. He said some laymen would be led astray without proper instruction. Others could profit and realize high stages of detachment if given the opportunity.

There is little evidence that this plea was answered during Sakyamuni's lifetime. But not very long after the Parinirvana, the same views were expressed with considerable force during the debate leading to the great schism. In fact it was the strength of the lay support that helped in the creation of the "party of the majority" (Mahasanghika). Nevertheless, in the time of the Master, most of the laypeople were simply encouraged to adopt a generous outlook and to abstain from immorality and violence. They were exhorted to behave with affection and kindness to all, particularly their own family and household, and to seek honestly to secure their future and livelihood. All this is contained in one of the suttas of the Digha collection called the Sigalovada.

It will have been noticed that if the layperson expressed faith in the Buddha, further teaching sometimes followed. This seems to hark back to Sakyamuni's insistence, from the time of his Enlightenment, on proper modes of respect to his person. The sharp rebuke to his first five disciples for addressing him as "friend" will be recalled. This factor of faith or confidence and the recognition of worthy qualities, lies at the heart of the establishment of the subordinate order of laymen and laywomen.

These were the upasakas (male) and the upasikas (female) who have taken refuge in the Three Jewels of Buddha, Dharma, and Samgha. This subordinate Order had, like the monks and nuns, its own code of behavior and formal acquiescence and it flourished mightily all over India for as long as the Dharma lasted there. Such lay devotees, or those who had made a public profession of adherence to the Buddha, his teaching, and his Order of monks and nuns, formed the body of the "faithful." They had, in fact, entered the outer court or assembly area at the entrance to the Path. Others, who gave generously but remained as they were, gained merit from the gift, but they stayed on the periphery of the Buddha's following, which was comprised of male and female lay devotees and the monks and nuns of the Order proper.

For the lay devotee who remained a householder and followed the norms of his or her society, the primary task was to support the clerical Samgha with food, clothing, shelter, and medical necessities. In so doing they practiced the giving whose karmic outflows would help to lay foundations for later development and eventual entry into the Order in a subsequent life. Those foundations consist of the engagement to renounce the basic acts of immorality (see List E) plus the fostering of and preliminary exercise in the Aids to Emancipation (see List D) and the good roots.

In many respects the lay devotee accepted a code of discipline (pratimoksa) and made a profession of faith similar to that of the monks and nuns. Entry into the status of upasaka or upasika was made before a panel of monks or of well-established upasakas, where the candidate made formal request for the rite to be administered to him. In the presence of this panel and of witnesses the candidate took formal refuge in the Three Jewels and then accepted, one by one, the precepts of conduct. Only then was he or she inaugurated into the lay Order for life.

Such a formal ceremony was regarded in the early Indian Samgha as an act of engagement to protective conduct. As such, the ritual itself was an exercise in renunciation that, because it involved acts of the body, speech, and mind with good intent, was a meritorious activity in itself, having propitious karmic results for the new entrant. This ceremonial consisted of two distinct parts: first, the "going for refuge" in each of the Three Jewels of Buddha, Dharma, and Samgha. To the careful minds of the Indian masters this first part of the rite actually endowed the candidate with the status of upasaka or upasika—a faithful lay follower. The second part, acceptance of precise rules of conduct, was the practical outflow or consequence of the first.

The five rules, or five-fold discipline, consists of five kinds of activity, which are formally renounced by the upasaka. They are given in List E. From this list it will be noticed that the five rules are simply the first part of the ten prescribed for novice monks who "go forth" entirely from the household life. This engagement on the part of the upasaka to a proportion of the full complement of ten rules serves to emphasize the preparatory nature of upasaka status. Once "inducted," he has passed through the outer gate and has turned toward the still distant Path proper.

For the most ardent lay follower, opportunities were provided for him to take a temporary step into the lifestyle of the "gone forth" monks and nuns. On full moon days or at certain festivals laymen and women could take "the fast of a day and night" (upavasastha). For this, the layperson left home and stayed within a temple or monastery precincts for twenty-four hours. During that period they adopted Precepts one through nine (excepting gold and silver), and they fasted. Also, of course, during this brief sojourn they had the opportunity to listen to monk discourses and practice certain basic meditations. Regular withdrawals of this nature kept alive the knowledge that their upasaka status was only a part of the fully disciplined lifestyle required for the practice of the Path. However, that status also, by the additional ceremonial and the even temporary adoption of the full code produced merit (vipakahetu) for the future.

Apart from the codes of conduct and engagement that conferred the status of upasaka or bhiksu, there was another set of abstentions that underlay all the codes and that were more closely aligned to the practice of the Path itself. They are called the

The Path: The Two Preparatory Stages

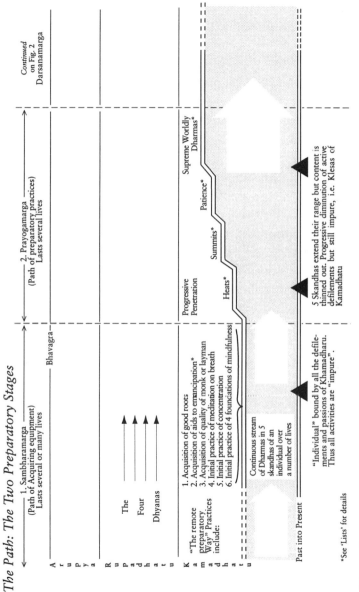

Figure 4

253

"Ten Bad Ways of Action" (see List F). To avoid all these was naturally called the "Ten Good Ways of Action." List F shows them grouped under their sections of bodily, speech, and mental activities. These ten were described as the most grave of worldly bad actions and were the minimum renunciations to be undertaken by anyone aiming to embark on progress toward the Path proper.

Several features of this list are worthy of comment. Notice that four of the ten are devoted to wrong conduct in speech. Of all the worldly habits, unrestrained speech is the most prevalent and constant type of serious misconduct. One doesn't meet with either the possibility or the desire for murder too often, but lying and other forms of wrong speech occur every day and are the most difficult to control entirely. Then there are the last three, of mind. This is another way of saying that the "three fires" of greed, hatred, and delusion have to be combated from the start and not understood as results which are attained at higher levels of practice. Finally, there is the total omission from this list of ten bad actions of the rule against drinking intoxicating liquor.

This omission is explained in the *Abhidharmakosa* as being due to its not having the same degree of gravity as the ten prohibitions. It may also have something to do with the use of certain fermented liquors for medicinal purposes in the ancient Indian Pharmacopoeia. Whatever the reason, the omission cannot be taken as an encouragement to indulgence and drunkenness. Hence the specific embargo in the upasaka's rules of conduct and the condemnation of "dicing and drinking" in the general advice to laymen in the Sigalovada sutta mentioned earlier.

From all this material on the layman's status within the wider Samgha, and his code of conduct and opportunity for stricter practice, the aim and purpose stand out with some clarity. The practice of this Path, even in its preliminaries, is incompatible with unrestrained everyday conduct in the world. The closer one moves toward the Path, the more one is necessarily drawn out of or away from worldly affairs and modes of behavior. The upasaka in this system is thus engaged in a partial discipline, which in its full range will require him to abandon family and society so as to detach himself from the grosser forms of misconduct for good. While he remains within the household and family his code of behavior and his cardinal virtue of generosity and care for his kin and their welfare protect him from future harm and build stores of good actions which will fructify for him later.

This is not all. He is also enjoined to visit the Samgha of monks frequently so as to benefit from listening to their preaching. In this way Dharma seeds are sown that he should ponder and put to use in everyday life. In effect, his practice of giving (dana) and moral conduct (sila) ensures him a favorable rebirth, either in the heaven worlds (svarga) or in well-endowed circumstances among humankind. His attention to the preaching reminded him of the higher life and its attainments as well as the acts of the Buddha and his Arhats. (Remember that in India during the first centuries after Sakyamuni's death there were no books containing Dharma for him to study; the whole of the teaching and practice was memorized by the monks and regularly recited or recalled for appropriate discourses to laymen.)

All this is contained in the general practice formula of listening (sruta), remembering and considering (cinta), and meditative penetration (bhavana). The third part of that formula, bhavana, was not, however, expected of laymen. Their worldly cares and activities were thought to be unconducive to the calm and recollected attention that bhavana requires. Nevertheless, if the layman could arrange his affairs so as to practice seclusion and meditation at times, so much the better for him. Ordinarily, the practice of concentrated attention was felt to be beyond him except on fast days.

Once the layperson takes the decisive step of leaving the world and enters into the monk or nun Samgha, the whole range and tenor of practice expands. In the first place, the doors onto worldly concerns and comforts firmly close with the required acceptance of over 200 rules of discipline when full ordination (upasampada) is conferred. The special rules of discipline for the fully ordained monk are grouped under various headings of declining gravity in the Pali Vinaya. The most grave are the four actions which incur "defeat" and expulsion from the monk Samgha. These are, in order: sexual intercourse, stealing, killing, and claiming a higher state of practice than is actually possessed. The other groupings concern acts that incur probation and reha-bilitation: either defeat or probation, forfeiture of wrongful acquisitions, expiation, confession, and further training.

Of course, keeping all these rules of conduct preserves the status of the monk and ensures his complete detachment from worldly passions and greed for possessions. But keeping such rules does not, by itself, constitute progress on the Path. The intention is that, by adopting such an ascetic mode of life, one clears away all obstructions to total application to the specific practices, particularly meditation, which bring about progres-sion through the stages.

In every age and in every place where the Samgha flourished there were monks who were "professionals," i.e., those who found the monk mode of life congenial and comfortable. Such people kept all the rules, preached when required, and generally maintained the accepted norms and standards of the ascetic life. But they went no further. They did not embark upon the graduated course of training in mindfulness leading to the higher attainments. Perhaps their practice was sporadic, lacking determination, or even unsuccessful and abandoned. In later times, others again became scholars, philosophers, and scribes— all necessary and admirable, particularly in times when the leisure essential to academic or scholarly pursuits could only be gained by entry into the monk Samgha. In a way, the monk is like the athlete who has joined the training camp, has stripped down to running gear, and has adopted the diet and the exercises, but who may or may not get out onto the track and run for real. So long as he maintains the regimen he is still a potential runner in a way no layman could ever be, but until he lines himself up on the start line and launches himself forth, he will remain a "reserve."

On the other hand, the monks by their very existence provide an opportunity for laymen to practice their giving and gain the consequent merit. Also, strict monastic rules of harmlessness and abstention ensure security to other beings inasmuch as they have nothing to fear from him. The monks and nuns also functioned as the repository and guardians of the Dharma teaching, because it was their memories and regular recitations that kept the corpus of the Teaching alive.

None of this, however, has to do with the veritable practice of the Path. None of these things, the pure keeping of the rules; the stainless moral life; the quiet, harmless behavior; or the maintenance of the Dharma recitations will by itself advance the monk on the Holy Path beyond the most preliminary stages. Without doubt, none of them will bring him within reach of the third Noble Truth and of Nirvana. Those goals require the practice of the successive stages and the meditative penetration of the practice formulas, all of which lead to ever-increasing insight. Thus the monk, in addition to his asceticism, has to go beyond it and complete the fundamental practice formula for progress in the Path: sila, samadhi, and prajna (morality, concentration, and wisdom).

Assuming, then, that the monk has a true vocation to the Path, we can say that all the rules and modes of life proper to the monk are simply the prerequisites for the special training he must undertake in order to approach the Path proper. As mentioned previously, sila or moral conduct is the basis of all productive practice in that it cuts off any further acts having painful or turbulent outflows. In its complete form, as in the case of the monk, sila induces a state of relative calm and unencumbered clarity necessary for the exercise of intense meditation.

But however important and necessary sila may be, from the point of view of the practice of the Path, it remains a preliminary, though in a negative sense the total or partial maintenance of the moral rules will determine the success or otherwise of any of the specific practices. In this way, the adoption and complete fulfillment of the Ten Precepts (List E, i and ii) and the full disciplinary code of the Vinaya satisfy the requirement of the first of the three-fold formula, sila. The samadhi (concentration) and the prajna (wisdom/insight) must then follow if the monk is to travel the Path itself.

In Part Three of this book, the graduated phases of that concentration and insight were set out as recorded in the Satipatthana sutta. Another Pali text, the Samannaphala sutta (the fruits of the life of the recluse) of the Digha collection also plots this sequence of practices and provides a body of supplementary detail. In this text, the Magadhan King Ajatasatru the successor to Bimbisara, questions Sakyamuni on the immediate results to be gained by the life and occupation of a monk in the Samgha. Sakyamuni replies at length and in so doing presents us with another route map of the Path, with the focus of attention on its upper extremities and its fulfillment. This authoritative description, in conjunction with the Satipatthana sutta and the expanded detail from the Sanskrit and Pali *Abhidharmas*, supply the material for the collation that follows.

So far we have been describing the elements of the first of the two preparatory stages, called, appropriately enough, the Path of Acquiring Equipment (sambharamarga). Here the phase of initial preparation may last for numerous lives (see Figure 1). All that has gone before concerning the first contact with the Dharma, weakening of greed and hatred as a result of experience, and the gentle skepticism towards the ways of the world would all add up to the initial "good roots." The consolidation of a person's attraction to the Dharma would follow, in the course of which the factors comprising the Aids to Emancipation (List D) would develop in proportion to his grasp and understanding of the Teaching.

Sooner or later our hypothetical candidate (male or female) will hear more, learn more, observe and apply more until a respect, a confidence, and an acquiescence in the Teaching and Practice are aroused. According to the strength of his perceptions and consequent acquiescence, he will eventually adopt the status of layman (upasaka) or monk (bhiksu). If he remains a layman, his practice of the limited Precepts and of giving will set in motion the future ripening that will project a disposition toward entering the Samgha later on in the present life or in a subsequent life.

On the other hand, if he possesses favorable karmic propensities from the past and can take on the quality of a monk, then the opportunity of more advanced practice is open to him. As we have seen, even as a monk, actual engagement in the practices of the Path are not automatic. If he lacks sufficient purpose, he will simply produce good acts of restraint and harmlessness which, like the layman, build toward a favorable rebirth with more motivation to embark upon the Path proper.

Alternatively, from his more favored stance as a monk he may begin the first steps on the Path leading to the higher stages. In the latter case, the first steps will be the practices concerned with the attention to breathing that, once acquired, bring in their wake a certain basic proficiency in concentrated attention. With the aid of the calm pacified breath and concentrated observation, the six triads of the sense impressions are gradually brought into view and stabilized. At this point, the practice formula of the Four Foundations of Mindfulness is the framework of the monk's exercise, and he gains proficiency in focusing upon and retaining the perception of the Five Skandhas. Needless to say, he is only a novice practitioner at this stage, and a proportion of his time will also be devoted to the study of the Teaching as a whole. This span of practice experience, from leaving the world up to and including the preliminary exercises is, when coupled with Dharma study, referred to as the "remote preparatory way."

Throughout this long period required to traverse the Path of Acquiring Equipment and beyond, as we shall see, our candidate is totally immersed in Kamadhatu, the world of all the passions and defilements. Despite his adherence to the monk precepts and his discipline, his whole personality stream (samtana) is dominated, more or less, by the root defilements of attachment, aversion, self-esteem, ignorance, false views, and doubts. Thus, in terms of the Path, all his practices and activities are "impure," inasmuch as these defilements (klesa) remain active to cloud his perceptions and obstruct the deep penetration of the profound Truths.

Nonetheless, he has taken the first positive steps on the Path itself, as he develops the five Faculties or Aids to Emancipation, begins the exercise of the Four Right Efforts, and gains preliminary mindfulness as part of the Four Foundations. All these, the Faculties, the Right Efforts, and the Four Foundations are constituents of the Path as set out in another vital formula, that of the Thirty-Seven Auxiliaries of the Enlightenment (bodhipaksika). This set of special practices and powers tells us just what is needful to reach the highest goal. The detail of this cardinal formula is given in Lists A and B and it should be understood that the sequence of groupings extends over the entire length of the Path.

With monk status and proficiency in the four types of mindfulness (on the body, feelings, thoughts, and dharmas), we approach the end of Sambharamarga. To complete the first of the Paths, the fourth type of mindfulness has to be mastered, so that Dharma elements can be brought into direct view. Then, and for the first time, an intimation of the real meaning of the Four Noble Truths is received. This intimation, together with the perception of Dharma activity, begins to absorb the whole of the monk's attention, so that his concentrated meditations become more acutely focused. It is just when the Dharma activity is directly related to the meaning of the Four Noble Truths in sharply focused interior concentration that the monk crosses the threshold of the Second Stage and enters the Path of Preparatory Practices (Prayogamarga).

THE PATH OF PREPARATORY PRACTICES
(PRAYOGAMARGA)

During his passage through Prayogamarga, the monk ascetic cultivates several modes of meditative practice in parallel. His interior concentration has various mutually supporting aspects, each having its own characteristics.

The first mode, and probably the best known, is the Four Dhyanas (Pali: jhanas) or meditative absorptions. These four "absorptions" were specified by Sakyamuni as part of the fruits of the religious life when undertaken according to his Doctrine and Discipline. For this the monk retires into seclusion and by means of the practice of mindfulness on breath and body begins to detach himself from the five hindrances of lust, anger, torpor, agitation, and doubt. If successful, he gains a state described as easeful, peaceful, and joyful, together with enhanced faculties of reasoning and investigation. This is the First Dhyana, in which his whole body is pervaded by joy and ease. From there he can proceed to the Second Dhyana, which stops reasoning and investigation but is marked by serene concentration. The Third Dhyana follows, in which joy subsides but he is fully mindful and equable, with his body totally at ease. Entry into the Fourth Dhyana brings detachment from both ease and discomfort and is marked by a pure equanimity in which mental concentration is both firm and supple.

As a meditative practice performed by a monk living (necessarily) in Kamadhatu, the Four Dhyanas are temporary states progressively acquired and then withdrawn from at the conclusion of a particular practice session. The Four Dhyanas are also realms of Samsara in their own right, and they comprise the second of the three tiers of existence called Rupadhatu. By a special meditational exercise the monk can, while belonging by birth, body, and faculties to the realm of Kamadhatu, reach up to and remain temporarily in the realm of the gods.

Hence the advocacy of these states by Sakyamuni as desirable fruits of the religious life. Fruits such as these, he explained to King Ajatasatru, bore comparison with and exceeded any of the pleasures and special perquisites of kings, princes, and rich men of the world. However, in terms of the Path, they are suitable conditions within which certain phases of the Path take place. The Four Dhyanas function in parallel with the other modes, because facility in gaining them helps to smooth the passage through the entrance to the Path proper and because the one-pointed concentration involved is the means to penetration of the practice formulas.

A more particular mode of practice which actually promotes passage along the Path also belongs to Prayogamarga and is called the Nirvedhabhagiyas or Aids to Penetration (see List D, ii). This too consists of four progressive stages but in this case their successful attainment bestows particular insights that counteract certain defilements. The Nirvedhabhagiya sequence develops from the attainment of a direct perception of dharmas achieved at the culmination of the previous Path.

By bringing the Dharma elements into view, the meditator perceives clearly and without mistake that all the composites of the body and mind are impermanent because their Dharma constituents are never stable for a moment. He not only understands this, he sees it for himself. For the same reason, he also sees how it is that no Self can be found and how all the compounds, including the sense impressions, are both suffering and turbulence. This deep inner experience locks his attention onto the formula of the Four Noble Truths. And from the moment when he turns his concentrated attention to this cardinal formula he enters the first phase of Prayogamarga, called Heats (usmagata).

Thus the meditator, by means of the clear perception of dharmas comes to an unfolding of the real meaning of the Four Noble Truths in their sixteen aspects. From now on and throughout the four phases of Prayogamarga, the monk ascetic holds his penetrating concentration upon the sixteen aspects, gaining a deeper and more acute insight as he proceeds. This growing acuteness of attention and insight is supported and developed by the Four Right Efforts (see List B), which are themselves the second factor of the Auxiliaries of the Path. As the effort grows to intensify the insight, the energy involved generates body heat, and this is why this first phase is called Heats. Despite all the effort, however, only brief moments of Dharma activity under sixteen aspects is perceived.

The expansion of the periods of deep penetration occupies the second phase, called Summits (murdhan). During this period of broadening the range of insight into the sixteen aspects, the Four Bases of Psychic Power are realized (see List B). And with that another group of the Auxiliaries of Enlightenment is gained.

The third phase, called Patience (ksanti), is reached when, as a result of the penetrating attention to the sixteen aspects, a preliminary recognition and acceptance of their validity is acquired. In addition, by a progressive weak, medium, and strong comprehension, the sixteen aspects are seen as applying to all three realms of Samsara. By the time of the "strong" stage, attention focuses on the suffering feature only belonging to the realm of Kamadhatu; that is to say, the deplorable state of his own realm of life. On reaching the limit of this third phase, the Five Faculties (see List B) are intensified to a higher degree and become the Powers. Also, because of the strength of the concentrated insight, certain defilements such as torpor and agitation are eliminated for good. For the same reason, once this stage is established rebirth into the lower destinies of animals and pretas is forever cut off.

From here the fourth and last phase of Prayogamarga can be reached. This phase is called Supreme Worldly Dharmas (laukikagradharma) and consists of the final refinement of concentrated penetration to the Duhkha (suffering) feature of Kamadhatu. By this time an intensely powerful one-pointed focus is brought to bear on the first of the Four Noble Truths as it applies to Kamadhatu. Now that focus results in a continuous, moment-by-moment direct perception. The successful attainment of this totally focused, intensely penetrating concentration brings with it the ability to make use of the so-called magical powers (rddhi). These are, at this point, the fully developed capabilities arising from one of the sets of the Auxiliaries of Enlightenment.

This set of factors, the Bases of Psychic Power (see List B), become established during the second phase of Prayogamarga, called the Summits, and are linked to the intensified practice of the Four Right Efforts. Now, during the last of the four phases, the magical powers become available. They are the ability to: multiply oneself into many replicas; to make oneself invisible; to pass through solid objects with ease; to penetrate the earth as if it were water; to walk on water; to fly through the air crosslegged; to touch the Sun and the Moon with one's hands; and to gain bodily access to the Brahma-heavens.

To Western minds these features of the Path are rather baffling, even bizarre. Yet it has to be said once more that this Path, and much else in the Buddha's Teaching as it has been preserved through the centuries, contains elements quite foreign to our accepted canons of the possible. The "magical powers" are a typical example of this.

Instances of the Buddha himself using his special powers are scattered throughout all the canons of scripture. We may recall the display of the pairs of fire and water and the pacification of the enraged elephant without any visible activity whatsoever. The Arhats too would demonstrate such abilities on rare occasions. Examples of this include the case of Gavampati repeating the fire and water display and Mahakasyapa walking into the solid rock of the mountaintop. However, although we have reached the phase of Supreme Worldly Dharmas, where these powers become accessible, we are still, in this narrative, a long way from the state of Arhat and even further from the state of a Buddha.

Despite all these attainments, the highest and last phase of Prayogamarga is still impure and mundane, as its title suggests. Although some of the defilements have been stopped and human rebirth assured, the ascetic is still bound by all the other bonds of the Kamadhatu defilements. Possibly this was one of the reasons why Sakyamuni forbade the public practice of the magical powers by his monks.

Another reason is also likely: All four of these phases comprising the Nirvedhabhagiya can be gained and lost again. Progress, even at this stage, is not necessarily definitive and lasting. As ascetic who reached this level and then got seduced by the exercise of the magical powers could find that his intensified concentration became clouded by thoughts of exhilaration and self-esteem. Then he would lose both his penetration to the First Noble Truth as well as his magical powers.

And it is not only thoughts of exhilaration and self-esteem that can cause the hard-won levels of the Path to disintegrate. There is a story told in the Treatise on the Great Perfection of

Wisdom (*Mahaprajnaparamitasastra*) concerning the fall from grace of a whole body of ascetics (non-Buddhist of course). We are presented with the intriguing picture of a squadron of 500 rshis (ascetics) flying cross-legged over a king's palace. As they cross the inner courtyard they see him entertaining himself with nude dancing girls. On seeing this, the whole squadron loses its power of flight and they fall to the ground. The king is not amused at this rain of rshis from the sky and he orders their hands and feet to be cut off. Both the moral and the warning implicit in this somewhat quaint story need no elaboration.

Thus there is a trap at this level for the unwary. The whole of Prayogamarga could slip from the ascetic's grasp, especially if he dabbles in the magical arts. But it could all be regained so long as he remains a monk with moral purity intact. Even so, for the monk who is ardent to gain the Path proper (and we are not there yet) the mere exercise of psychic tricks is not worth the loss of proximity to the Pure stages. In the event that the monk gains and retains the fourth phase without mishap, or that he eventually regains this level after losing it, by completing the four phases of Prayogamarga the ascetic arrives at one of the most crucial and decisive experiences of his long journey. He then confronts the gateway to the third of the Five Paths, Darsanamarga, which is a pure stage marking the beginning of the Path proper, the Aryamarga, sometimes rendered as the Holy Path.

Before we leave the Prayogamarga and move away from the two preparatory stages in this chapter, it may be well to recapitulate the contents of the Path of Preparatory Practices. Our narrative has been devoted in large degree to the operative features of the second of the Paths, the Nirvedhabhagiyas, which actually propels the practitioner onwards and upwards along the route.

However, as we remarked at the beginning of this section, several modes of practice are cultivated in parallel during this stage. In addition to the Nirvedhabhagiyas, all four of the dhyanas are reached and used throughout this Path. Equally, if not of more importance, the first five groups of factors of the seven that comprise the Auxiliaries of Enlightenment (bodhipaksikas) are also fully activated (see List B). These first five groups are the ones classified as either pure or impure. When put into operation in the second of the Paths, they are impure, because the ascetic at that stage has not yet shed the bonds of defilements belonging to Kamadhatu. Therefore, from the moment when the ascetic brings dharmas into view and proceeds with the deepening penetration of the sixteen aspects of the Four Noble Truths, these three major modes of cultivation move on together in parallel. In a manner of speaking they intertwine by supporting each other and by providing the necessary conditions for the Nirvedhabhagiyas to develop to full strength. A careful study of Lists B and D, ii, in combination with this narrative will give the reader some idea of what takes place.

Moreover, it should not be thought that this process of intertwined cultivation is always possible during a single retreat or in even a lifetime of seclusion, though for the particularly well-endowed it can be so. All this can take several lifetimes to achieve in full, and every existence will need to have those favorable conditions allowing entry into the monk Samgha and trained guidance therein in the special practices.

However, as we learned earlier, the version of the Path expounded in the *Satipatthana* holds out the promise of entry and total traversal of the Path in seven years or less. In such a case, where conditions of maximum ardor and potentiality combine, the Prayogamarga stage proceeds uninterruptedly after completing the Four Foundations of Mindfulness. It will be recalled that the *Satipatthana* describes the meditating monk becoming aware that he had acquired the certain factors of Enlightenment; and then he could move on to the special insight of knowing the Four Noble Truths "according to reality."

This is exactly what now takes place following upon the attainment of the fourth phase of Prayogamarga. From the series of continuous, moment-by-moment concentrations on the suffering aspect of Kamadhatu there arises a pure moment of thought that launches a sequence of specially charged insights concerning the true nature of the Four Noble Truths. That pure thought carries the monk out of Prayogamarga and into Darsanamarga. Once he enters Darsanamarga, he becomes an Arya or Holy Person imbued with pure states and divested of many defilements. Entrance into this Path takes place in the first dhyana, the state of joyful ease and detachment plus reasoning and investigation.

14. The Path Proper: Darsanamarga, Bhavanamarga, and Asaiksmarga

THE PATH OF VISION (DANANAMARGA)

The Path of Vision is a very short but critical passage that decisively propels the practitioner towards the final goal of Nirvana. From this point on the monk is no longer a worldly person (prthagjana); he has gained the pure Path, the Path proper. In fact, this stage lasts for only fifteen moments of a sixteen-moment sequence of highly charged insights called comprehension (abhisamaya). The sixteenth moment marks the beginning of the next Path, Bhavanamarga (see Figure 5).

These fifteen moments of intense, brilliant, utterly convincing comprehensions open out as a result of the four-phased concentration upon the sixteen aspects of the Four Noble Truths of the immediately preceding stage. They are the final penetration to the full meaning and essence of the Four Noble Truths, to the point where the meditator knows "according to reality" the origination and stopping of suffering and the Path as they really are. This is a state in which the meditating monk is sometimes heard to exclaim, quite involuntarily, "What suffering!"

Here the ascetic perceives directly, for the first time, the turbulence and pain of Samsara on all of its levels, and he sees, too, how it arises and reproduces itself. With equal intensity and clarity he sees how to stop it all, and that perception of the Way of stopping confirms the detail of the true Path, which he can now undertake in the full knowledge of its efficacy.

Once that visionary comprehension is gained, he becomes a "Stream Entrant" (Srota-apanna). He has set foot on the real Path, and on completion of the fifteen moments of vision, he will have no more than seven further births before he gains final Nirvana. In this way he is sometimes described as "assured of the Supreme Good" (samyaktva), in that an upper limit is set on the time remaining to him before he reaches Nirvana. Entrance into the Stream—that is to say, the acquisition of the first of the four fruits of the religious life, which brings all the others within reach in due order—brings into play a different mode of practice having to do with the pure exercise of stopping, the third Noble Truth.

Apart from its crucial role marking the entrance to the Path proper, the fifteen moments of Darsanamarga have an associated function that from here on begins to dominate the remaining higher stages. Each of the momentary comprehensions either halts or extirpates certain categories of passions and defilements (klesa). The detail of this full sequence of the sixteen-moment abhisamaya is heavily loaded with a technical apparatus of specialized terminology, which is too involved to present here. However, its outline and function have to be described in order to understand what follows.

In brief, then, the sixteen moments (not to be confused with the sixteen aspects of the Four Noble Truths) comprise pairs of ksanti (recognition/acceptance) and jnana (knowledge/comprehension), which bring about the directly perceived certainty concerning each of the Four Noble Truths and are applied to the three realms of Samsara (Kamadhatu, Rupadhatu, and Arupyadhatu). The full sequence of the pairs of ksanti and jnana produces the unshakable knowledge of the nature of Samsara and how it is to be surmounted. Following in the wake of each of the ksantis the possession of certain defilements is dislodged. In a similar manner, each of the jnanas produces the final stopping of these defilements.

In other words, the visionary penetration of the Four Noble Truths activates the separate parts of the formula into a powerful instrument. Suffering and turbulence are not only understood but are felt and experienced in Samsara as a whole. The same occurs with origination and passing away. In the case of stopping (nirodha), it actually begins to function according to its nature so that certain categories of defilements of Kamadhatu are finally relinquished. The Truth of the Path is also activated, because the Path proper has been reached, and the process leading directly to Nirvana has been set in motion, allowing this goal to be gained in no more than seven further births. The Path proper, now clearly perceived and understood, involves the abandonment of more and more passions and defilements from this point onward.

As a general example of this process of abandoning certain passions during the fifteen-moment sequence of Darsanamarga, a substantial part of the stopping process concerns the defilements (klesa) of doubt (vicikitsa) and false views (drsti) relating to Kamadhatu, which are all relinquished forever. Of course, there still remain the same categories of klesas relating to the two higher realms of Samsara. Similarly, the major part, but not all, of the klesas of attachment (raga), aversion or hostility (pratigha), self-regard (mana), and ignorance (avidya) relating to Kamadhatu are abandoned. All these abandonings of klesas occur during the fifteen-moment process and purify the ascetic of them. Only the most deep-seated parts of the klesa-categories of Kamadhatu remain after this visionary experience, and they, together with the defilements specific to Rupaand Arupydhatu, require long periods of continuous concentrated cultivation (bhavana) in the fourth Path (Bhavanamarga) to stop them.

By the time of the sixteenth moment of the abhisamaya, the ascetic will have stopped and rendered totally inoperative thirty-two of the thirty-six categories of Kamadhatu defilements, including satkayadrsti, the wrong view of a "self." There still remain sixty-six more kinds of the deep-seated or more refined defilements to eradicate. And it should be clearly understood that it is just this eradication of the klesas that will necessitate the several series of lives required to traverse the highest Paths of Bhavanamarga and Asaiksamarga (see Figure 5). But at this point, at the gaining of the sixteenth moment of the abhisamaya, our monk ascetic has moved on.

THE PATH OF REPEATED MEDITATIVE CULTIVATION (BHAVANAMARGA)

Having arrived at the Aryamarga, or Path proper, and having passed through the stage of vision, we must pause briefly to consider the consequences of that passage.

Our hypothetical monk ascetic has entered the Stream after a long period of meditational effort based upon and supported by his practice of strict morality. We have taken no account of the possibility that he could have special endowment and thus the capacity for realizing the full depth of the Four Noble Truths briefly or suddenly. In such a case, his progress to this stage would have been much less arduous, of course. But however rapidly or easily attained, the progressive stages of his realization are the same.

Having gained the Holy Path by the visionary experience of the fundamental doctrinal formula, he has before him a similar possibility of faster or slower traversal through the last two stages. His onward movement takes place, generally speaking, within one of two main doctrinal frameworks. The shortest scheme, that of the *Satipatthana*, allows for complete traversal in seven or fewer years. The Indian masters of Mainstream Indian Hinayana, however, favored the slower scheme, which involves a maximum of seven further births from completion of Darsanamarga to final attainment of Nirvana.

Whichever it is to be will not be a matter of choice under normal circumstances. The speed of progress will largely depend on the ascetic's inherent capacities (vipakaphala) and on the prevailing conditions (pratyaya) that support or retard the meditational practices in seclusion. For the purposes of this exposition, the relative speed of full attainment can be ignored because, once again, the principal features of the last two stages will be similar whether in quick time or slow time.

Another matter worthy of consideration before describing the last two stages is, what kind of person is this monk ascetic who has reached and passed through Darsanamarga? He is above all a meditative recluse. The intense introspective concentration he has forged and used to realize the Truths of the formula has occupied most of his waking time. Only the regular meal times or begging rounds plus the obligatory attendance at the Order's confessional (uposatha) would interrupt his long sessions of meditation practice. He may be prevailed upon to preach or teach on occasion. It is unlikely, however, that he would do this from choice, especially if his visionary experience was of the highest grade of the weak, middling, or strong categories that apply to all stages of this practice. In this case he is more likely to devote himself exclusively to further effort into the fourth stage of the Path.

It has to be remembered that he now lives and abides in the mode of perception that operates at the Dharma level of experience. He no longer perceives people and external surroundings as we do. His sensory faculties are strictly controlled to register only "visual objects," for instance, or the five groups of elements comprising the personality (skandhas), all in permutations of rapidly changing combinations. Under this aspect, his entire receptive sensory apparatus impresses him as distasteful in the extreme, marked by suffering and turbulence. His joy and delight is only to be found in the absorptions (dhyana) of easeful detachment. Of course, at this stage these represent the refined forms of attachment he yet has to conquer, but for the present they are infinitely preferable to any worldly activities, even of the restricted kind within the monk Samgha.

A most telling illustration of this state of mind is to be found in Buddhaghosa's *Visuddhimagga*. He relates how such a monk was approached on his begging round by a husband out searching for his wife who had disappeared from home. The husband, describing his wife, asked the monk if he had seen her in his travels. The monk replied that he had seen no such person but he had passed a "bag of bones" a little way back up the road!

To conclude our brief review of past progress and present stance, we can do no better than to trace the development of the Auxiliaries of Enlightenment up to Darsanamarga. The gaining of the fruit of Srota-apanna and passage through the successive moments of Darsanamarga presuppose the acquisition of six of the seven groups of the Bodhipaksikas (see List B). By this stage also there should be ease of access to all four absorptions (dhyana), though this is peripheral to the Path itself. The Bodhipaksikas, on the other hand, are indispensable, and the first group of these, the Four Foundations of Mindfulness, our monk gained on completion of Sambharamarga, when he was a mere beginner (adikarmika) on the Path. Then, during the Prayogamarga in four steps, he acquired in turn, the Four Right Efforts, the Four Bases of Psychic Power, the Five Faculties, and the Five Powers, but all of these were still impure. On his entry into Darsanamarga, he acquired the Eight Constituents of the Noble Path that, although practiced before, were now pure for the first time. This purity comes with entry into the Path proper, which is not contaminated with any of the defilements of the mundane world, Kamadhatu. The ongoing repercussions of this visionary experience will almost certainly propel him forward into the fourth of the five Paths, Bhavanamarga.

From his present stance, therefore, our ascetic has only the last group of the Bodhipaksikas to gain, and they are the seven pure Constituents of Enlightenment (see List B). These are the special characteristics of the fourth Path, that of Repeated Meditative Cultivation. It is in the fourth of the Paths that the refined defilements of the higher spheres are countered, and by means of a continuous investigation of Dharma activity, the second and third Noble Truths (of origination and of stopping) come into decisive operation.

It will be remembered that, when Darsanamarga was reached, all four Noble Truths were experienced in actual reality. The first Noble Truth of suffering destroyed certain categories of defilements, divesting the fourth Noble Truth of its impurities and allowing its eight factors to activate in the "pure" sphere of Rupadhatu. By the same process, the second Noble Truth of origination and the third of stopping now predominate

The Path Proper: The Holy Path (Aryamarga)

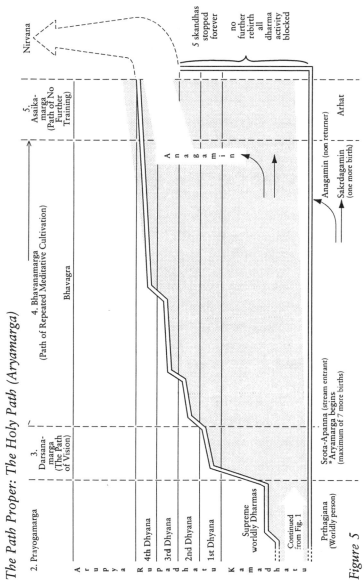

Figure 5

277

in the Bhavanamarga. By a skillful and powerful concentrated meditation all seven Constituents of Enlightenment are focused around the investigation into dharmas. That clearly concentrated investigation, free of impurities, brings about the unerring recognition of the pattern of their origination. With this profound insight that other great formula at last comes within reach as experienced reality: the formula of Arising Due to Conditions (Pratityasamutpada).

As we have seen, the formula of Arising Due to Conditions involves Dharma-clusters coming into existence because of past actions and then acting as conditions that allow other Dharma-clusters to arise and establish. Now that activity in causal sequence is directly perceived as it really is, and because it is thus seen and understood, its reverse process, the stopping of this activity link by link, can actually be brought into play. Once that eliminating process is started, the third Noble Truth of Stopping (nirodha) functions according to its nature.

Again we see how the doctrinal formulas, which are at first verbal or written descriptions, are transformed by the practice of the Path into dynamic phases of the true nature of things (dharmanam dharmata). It is just this dynamic in its pure form, begun in Darsanamarga by the onset of a penetrating insight, that occupies the whole of Bhavanamarga, a stage that can last up to seven lives, or as little as seven days.

What takes places is the progressive elimination of all the categories of defilements of the two higher spheres, there being nine major categories of klesa in all three spheres of Samsara. In addition, and toward the end of this long period of practice, there is a gradual reduction of all Dharma activity by a continuous, increasingly decisive reversal of the links of the Pratityasamutpada. Hence the title of this fourth Path translates as "Path of Repeated Meditative Cultivation." What is cultivated in ever increasing degree is the third Noble Truth of stopping.

In the course of this progressive elimination, and by the destruction of the sixth major category of defilements (those of Rupadhatu) and the severe attenuation of the three fires of greed/attachment (raga), hatred/aversion (dvesa), and delusion/ignorance (moha), the ascetic gains the second fruit, that of Sakrdagamin. The name specifies the six categories that are disposed of when this fruit is gained. This second fruit marks the environs of the conclusion of Bhavanamarga and is the state in which the ascetic has only one more birth to undergo. The reduction in the number of births is the direct result of the process of stopping and eradication that has occupied this entire stage.

There is another possible alternative for the Holy Person at this very advanced stage upon the pure Path. Depending upon the precise number and type of defilements suppressed during the cultivation of stopping, he may be able to eliminate all the dharmas that project a human birth. In such a case, the ascetic will expire toward the end of the Bhavanamarga, and his last birth will be among the gods of Rupadhatu, where his very nature will be meditative. From there, unseen and unknown to the denizens of the mundane world of Kamadhatu, he will achieve the final destruction of ignorance (avidya) and all other outflows and reach Nirvana. Such an alternative is the third fruit, the Anagamin or Non-Returner, meaning one who is not again born into the human realm of Kamadhatu.

The Sakrdagamin who does not succeed in eliminating the outflow into Kamadhatu will be reborn there once more, at most. In the course of that last birth he will enter the fifth and last Path, the Path of No Further Training (Asaiksamarga). All the sudden attainers to Asaiksamarga, apparently in a single life-time, such as the Arhats at Lake Anavatapta, would have heard the Four Noble Truths for the first time from Sakyamuni, hav-ing fulfilled a version of the Two Preparatory Stages in their pre-vious lives. That first hearing would have produced an immediate abhisamaya (the Darsanamarga) with the two final Paths following in rapid succession.

THE PATH OF NO FURTHER TRAINING (ASAIKSAMARGA)

In order to gain this final fruit and the summit of the pure Path, the Holy Person succeeds in breaking all the links of the Pratityasamutpada, up to and including numbers ten and eleven, Becoming and Future Birth. His "diamond-like" concentration is so potent and his residue of defilement is so meager that he finally succeeds in preventing any further "outflow" (asrava) from taking place. His skandhas become completely purified in the sense that his sensory apparatus, feelings, and consciousness are entirely disjoined from any defilements whatever, and his Dharma composition consists exclusively of the ripening fruits of the past good and pure actions performed by him during his long and sustained practice of the Path.

Because he is devoid of all passion and all karmically potent activity, and because he has uprooted the last obstruction, igno-rance (avidya), no further thoughts and actions have any re-tributive power (hetu). He simply lives on by the declining momentum of his last series (samtana). This is the fourth and last fruit, that of Arhat (Pali: Arahant). At last, at death, there is nothing left to reproduce, and his Dharma samtana is finally and completely extinguished in Nirvana. This last and highest attainment of the Path of Purity can only be authoritatively described by the Buddha himself, as recorded in the second sutta of the *Digha Nikaya* in the Pali collection:

> . . . To him, thus knowing, thus seeing, the heart is set free from the deadly Taint of Lust, is set free from the deadly Taint of Becomings, is set free from the deadly Taint of Ignorance. In him, thus set free, there arises the knowledge of his emancipation, and he knows: rebirth has been destroyed. The higher life has been fulfilled. What had to be done has been accomplished. After this present life there will be no beyond.

Thus the Arhat has travelled the Holy Path to the end, in accordance with his great Teacher's directions. By fulfilling what had to be done, he gained the highest fruit and entered Nirvana, which precludes all rebirth in any of the spheres of Samsara.

What else awaits? Only silence and the most profound respect.

15. The Three Ways

THE BODHISATTVAYANA, THE PRATYEBUDDHAYANA, AND THE SRAVAKAYANA

In this exposition of the Three Ways of Mainstream Hinayana, we seek to identify some of the primary differences between the Buddha and the Arhats. We can also explain, in brief, that rather elusive category of the fulfilled Saints, the Pratyekabuddha.

Dealing with the Arhats first, as they are fresh in the reader's mind, we can see with some clarity, perhaps, how they are described in the texts as "having laid down the burden" and destroyed rebirth forever. In order to do this they need to purify their whole personality base of Dharma activity by bringing it all to a permanent stop. That radical purification is achieved by ever more intense meditative concentration over long periods, during which time they are necessarily withdrawn and secluded from most, if not all, worldly activity.

Their gradual development depends upon the penetration to the real meaning of several major practice formulas, notably the Four Noble Truths and the Arising Due to Conditions. All these practice formulas were formulated and taught for the first time by Sakyamuni. In this way the Arhats followed the directions and guidance of the original "Pathfinder," and so these followers are often referred to as Sravakas (Listeners). Thus their "way" or progress to their goal of Nirvana became known as the Way of the Listeners (Sravakayana).

The first difference is therefore one of status, as between master and pupil. The prospective Arhat follows an already marked out Path and in the initial stages is under the close supervision of a teacher who has preceded him along it. In the case of the Buddha, however, no Path existed for him to follow. It had to be rediscovered on its own, and once he had found it, the Buddha had to devise the means and methods that would enable others to pursue it with certainty to a successful conclusion.

Another, more fundamental difference concerns the nature of the Buddha's Enlightenment itself. Although the experience and quality of Arhatship is the same for the Buddha and his disciples, the Buddha's Enlightenment is "supreme and perfect" and involves powers and qualities that Arhats do not possess. These special powers and qualities result from his altogether different line of development going back into the depths of his past. That past is characterized by the individual prediction to Buddhahood by a previous Buddha and his fulfillment of the Paramitas, such as giving and patience, during an innumerable succession of past lives. Here that special being proceeds along a unique way, as a Bodhisattva destined to "supreme and perfect Enlightenment." This became known as the Way of the Bodhisattva (Bodhisattvayana).

Again, because of his unique status in rediscovering the Path on his own and leading others to it, he established the Three Jewels of Buddha, Dharma, and Samgha where none existed before. Arhats are a part of the Three Jewels, but they only help to preserve and maintain what was produced for them.

There is also that mysterious nature of the Buddha that rendered it undesirable (or impossible?) for any physical representation of him to be made. On his own declared statement, he was neither god nor man but the supreme teacher of all beings. His birth and childhood were accompanied by prodigies, and his future was predicted precisely. Little of this applied to any of the Arhats. As time went by in India, these crucial differences were codified by the *Abhidharma* masters into what is now known as the Buddha's Ten Powers, his Four Assurances, his Eighteen Exclusive Attributes, and his possession of great compassion and great benevolence. The only parity ever envisaged between a Buddha and the Arhats consisted in the fact that both had completed the Path of purity and destroyed all the defilements as well as any further birth. Some of the earliest schools even maintained that the Buddha had never had any defilements in the first place and that his particular Path of Purity was simply an exercise of expedient means to demonstrate what was necessary and possible.

A third difference, and one that caused a degree of disturbance and dissension in the early Indian Order, concerns the attitude of Arhats to their fellow beings, compared with that of the Buddha. Our earlier tracing of the traditional detail of Sakyamuni's life showed that he devoted his entire remaining life of forty-five years after his Enlightenment to a constant preaching and propagation of his Teaching, as well as to the care and direction of his numerous monks, as well as of everyone and anyone who came to him. Very few of the Arhats, other than Sariputra, did the same, and none so continuously and for as long as the Master himself.

This perpetual care and attention to others arose from the compassionate nature of his supreme Enlightenment, which revealed the true nature of the world and its beings in far greater depth and range than the insight of the Arhats allowed. Indeed, the incident of the immediate departure into Nirvana of many of the Arhats at the time of the Buddha's Parinirvana, and in particular the lack of concern on the part of Gavampati to make any effort to preserve the Dharma, even when asked to do so, came to be regarded as symptomatic of their insularity and was long remembered by both early masters and laity. Only Mahakasyapa comes out of that story with any credit and he had to be prompted to act and call the First Council.

The fact is that the Holy Path leading to Arhatship detaches the practitioner from the world in such a decisive and fundamental way that he lets go of it altogether. The total and unmitigated suffering he perceives is too much to endure, and the concern to distance himself from it overrides any ideas of helping anyone else, especially if that help diverts his energies from the Path. Moreover, and this is not readily appreciated by some, his very perceptions at Dharma-level blur the normal distinctions of this one and that one because it is all seen as a welter of interacting elements and not "people" at all. Certainly Arhats did teach; there would not be any Dharma today if they had not. And we know, too, that sixty new Arhats were sent out in all directions by the Buddha at the very beginning of his ministry to teach Dharma in the world. But nothing was ever heard of them again and there is no certainty that any of them did as they were bid.

Another celebrated episode of the Samgha's very early history illustrates the point in another way. The persuasion of the scattered Arhats by a wandering monk to assemble and convene the Second Council of Vaisali was a formidable enterprise, because several of them were unwilling to be disturbed. Even the most venerable Arhat Sarvagamin, who lived a stone's throw from the regular public spectacle of the Vaisali monks accepting money donations from the laity, was totally unaware of the situation until told about it. Then he prevaricated when asked to deliver an authoritative opinion on whether the acceptance of gold and silver by monks was permissible. And this was the norm.

The forest dwellers of the time certainly devoted themselves to their bands of devotees, those who had forsaken the world altogether, but consequently their teaching was directly concerned with the stages of the Path out of Samsara forever. They had little or no interest in the affairs of the world and in particular no interest in the events taking place in the larger urban centers, which they never visited. Compared with the Buddha, who was constantly involved with all kinds of persons, from the murderous brigand Angulimala to peasant farmers plowing their fields and to kings, queens, and princes of all the local realms, the Arhats and their secluded monk pupils were increasingly seen at the time as an exclusive elite.

This characteristic of withdrawn detachment and non-involvement on the part of the early Arhats was resented and condemned by the growing body of lay adherents and other monks, especially when, after the conclusion of the Second Council at Vaisah, the Arhats are believed to have attempted to tighten up the rules of conduct laid down by Sakyamuni himself. This, among other things, led directly to the schismatic Third Council after Arhats were openly accused of certain failings by a widely renowned monk called Mahadeva. At this traumatic event in the Samgha's history, the Arhats were reprimanded by the majority party as being unworthy to amend the canon of conduct promulgated by the Buddha himself.

Thus we have a very early case of Arhats being seen as distinct from and less worthy than the Buddha. Somehow, something was felt to be missing in the observed conduct of the Arhats compared with their Master. And that something may well have to do with the inherent nature of the Path of Purity, which disdains and rejects all worldly activity as well as (and more to the point) the people who remained in the world.

All the above is a reading of the attitudes and incidents preserved in our most ancient records of the situation dating from the time of the Buddha's death and to about 200 years after. Anyone reading and understanding the foregoing account of the Path could readily perceive that those who reach the upper levels are very likely to become totally uninterested in anyone not practicing as they are. To ordinary mortals they, in turn, would appear completely self-engrossed and lacking in human warmth. Of course, if the ordinary mortal has some idea of what that Path consists of he would know the reason. But that would not alter the case.

Mahakasyapa typifies this apparent hauteur. His cold and inflexible treatment of Ananda at the door of the First Council illustrates this well. The Arhats are necessarily the product of the Path they followed. One wonders if it is the same today, though it is difficult to judge, because it is not easy to ascertain whether there are any living or recent Arhats whose conduct could be objectively observed. Nevertheless, the criticisms of them at the time of the Third Council were acute and public.

Such distinctions in the quality and behavior of Arhats compared with Sakyamuni added to the worries on the part of some early Indian masters that led them to believe that the Path of Purity was not and never had been the whole of the Dharma. The Buddha himself was the supreme example and so perhaps there was teaching that included practices designed to emulate his own benevolent, wide-ranging compassionate care for all.

Indeed there was, and gradually over the years it emerged into the light thanks to careful collection of scattered fragments of doctrine that had either not been presented or had been set aside at the time of the first recitations.

However, that is another tale altogether and involves contentious issues and the slow consolidation of what became known later as Mahayana themes. With regard to Arhats and the Buddha, then, the differences between them concern the qualities of the original discoverer and of those who follow after, then the relative depth and range of insight into the nature of Samsara and its beings, and finally the special compassion for and constant assistance to those who are unfavorably placed and constrained in the world.

This lack of compassionate outreach is even more marked in the case of the Pratyekabuddha. The name itself means one who is enlightened by and for himself, and it carries strong undertones of solitary, isolated habits. Perhaps the best and most detailed description of such an inwardly turned ascetic is that contained in the third section of the *Sutta Nipata*. There all forty-one verses praise wandering alone like a rhinoceros. Verse three states categorically:

> He who has compassion on his friends and companions loses his own advantage, having a fettered mind; seeing the danger in friendship, let one wander alone like a rhinoceros. . . .

Generally speaking, then, the ascetic who has gone forth and who pursues the Path or Way of the Pratyekabuddha (Pratyekabuddhayana) is one who does not congregate or live with other monks and who seeks no teacher. He is the recluse par excellence, living in wild inaccessible places or in forest clearings. He is even unlikely to beg his food but subsists on what he can collect around his retreat. Sometimes, as we have seen in the stories related by the Arhats at Lake Anavatapta, pious people travel to visit him, bringing food as a gift of devotion. But as the *Abhidharmakosa* says, "he dreads being distracted from his meditations and of coming into contact with men." His Path is characterized by the search for and discovery of the reality of causal production, and thus he discovers the formula of the Pratityasamutpada all by himself. When he has gained what he seeks he proceeds to realize it, piece by piece, mainly from the calm absorption of the fourth dhyana. And having realized it he acquires a form of Bodhi (Enlightenment) that stops all defilements and future rebirth. His attainment, however, conveys no impulse to share his achievement with others. He usually passes into Nirvana after a life lived largely in solitude and silence.

These three types of personage, the Arhat, the Pratyekabuddha, and the Bodhisattva destined to become the Buddha of a particular era comprise the three Ways (yana) of Indian Mainstream Buddhism. Both Arhats and Pratyekabuddhas display tendencies toward withdrawal and isolation, the latter to an extreme degree. The Buddha, on the other hand, with his immense prehistory of devotion to special feats of training as a Bodhisattva, selects his last birth and becomes a being unlike any other. He discovers what has been lost for ages; he penetrates the reality of all existences to an unimaginable depth; and he devises innumerable means and devices to guide all manner of people toward liberation from Samsara in a way suitable to their capacities and conditions. Secure and unperturbed in his supreme and perfect Enlightenment, he reaches out to all and sundry with compassionate help. The Pratyekabuddhas rarely, if ever, help anyone else. The Arhat does so, but his efforts in this direction are prone to be selective and restricted and much reduced in range compared to the Buddha's.

From such austere beginnings on the part of the Buddha's principal followers, Indian Buddhist masters persevered in their efforts to regain the whole of the Dharma dispensed by Sakyamuni and to plumb to the depths his most profound and little understood pronouncements. In the course of time, the Samgha came to provide greater sustenance and support for all kinds of people as the deeper implications of the Dharma were drawn out. The schools of the Great Assembly (Mahasanghika) were the front runners in this process, and eventually they brought together parts of the original deep Dharma, wherein later masters were to perceive and understand that the aversion for and the thrust out of Samsara was only a preliminary insight. That aversion had its place but was like medicine, too strong a dose too often repeated could lead some patients to die.

In their turn, the orthodox (Sthavira) schools of Mainstream Hinayana, particularly the immensely powerful Sarvastivadins, came to reconsider and adjust their modes of living so that monks and nuns did not take themselves off into quiet viharas away from the town. By the time of the beginning of our era, most of the main city centers of north India and Kashmir were served by temples, not just monasteries, where the monks and the nuns were more accessible to the public for guidance and for the great devotional ceremonial so dear to lay people's hearts. By those means of greater accessibility the Hinayana form of the Dharma far outstripped the infant Mahayana in general popularity in northern India by the third century A.D.

Despite this, the Path of Purity has never been drastically modified, nor is it likely to be. The highest fruit of that Path, in the shape of recognized Arhats, was still being produced here and there around Taxila, in northwest India, even at the height of the popularization process. Several stupa remains have been found in small monastic cells in the vicinity of Taxila, dating from about 100 A.D. They are thought to commemorate Arhats or specially revered holy persons who lived there.

One commemorative cell-stupa was found within the Dharmarajika temple-complex less than a mile from Taxila city (Sirkap). That cell, with its stupa, is sited right next to the processional route inside one of the entrances to the main temple area. The temple-complex itself contains the great stupa reputedly built by Asoka and therefore would have been visited regularly by hordes of pilgrims and by the pious inhabitants of Taxila itself. All these visitors would have passed within an arm's reach of this particular cell and its special occupant. Without doubt, during his lifetime this holy person would himself have been the object of veneration by the multitude. Specially favored dignitaries, both clerical and lay, would have sought interviews with him. Hardly a day would have passed without large numbers of laypeople seeking to make offerings to him or to question him.

This mode of life for holy persons of the highest attainment is a far cry from the seclusion and the forest retreats sought by the Arhat masters of earlier centuries. Such a mode of life, in the midst of the turmoil and hubbub of an open and much frequented shrine, conveys more clearly than words can what a transformation had been brought about among some of the leading figures of the Hinayana Samgha. Withdrawal and solitary detachment had been replaced by a willingness to be

291

involved, even immersed, in everyday affairs, albeit in a setting of deep piety.

NIRVANA AND THE THREE WAYS

No exposition of the fundamental doctrines of Indian Buddhism would be complete without some discussion of Nirvana. The obligatory exposition here, however, will be brief and suggestive rather than elaborate and exhaustive.

The reasons for this are several and of some consequence. First, an in-depth discussion would require an array of textual quotations, which would extend this book beyond reasonable bounds. Second, the subject is a minefield of explosive opinion that is beside our purpose. Third, when giants of Buddhist scholarship such as L. de la Vallée Poussin and T. Stcherbatsky can engage in public controversy for a considerable period, as they did several decades ago, and still not put the matter to rest, smaller minds had best hold their peace.

Here, then, we shall confine ourselves to a few primary source quotations, some guidance from Vasubandhu and, lastly, to some implications drawn from the final stages of the Path we have set out.

The word Nirvana carries a strong clue to its import. The first half of the word consists of the prefix "nir-," which is a negative. Generally speaking, the basic meaning of Nirvana is to be extinguished or put out, as with a fire or a candle. A useful collection of short statements about Nirvana, extracted from the Pali records of the Buddha's words, can be found in *Buddhist Texts through the Ages* by Conze, et. al. There we find such phrases as "stopping of Becoming," "getting rid of craving," "going out of the flame," "deathlessness," "peace," and "the un-changing state." Some of the more positive statements often include the word "bliss" in connection with the release and liberation from desire of all kinds. Even the most emphatic declaration of all the earliest sutta references from the *Udana* refers to the fact that there is a plane or state, but here too the descriptions are all negative: it is unborn, not become, not made, uncompounded, etc.

If we consider such terms in conjunction with the stopping process enshrined in the two cardinal practice formulas of the Four Noble Truths and the Arising Due to Conditions, we can readily appreciate that the gradual elimination of all the defilements throughout the upper stages of the Path would result in a final expiration well meriting negative terminology. Such is the word Nirvana. It stands at the end of the Path of Purity and has to be rightly understood as associated with the practices and conditions that apply only to the last of the Paths, that of No Further Training. However, all shades of opinion among Mainstream Indian Buddhists agree that Nirvana is not caused or produced by anything, least of all the Path. Buddhaghosa makes a fine distinction when he says that Nirvana cannot be produced by means of the Path, but it is attainable by means of the Path, just as a path leads to the top of a mountain but does not produce it.

Another generally agreed dictum is that Nirvana has nothing whatsoever to do with Samsara. It is not located in any part of the three-realm world-system, and its nature is exactly and completely the opposite of all the functions and operations that take place in Samsara. For example, it is unborn, so it is deathless. It is uncompounded and therefore remains isolated and enters into no relationship whatever. In philosophical terms it is absolute in the strict sense of the word. Yet for all that, an Arhat is an Arhat because he attains it.

This is understandable because the Arhat has also become Arhat due to his having stopped and extinguished in himself all the characteristics of Samsara. He has no further outflows; Karman for him is switched off. He is in his last birth, and so there will be no further rebirth in any part of Samsara for him. What happens to him after death is impossible to specify, except in negative terms, just as is the case for Nirvana also.

Turning briefly to Vasubandhu's *Abhidharmakosa*, we find that he quotes the root text of his mentors, the Sarvastivadin/Vaibhasikas, which deploys another array of negatives to describe Nirvana.

It is called Nirvana because:
of the destruction of the passions (klesa)
of the pacification of the three fires (raga, dvesa, and moha)
of the destruction of the three characteristics (birth, growth, and death)
of the disjunction from all impurities
of the disjunction from all the destinies (gati)
of the exit from the forest of the skandhas
of the liberation from all the sufferings of rebirth

These seven statements about Nirvana amount to a denial of the elements and features of Samsara. In fact, they add up to the total stopping of the third Noble Truth.

So far, the picture is all of a piece with what the completion of the Path of Purity would lead us to expect. But there is one little difficulty. This difficulty is one that, like several others in the corpus of doctrine and practice making up the early

Mainstream Hinayana, began to grow as time went on. It is this: the final goal of the Path is described in the earliest texts by the use of two special terms, not one. The final goal consists, not only of Nirvana, but of Nirvana and Bodhi. This other term for full attainment, Bodhi, is certainly not negative; its basic meaning is to awake, or to know.

To give two examples. The goal of Buddhahood, which Sakyamuni attained, included the status of Arhatship. Arhat is one of the Buddha's titles, but in his case it is called "supreme and perfect Enlightenment" (anuttarasamyaksambodhi). In addition, one of the most important formulas of the practice of the Path is called the Thirty-Seven Auxiliaries of Enlightenment (bodhipaksika). It is not called the Thirty-Seven Auxiliaries of Nirvana. And a glance at the constituents of this formula (see Lists A and B) will show that its contents are far from negative.

Nevertheless, Arhats are almost always spoken of as attaining Nirvana, not Bodhi. Buddhas are always spoken of as attaining to Anuttarasamyaksambodhi under the Bodhi tree and of passing into Parinirvana at death. What have we here? Are there two distant goals that differ from each other? Is the "only way" of the Satipatthana a way with more than one outcome? The marked distinctions made between the status of the Buddha and the Arhats lends weight to the possibility. Not only that but the Three Ways (yanas) that we have discussed earlier are described in the *Abdhidharmakosa* as having three separate Bodhis. They are specified as Sravakabodhi, Pratyakabuddhabodhi, and Anuttarasamyaksambodhi. Each of them has special distinguishing features; we have mentioned a few of them in the above section on the Three Ways. The interesting thing is that the supreme Bodhi of the Buddha incorporates all the features of the other two, plus his own exclusive attributes. And those attributes are distinctly positive super-knowledges, powers, and faculties.

In this scheme, which is still firmly within the boundaries of Mainstream Hinayana, we see that the predominantly negative Nirvana takes its place beside the much more positive features of Bodhi. All of them together comprise the "supreme and perfect Enlightenment" of the Buddha. In this context it is little to be wondered that some of the Indian masters came to feel that the Path of Purity was not the whole story. As we have seen, the return to the example of the Buddha himself served as a corrective to the "withdrawal symptoms" of the early Arhats. Several centuries later, when the problem had intensified and clarified as a result of deep and consistent attention to the Buddha's more profound statements, the theme was developed into altogether larger proportions. That was part of the gradual emergence of the Mahayana from the original Dharma, taken as a whole.

16. CONCLUSION

I t may be now be useful to bring together several matters that
have been referred to in passing throughout this book. In
addition to this, the subject of the Path will be commented
upon without the careful constraints necessary for expounding
Mainstream consensus doctrine. The comments will not detain
us long, as they will be concerned only with an ancient uncertainty and a few present-day questions.

In the chapter on the first two Paths we saw a marked reluctance in the early Samgha to divulging much of the higher levels
of training and doctrine to laypeople. Sakyamuni was very particular about this and seemed to judge the layman's inner development and capacities before saying anything to him about the
special practices of the Path. Doubtless this was done in order to
avoid frustration and feelings of inadequacy in lay people unable
or unwilling, for various reasons, to enter the Order. Other reasons also had a hand in the matter, such as the difficult and subtle nature of the higher reaches of the Path and the need for close
supervision of the doctrine-practice amalgam, a supervision not
easy to sustain in the case of a layman immersed in family and
worldly pursuits. Sariputra was quite blunt to Anathapindika on
the subject.

It may be objected here that Sakyamuni also said that he held nothing back and did not have the closed fist of the teacher. That is true, but he said that to Ananda with reference to the Order, not to lay people. The reticence toward the majority of laymen and laywomen produced an uncertainty among Indian masters of later times as to whether lay people could complete the final stages of the Path and attain Nirvana while remaining lay people.

Even today, after decades of modern critical scholarship devoted to the content of the texts, there is no generally agreed upon, unambiguous certainty based on the traditional source material. Several Pali texts contain cases of lay followers attaining Arhatship just before death or immediately prior to joining the Order. On the other hand, there does seem to be general agreement that lay people can sometimes quickly gain the first three of the four Fruits: Srota-apanna, Sakrdagamin, and Anagamin.

But according to one of the most renowned European Buddhist scholars and translators of modern times, Professor E. Lamotte, "the crucial point is to know if the upasaka can gain the state of Arhat, the fourth and last fruit of the religious life." Lamotte goes on to quote an extract from the Majjima collection of the Pali texts wherein the Buddha is asked the question by Todeyaputta. The Buddha replies that on this subject he makes distinctions (vibhajyavada); he makes no categorical statement regarding layman or monk—it is what he does that counts.

After the Buddha's time, during the period of the early schools, at least one school of mainland India, the Uttarapathakas, claimed unequivocally that laymen, as laymen, could gain Arhatship. This opinion is recorded in the Pali collection of controversies, the *Kathavatthu*, but is disputed by the Theravadins. Also, as we have seen, the majority party, strongly supported by laymen at the time of the great schism, turned the argument around by asserting that the Arhats themselves were still liable to certain serious faults. Other schools claimed that Arhats could fall away from the fourth Fruit.

What seems to emerge from the several views is that the prime matter concerns the capacity to fulfill the practices that develop into the four Fruits. The monk or nun in the Samgha is particularly well-placed to sustain the effort, without distraction, for long periods of meditative seclusion. The layman is not so well-placed in this regard, for reasons that are obvious. And as the highest levels of this Path take place in the stage of Repeated Meditative Cultivation, leading into the stage of No Further Training, it is the capacity for intense and uninterrupted meditation that is crucial. Not only this, but for the intense meditation to be successful, all the moral precepts of conduct have to be preserved intact. That, too, places the layman at a relative disadvantage.

Perhaps it comes to this: the monk's mode of life, detached, ascetic, morally and sexually "pure," is the ideal basis for completing the practices leading to all four Fruits. If the layman can follow the same mode of life and still remain a layman then he too has the same basis for achievement. The real question is, can he?

The answer is, in some respects, more difficult today in the West, than it ever was over 2,000 years ago in India. The present-day phenomenon of urban life en masse makes the detached, ascetic life very hard to adopt, let alone sustain, for lay people. On the other hand, for some, the Western economic systems have brought leisure time and independence to a degree unknown and unheard of in the ancient cultures of the East. So, on balance, the specific conditions of modernity may cancel each other out, but the possibility of lay fulfillment of this Path will still remain as doubtful as it was in the past.

A question more relevant to our times may possibly be: is the Path of purity a practical option for Westerners? Is this Path of total stopping one that can persuade and attract devoted practitioners? That is a question answered by different people in different ways. The answers will probably reveal more about the person answering than about the substance of the problem. At least the detailed expositions in this book of the fundamentals of that Path may serve to clarify what is involved so that a valid answer can be arrived at.

One can proceed a little further and say that if the clerical Samgha is the proper means of embarking upon this Path, then it is the Samgha itself that has also to be considered in the Western context. To put this plainly: if the Path of Purity is sufficiently attractive to the urban Westerner, and if the Samgha of monks and nuns is the right vehicle for it, then the Samgha will have a recognizable role in our society. But if not, what is the role of that Samgha? Is it teaching? If so, of what kind? Is it as exemplars? If so, of what?

These are some of the questions that naturally arise from an acquaintance with the traditional detail of the Path of Purity today. For the Buddhists of India and Ceylon in ancient times, there is little doubt that this Path, and therefore the Samgha itself, was mightily attractive for centuries. And in certain areas the Samgha still is today.

During the course of the present century in the West, the Path of Purity has emerged from its Oriental languages and traditions so that it can now be seen by us with considerable clarity. One wonders how it impresses the present-day Western man and woman of this world. Does it, will it, have the "pull" it had in times gone by for other people in other places? If its attraction is to the few, to the small minority, it will necessarily be confined to the very fringes of modern society. And we all know what happens to fringe activities. If that is to be its fate, then other Paths will need to be expounded and mapped out that are just as much a part of the Buddhadharma and that may be more amenable and more adaptable to modern conditions. Or perhaps the Path of Purity itself can be adapted, though this has very limited possibilities, as can be seen.

In any event, we shall need to become more familiar with the scriptural canons to ensure that we are dealing with the true Dharma and not with some concoction that involving extraneous material and other ends. This need applies whether we are considering the Dharma as a phenomenon in society or whether we are seeking to practice some of its teaching. The intimate connection between doctrines and practices has been demonstrated in these pages, especially in the cases of the major formulas like the Four Noble Truths and the Arising Due to Conditions. Practice divorced from traditional doctrinal knowledge or instructions, and vice versa, will be equally unproductive. Not only will the one without the other not produce real progress on this Path, or any other Dharma Path; it will also lead to distorted views of what the Path actually consists of, with stagnant results for both the practitioner and the theoretician. Our predecessors in the great Buddhist civilizations of India and China achieved such modifications in a variety of ways, but we, in general, remain ignorant of them. That is our great disadvantage. We tend to believe that we and our conditions are unique in the world and that the ancients have little or nothing to tell us of any consequence. That may well be in the spheres of science and technology, but on questions of religion and spiritual need we are dwarfs trying to look down upon giants. As we have said before, models are necessary, so that we can compare our own efforts at adaptation with the Dharma itself and with successful reproductions of the past. Without such models for comparison and because what we seek to pursue is "foreign," with little paralleling our own norms of behavior, our self-imposed and ignorant isolation from past masterly reproductions will, in all likelihood, lead to jerrybuilding or weird invention.

The final comments of this chapter also have to do with the essentials of the Dharma, but in a more technical sense. They concern the profusion of Sanskrit terms that adorn (or disfigure, as you will) the pages of this book. In the Introduction it was said that the appropriate terminology would be included in the body of the narrative but that it would be kept to a minimum. That intention of minimal use of terminology has proved impossible to achieve. Like Pandora's Box, once the lid is opened all floods out.

One of the principal reasons why the terms became so profuse is because the English renderings of important terms already in circulation are so varied. The prime example of this is the many different equivalents for the vital term Pratityasamutpada. To ensure the certain identification of the matter under discussion, the only sure recourse is the original word itself. Any likely disruption of smooth reading is far outweighed by the advantage of frequent contact with the terms in context, without having to resort to glossaries.

The frequent appearance of the Sanskrit and Pali terms in the narrative and in the charts and diagrams has already drawn some quite proper criticism from recognized experts and scholars, who complain that the terminology as given lacks diacritical marks. These marks rightly belong to any transliteration of Sanskrit into the roman alphabet, because they indicate both the correct pronunciation and construction of the word. However, as this author is addressing non-specialist general readers, who may well be seeing such terms for the first time, at least in such profusion, the diacriticals have been omitted deliberately. The reason is simply that the terms are shown as an aid to later recognition elsewhere and to identify the English equivalent exactly. To insert the diacriticals also would add little or nothing to the purpose and might have proved to be an unnecessary complication in an already complex body of material. There will be time enough for the full panoply of Sanskrit and Pali if and when the reader wishes to proceed to the textual translations or to more detailed studies. Meantime, in this author's opinion, it is better to have the terms "stripped to the waist" than "overdressed" at this stage.

And so, at long last, the author takes his leave of the readers of this book. A word of thanks and appreciation is due to those who have struggled through this four-fold maze to the end. It has to be said, albeit without regret, that this author has shared in the struggle. Coming to grips with the Dharma as given is no small matter. Yet, if some inkling of the grandeur and inspiration emanating from the original themes has been glimpsed, even momentarily, then the effort and the patience will have been worthwhile. These presentations, by their very nature, are just intermediaries. When the actual texts are studied, the impression of grandeur is quite stunning. Perhaps the reader has this great experience to come. If so, bon voyage!

LISTS

LIST A

(i) The Path = Thirty-Seven Auxiliaries of Enlightenment (Bodhipaksika)

4	Foundations of Mindfulness (Skt. Smrtyupasthana; Pali: Satipatthana)
4	Right Efforts (Samyakpradhana)
4	Bases of Psychic Power (Rddhipada)
5	Faculties (Indriya)
5	Powers (Bala)
7	Constituents of Enlightenment (Bodhyanga)
8	Constituents of the Noble Path (Aryamarganga)
37	

(ii) These thirty-seven names comprise ten things:

Faith (Sraddha)
Energy (Virya)
Memory/Mindfulness (Smrti)
Wisdom (Prajna)
Concentration (Samadhi)
Even-mindedness (Upeksa)
Joy (Priti)
Resolution (Samkalpa)
Moral conduct (Sila)
Aptitude (Prasrabdhi)

LIST B
37 Bodhipaksikas in Detail

4 Foundations of Mindfulness (pure or impure)	The body Feelings Thoughts Dharmas
4 Right Efforts (pure or impure)	Dispelling bad Dharmas present Stopping further bad Dharmas arising Sustaining good Dharmas present Producing good Dharmas not present
4 Bases of Psychic Power (pure or impure)	Concentrated intention for action Concentrated thought Concentrated energy Concentrated examination
5 Faculties (pure or impure)	Faith Energy Mindfulness Concentration Wisdom
5 Powers (pure or impure)	—the 5 faculties increased to full strength
7 Constituents of Enlightenment (pure only)	Investigation into Dharmas Energy Concentration Mindfulness Joyous zest Aptitude Even-mindedness
8 Constituents of the Noble Path (pure only)	Right views Right livelihood Right intentions Right energy Right speech Right mindfulness Right action Right concentration

LIST C

(i) The Basic Defilements (Klesa/Anusaya)
    Attachment/Greed (Raga)
    Hostility (Pratigha)
    Pride (Mana)
    Ignorance (Avidya)
    False views (Drsti)
    Doubt (Vicikitsa)

(ii) Types of Defilements in Each of The Realms of Samsara

	Kamadhatu	Rupadhatu	Arupyadhatu
Ragas	5	5	5
Pratighas	5	NIL	NIL
Manas	5	5	5
Avidyas	5	5	5
Drstis	12	12	12
Vickitsas	4	4	4
	36	31	31

Total: Ninety-eight kinds of defilement in Samsara
All have to be stopped and abandoned before the Path is
complete.

LIST D

(i) The Aids to Emancipation (Moksabhagiya)

Faith (Sraddha)

Energy (Virya)

Mindfulness (Smrti)

Concentration (Samadhi)

Wisdom (Prajna)

These are the same as "The Faculties" of List B.

(ii) The Aids to Penetration (Nirvedhabhagiya)

	Intensified Practice of:	Progressive Penetration
Heats (Usmagata)	4 Right Efforts	4 Noble Truths in 16 Aspects
Summits (Murdhan)	4 Bases of Psychic Power	More intense focus on 16 Aspects
Patiences (Ksanti)	5 Faculties	Intense focus on first Noble Truth of Kamadhatu (first Klesas stopped)
Supreme Worldly Dharmas (Laukikagradharma)	5 Powers	Highest Intensity of impure focus on 1st Noble Truth of Kamadhatu (lead directly to stage of Darsanamarga)

These are "Four Good Roots" (Kusalamula)

LIST E

(i) The Five-Fold Discipline of Engagement for Laypeople

The Upsaka or Upasika formally undertakes to renounce and avoid five actions. This formal renunciation constitutes the "morality of Engagement."

1. Murder or taking life (Pranatipata)
2. Theft (Adattadana)
3. Prohibited Sexual Conduct (Kamamithyacara)
4. Lying (Mrsavada)
5. Drinking Intoxicating Liquor (Suramaireyapramadasthana)

(ii) The Novice Monk Formally Undertakes Five More

Number three is amended to "All sexual activity" (Abrahmacarya)

6. Use of perfumes, garlands, unguents (Gandhamalyavilepana)
7. Dancing, singing, music (Nrtyagitavadita)
8. Use of high or large beds (Uccasayana, Mahasayanna)
9. Meals after time (Vikalabhojana)
10. Receiving gold and silver

LIST F

The Ten Bad Ways of Action (Akusalakarmapatha)

Defined as the most weighty and grave among the bad practices. The practice of the Path requires abstention from all of these as a minimum.

3	1. Murder or taking life (Pranatipata)
of	2. Theft (Adattadana)
body	3. Prohibited sexual conduct (Kamamithyacara)
4	4. False speech or lying (Mrsavada)
of	5. Malicious or slanderous speech (Paisunya)
speech	6. Injurious or insulting speech (Parusya)
	7. Thoughtless speech (Sambhinnapralapa)
3	8. Covetousness (Abhidya)
of	9. Malice (Vyapada)
mind	10. False view (Mithyadrsti)

GLOSSARY/INDEX OF FORMULAS

INDEX OF FORMULAS AND TERMS

The two-part Index that now follows provides references to the use of special Sanskrit terms.

No proper names, titles or place names are given in either Index, because the purpose is to pick out the technical terms and teaching formulas only. In one case however an exception is made. This exception concerns the three dhatu (tri-dhatu) or realms of Samsara, which figure prominently in the exposition of the higher stages of the Path.

Contrary to the practice adopted within the text, here in the two-part Index, all the Sanskrit terms have their proper diacritical marks. On this subject, however, there are variations in the current English renderings of some of the more commonly used terms and diacriticals. The style of terminological rendering followed by this author is that of E. Conze in his *Vocabulary to the Prajnaparamita Sutras* (Ts 1952) and Edgerton's *Buddhist Hybrid Sanskrit Dictionary* (Indian edition 1970). This particular style, i.e., Samgha instead of Sangha, coincides with current usage among the Sanskrit specialists of the Continent, where much work has been done in the detailed study and translation of texts of Sanskrit origin.

As stated earlier, diacritical marks in Sanskrit indicate pronunciation, among other things, so as an aid to proper spoken usage the principal vowels and consonants controlled by diacriticals are listed together with approximate pronunciation values for each.

ā	as in father	ñ	as in hinge
ī	as in marina	ṇ	as in not
ū	as in rude	ṛ	as in river
ḍ	as in drum	ṣ and ś	as in shut or hush
ṃ or ṅ	as in bang	ṭ	as in true

The first part of the Index consists of a collection of the main formulas. Apart from their main purpose, which is to serve as an aide memoire of the expositions already made, all the formulas, taken together, provide an expression in shorthand, so to speak, of some of the central themes of Mainstream doctrine and practice. To facilitate their use in this manner the formulas have been grouped under three headings: Practice Formulas, Doctrinal Formulas, and Disciplinary Formulas.

Also in the groups of formulas it will be seen that brief English equivalents of most of the terminology is given, whereas in the second part of the Index, equivalents are omitted for the technical terms themselves. The reason for this is important. In no case should any English equivalent, where given, be regarded as a definition. The intention throughout both parts of the Index is that the references to the detailed expositions and usage should combine to produce a more accurate understanding of the meanings of the particular terms and formulas. It has already been remarked upon that single word or short phrase English definitions are all too often misleading and sometimes downright inaccurate. It is only by gaining a familiarity with how the terms are used in their various contexts that a valid understanding of their meanings is acquired. In view of this, the English equivalents given for the constituents of the Formulas should only be regarded as indicators, no more, of the detailed treatment embodied in the book.

Needless to say, not all the technical vocabulary finds a place in this two-part Index. Much of the Abhidharma terminology that comes into play in most of the doctrinal texts is set aside as inappropriate for present purposes.

GLOSSARY/INDEX OF FORMULAS

A. Practice Formulas

Index and Reference	*Glossary*

Practice Formula I
Three Bases of Insight.
śruta, cintā, bhāvanā
137 (expo), 256

śruta = listen or read.
cintā = ponder, consider.
bhāvanā = apply repeated meditative concentration to what has been heard or read and then considered.

Practice Formula II
General Guidance for
  Laypeople.
dāna, śīla, svarga.
139 (expo. of "slow gradual"),
248, 255

dāna = generosity and supportive action.
śīla = moral conduct (basic).
svarga = heaven; sufficient practice of dana and sila results in favorable rebirth.

Practice Formula III
Practices Essential for All the
  Higher Stages.
śīla, samādhi, prajñā
138 (expo. of "fast gradual"),
258-259

śīla = moral conduct (strict).
samādhi = one-pointed concentration.
prajñā = insight-wisdom.

Practice Formula IV
The Four Foundations of
  Mindfulness.
Satipaṭṭhāna (Pali), Smṛtyupasthāna (Skt.).
161-163 (expo.), 164-166,
260-261, 269, 276; in the
Pratityasamutpada, 213-215

rūpa = the body and sense objects.
vedanā = feelings.
citta = thoughts.
dharmas = mental objects.

Practice Formula V
The Four Absorptions.
dhyāna.
262-263 (expo.), 268, 275;
4th, 289

lst - easeful, peaceful, and joyful, with enhanced faculties of reasoning and investigation.
2nd - serene concentration without reasoning and investigation.

Index and Reference

Glossary

3rd - joy subsides, but fully mind
ful, with the body at ease.
4th - detachment from ease and
discomfort with pure equanimity
and with mental concentration
firm and supple.

Practice Formula VI
The Five Aids to Emancipation.
moksabhagiya.
251, 259, 261, 307 (List D, i)

śraddhā = faith, confidence.
vīrya = energy, vigor.
smṛti = mindfulness, recollection,
memory.
samādhi = one-pointed concentra
tion.
prajñā = insight, wisdom.

Practice Formula VII
The Four Right Exertions or
Efforts.
samyakpradhānas.
134-135 (expo. under Right
Energy), 193-194, 261, 265,
276, 304 (List A), 305 (List B,
second of Bodhipaksikas)

1) abandoning bad dharmas
already produced.
2) non-production of bad dharmas
not yet produced.
3) maintaining good dharmas already produced.
4) producing good dharmas not yet
produced.

Practice Formula VIII
The Thirty-Seven Auxiliaries of
Enlightenment.
bodhipākṣika.
261, 265, 268, 275, 276, 295,
304-306 (List A, B)

4 smṛtyupasthāna (satipatthāna) =
Foundations of Mindfulness.
4 samyakpradhāna = Right Exertions.
4 ṛddhipāda = basis of psychic
power.
5 indriya = faculties.
5 bala = powers.
7 bodhyaṅgas = constituents of
Enlightenment.
8 āryamārgaṅga = constituents of
the Noble Path.

313

B. Doctrinal Formulas

Index and Reference	*Glossary*
Doctrinal Formula I	
The Middle Way.	Avoiding both;
mahyamā pratipad.	1)unrestrained passion and
76 (expo. of first preaching),	worldly indulgence.
79, 234	2)unrestrained self-torture and
	severe austerities.
Doctrinal Formula II	
The Three Fires.	rāga = attachment/greed.
rāga, dveṣa, moha.	dveṣa = hatred/aversion.
136, 160, 279, 294	moha = ignorance/delusion.
Doctrinal Formula III	
Three (or Four) Signs (Seals).	1) sarvasaṃskāra anityāḥ = all
anityatā, duḥkha, anātman,	composites are impermanent.
Nirvāṇa.	2) sarvasaṃskāra duhkhāḥ = all
125, 143-147 (expo.), 168;	composites are suffering/turbu-
anātman, 177, 225	lent.
	3) sarvadharmā anātmānaḥ = all
	the elements are without a Self.
	4) śāntam nirvāṇam = Nirvana is
	peace.
Doctrinal Formula IV	
The Three Jewels	The Buddha = the Enlightened One.
Tri-ratna.	The Dharma = the Doctrine/
112, 139, 250, 283	Practice amalgam.
	The Samgha - the practitioners of
	the Path (strictly, the Order of
	monks, nuns, and probationers).

Index and Reference

Glossary

Doctrinal Formula V
The Four Noble Truths.
catur āryasatya.
64, 79, 129-136 (full formula
and expo.), 150, 151-152, 166,
169, 248, 261-262, 265, 276,
271, 272, 273, 276, 280, 282,
293, 301; first preaching of, 76;
last preaching of, 111; Nos. 1
and 2 in the Three Signs, 144;
with the Pratityasamutada, 212-
213; Third Noble Truth, 258;
Sixteen Aspects of, 264, 268

1) duḥkha = suffering/turbulence.
2) samudaya = origination of suffering.
3) nirodha = stopping of suffering.
4) mārga = the Way or Path (in
   eight parts):
   a) samyagdṛṣṭi = Right View.
   b) samyaksaṃkalpa = Right
      Intentions.
   c) samyagvāc = Right Speech.
   d) samyakkarmānta = Right
      Action.
   e) samyagājīva = Right Liveli-
      hood.
   d) samyagvāyāma = Right
      Effort.
   e) samyaksmṛti = Right Mind-
      fulness.
   f) samyaksamādhi = Right
      Concentration.

The Sixteen Aspects (see 135-136)
1) duḥkha
   a) painful.
   b) dependence on causes.
   c) emptiness.
   d) impersonality.
2) samudaya
   a) seeds become causes.
   b) immediate causes.
   c) successive appearance.
   d) concurrence of conditions.

Glossary

3) nirodha
   a) extinction of skandhas.
   b) calmness.
   c) sublimity.
   d) escape.
4) mārga
   a) the route to Nirvana.
   b) correct method and means.
   c) security.
   d) release.

1) uṣmagata = heats.
2) mūrdhān = summits.
3) kṣānti = patiences.
4) agradharma (laukikagradha-
   ma) = supreme worldly dharmas.

1) srota-āpanna = entrant into the
   Stream.
2) sakṛdāgāmin = gainer of the
   sixth category (once-returner).
3) anāgāmin = never-returner.
4) arhat = one who completes the
   Path to Nirvana.

1) rūpa   = bodily faculties and
   sense objects.
2) vedanā = feelings.
3) saṃjñā = perceptions.
4) saṃskaras = composites.
5) vijñāna = consciousness.

Glossary

1) Prophesies a future Buddha.
2) Arouses in someone the desire
   for Buddhahood.
3) Makes the necessary converts.
4) Designates a model pair of disciples.
5) Establishes rules of morality.
6) Completes five-sixths of normal
   life span.
7) Performs the miracle of the
   pairs.
8) Descends from the heavens at
   Samkhasya.
9) Converts father and mother.
10) Unravels karman at Lake
    Anavatapta.

1) avidyā = ignorance. (204)
2) saṃskāra = composites. (207)
3) vijñana = consciousness. (207)
4) nāma-rūpa = mental and physical embryo. (208)
5) ṣaḍāyatana = the six faculties.
   (208)
6) sparśa = contact. (209)
7) vedanā = feelings. (209)
8) tṛṣṇā = craving/thirst (209)
9) upādāna = grasping. (210)
10) bhava = becoming. (210)
11) jāti = birth. (211)
12) jarāmaraṇa = decline and
    death. (212)

Glossary

1) rūpa-āyatana = visual objects and colors.
2) śabda-āyatana = sound objects.
3) gandha-āyatana = odorous objects.
4) rasa-āyatana = taste objects.
5) spraṣṭavya-āyatana = tangible objects.
6) dharma-āyatana = mental objects.
7) cakṣur-āyatana/indriya = eye faculty.
8) śrotra-āyatana/indriya = ear faculty.
9) ghrāṇa-āyatana/indriya = nose faculty.
10) jihvā-āyatana/indriya = tongue faculty.
11) kāya-āyatana/indriya = bodily faculty.
12) mana-āyatana/indriya = mental faculty.
13) caksur-vijñāna = visual consciousness.
14) śrotra-vijñāna = sound consciousness.
15) ghrāṇa-vijñāna = smell consciousness.
16) jihvā-vijñāna = taste consciousness.
17) kāya-vijñāna = touch consciousness.
18) mano-vijñāna = mental-object consciousness.

C. Disciplinary Formulas

Index and Reference

Disciplinary Formula I
a) Laymens' Five-Fold Discipline
of Engagement.
samādānasīla.
251-252 (expo.), 308 (List E, i)

b) The Ten Rules of the Novice
and Fully Ordained Monk. All
the above with Now. 3 increased
to total abstention (brah-
macarya) plus 6 through 10
daśaśikṣapadika.
254, 258, 308 (List E,ii)

Disciplinary Formula II
The Ten Bad Ways of Action
akuśalakarmapatha
254-255 (expo.), 308-310 (List F)

Glossary

1) prāṇātipāta = renouncing murder or the taking of life.
2) adattādāna = renouncing theft.
3) kāmamithyācāra = renouncing
prohibited sexual conduct.
4) mṛṣāvāda= renouncing lying.
5) surāmaireyapramādasthāna =
renouncing drinking intoxicating
liquor.
6) gandhamālyavilepana =
renouncing use of perfumes, etc.
7) nṛtyagītavādita = renouncing
dancing and music.
8) uccaśayana/mahāśayana =
renouncing use of large or high
beds.
9) vikālabhojana = renouncing the
taking of meals after time.
10) ? = renouncing gold and silver.

Three of Body:
1) prāṇātipāta = murder or taking
life.
2) adattādāna = theft.
3) kāmamithyācāra = prohibited
sexual conduct.

Four of Speech:
4) mṛṣāvāda = lying.
5) paiśunya = slander.
6) pāruṣya = insulting speech.
7) saṃbhinnapralāpa = thoughtless
speech.

Three of Mind:
8) abhidhyā = covetousness.
9) vyāpāda = malice.
10) mithyādṛṣṭī = false views.

REFERENCES

Primary Sources
Buddhism in Translation by H.C. Warren. (Harvard Oriental Series) Cambridge, Mass. 1906.
Buddhist Scriptures by E. Conze. (Penguin), Harmondsworth 1959.
Buddhist Texts through the Ages by Conze, Horner, Snellgrove, and Waley. Oxford 1954.
Le Concile de Rajaghra by J. Przyluski. Paris 1926.
Early Buddhist Scriptures by E. J. Thomas. London 1935.
The Life of Buddha as Legend and History by E.J. Thomas. London 1949.

Secondary Sources
Philosophies of India, by H. Zimmer (edited J. Campbell) London 1951.
La Vie du Bouddha, by A. Foucher, Paris 1949.

Texts in Translation and Studies
Primary Sources
Le Congrès du Lac Anavatapta, (Extrait du Vinaya des Mulasarvastivadin) translated and annotated by M. Hofinger. Louvain 1954.
L'Abhidharmakosa de Vasubandhu, translated and annotated by L. de la Vallée Poussin. Second edition. Brussels 1980. 6 volumes.
Le Traité de la Grande Vertu de Sagesse (Mahaprajnaparamitasastra) Nagarjuna/Kumarajiva, translated and annotated by E. Lamotte. Louvain 1944-80. 5 volumes.
Pali Texts in various English translations.

Secondary sources
Analytical Study of the Abhidharmakosa, by S. Chaudhuri. Calcutta 1976.
Buddhist Dictionary by Nyanatiloka. Colombo 1950.
The Heart of Buddhist Meditation (Satipatthana), by Nyanaponika Thera, Colombo 1954
Histoire du Bouddhisme Indien, by E. Lamotte. 2nd. edition Louvain 1967.
Indian Buddhism, by A.K. Warder. Delhi 1970.
Indian Philosophy, by S. Radhakrishnan (2 vols) London, 1923 (Reprint 1948)
La Lumière sur les Six Voies (Sadgatikarika), by P. Mus, Paris 1939.
Les Sectes Bouddhiques du Petit Véhicule, by A. Bareau. Saigon 1955.
Les Premiers Conciles Bouddhiques, by A. Bareau. Paris 1955.
The Upanishads, trans. by F. Max Muller (2 vols) S.B.E. Oxford 1900.
The Visuddhimagga, by Buddhagosa, trans. by Nanamoli Bhikkhu Ceylon, 1956.

The Buddhist Society, London

Founded in 1924 by Christmas Humphreys, Q. C. The Buddhist Society is one of the original centers for Buddhist teaching and practice in the Western world. Since its inception, the Society has provided a program of talks, study classes, and meditation under the guidance of teachers trained in the traditions of Buddhism.

The Society's objectives are to publish and make known the principles of Buddhism, and to encourage the study and application of these principles. The Society adheres to no one school of Buddhism, and gives the newcomer an impartial introduction to the many branches of Buddhism practiced today.

For further information contact:

The Buddhist Society, London
58, Eccleston Square,
London SW1V 1PH, United Kingdom
Tel: 071–834–5858

Beyond Sanity and Madness
The Way of Zen Master Dogen
by Dennis Genpo Merzel
Introduction and calligraphy by Hakuyu Taizan Maezumi, Roshi

Dennis Genpo Merzel provides commentary and insight to three of
Dogen Zenji's most significant works: "Gakudo Yojinshu," "Bodaisatta
Shishobo," and *Yuibutsu Yobutsu,* a lost chapter from the Shobogenzo.
In so doing Genpo sensei puts forth an understanding of Zen practice in
a way rarely done before in our time. He speaks directly to the reader
with a wide range of voices and tones, with the killing and life-giving
sword of the true Zen master.

Dennis Genpo Merzel is the founder of Kanzeon Sangha and the abbot
of Kanzeon Zen Center Utah. He is a dharma successor of
Hakuyu Taizan Maezumi, Roshi.

ISBN: 0–8048–3035–5, 304 pages

The Butterfly's Dream
In Search of the Roots of Zen
by Albert Low

This is a lucid treatise on the spirituality of Zen, which also explores the
origin, consequences and the way beyond the continuing cycle of human
suffering. The author uses Christian, Sufi, and Hindu as well as Buddhist
sources and explains Zen in Western terms, making it accessible both in
theory and in practice.

Albert Low is the teacher and director of the Montreal Zen Centre.
He started Zen practice in 1961 and in 1966 began study with
Yasutani, Roshi. In 1986 he received full transmission as teacher of
Zen from Philip Kapleau, Roshi.

ISBN: 0–8048–1822–3, 184 pages

Free Yourself of Everything
Radical Guidance in the Spirit of Zen
and Christian Mysticism
by Wolfgang Kopp
Translated from the German by Barbara Wittenberg-Hasenauer

Intended for those who earnestly seek spiritual guidance, this book
conveys the deepest wisdom of eastern and western mysticism. Drawing
from his vast experience as a practicing meditation master, and using
examples from the great masters of Zen and Christian mysticism, the
author presents the fundamental elements necessary for a successful
journey to inner freedom.

Wolfgang Kopp was a student of the Soji Enku, Roshi. As Enku Roshi's
dharma successor, he directs the Tao-Ch'an Center in Wiesbaden, Germany

ISBN: 0–8048–1989–0, 144 pages

The Tao of Zen
by Ray Grigg

This dynamic book systematically links Taoism and Zen. The author
traces the evolution of Ch'an (Zen) in China and later in Japan, where
the Way was a term used interchangeably to describe the essence of both
Taoism and Zen.

Ray Grigg lives and teaches on Quadra Island off the coast of British
Columbia. He is the author of acclaimed books on Taoism as well as
Zen Brushpoems.

ISBN: 0–8048–1988–2, 376 pages

Two Arrows Meeting in Mid-Air
The Zen Koan
by John Daido Loori

Through a comprehensive introduction and twenty-one chapters centered on koans from classic collections and modern encounters, this book presents the relevance of koan study as it related to modern Zen training. The author draws on his many dharma discourses to provide a detailed examination of each koan, connecting the contemporary reader to the traditional Zen lineages.

John Daido Loori is the spiritual leader and abbot of the Zen Mountain Monastery in Mt. Tremper, New York. Trained in koan Zen as well as in the subtle school of Master Dogen's Zen, he is a dharma heir to Hakuyu Taizan Maezumi, Roshi.

ISBN: 0–8048–3012–6, 392 pages

The Whole World is a Single Flower
365 Kong-ans for Everyday Life
by Zen Master Seung Sahn
Foreword by Stephen Mitchell

"One of greatest collection of koans since the dawn of Zen in the West."
—*Tricycle,* The Buddhist Review

Korean Zen Master Seung Sahn provides 365 kong-ans (koans), which are practice for life—practice for answering the profound and practical questions that arise every day. The kong-ans come from traditional Chinese and Korean Zen as well as from Lao-tzu and the Christian tradition. Master Seung Sahn provides additional questions and commentary to each kong-an that will serve as guideposts on the reader's path to enlightenment.

ISBN: 0–8048–1782–0, 256 pages

For further information and to order copies of any of these titles please write to:
Charles E. Tuttle Co., Inc.
P.O Box 410
Rutland, VT 05702–0410, USA
or call toll-free within the United States 1–800–526–2778
outside of the United States call 802–773–8930